BI P9-AOO-180 HOOL

CREATING THE BEST LITERACY BLOCK EVER

A Framework for Successfully Managing, Teaching, and Assessing in an Extended Literacy Block

Maryann Manning | Gayle Morrison | Deborah Camp

SCHOLASTIC

New York • Toronto • London • Auckland • Sydney
Mexico City • New Delhi • Hong Kong • Buenos Aires

DEDICATION

This book is dedicated to teachers, who belong to the noblest profession in the world. They go to school each day with only one thought in mind— to improve the lives of their students. We single out those teachers who are improving literacy because without reading and writing, life isn't complete.

We also remember our parents as we continue to improve our teaching of literacy. We are all blessed with parents who were proud that we were teachers and encouraged us to learn as much as we could so we could be the best we could be.

Credits

Page 255, Appendix from McKenna, M.C., & Kear, D. J. (1990, May). Measuring attitude toward reading: A new tool for teachers. The Reading Teacher, 43(9), 626-639. Reprinted with permission of the International Reading Association.

© Paws, Inc. The Garfield character is incorporated in this test with permission of Paws, Inc., and may be reproduced only in connection with the reproduction of the test in its entirety for classroom use until further notice by Paws, Inc., and any other reproduction or use without the express prior written consent of Paws is prohibited.

Page 291, special thanks to Rigby Education, Scholastics Lexiles, and Weaver, B. M. (2000). *Leveling books K–6: Matching readers to text*. Newark, DE: International Reading Association.

The authors and publisher wish to thank those who have generously given their permission to use borrowed material.

Scholastic Inc. grants teachers permission to photocopy material in the appendices for personal classroom use. No other part of this publication may be reproduced in whole or in part or stored in a retrieval system, or transmitted in any form or by any means, electronic, mechanical, photocopying, recording, or otherwise, without written permission of the publishers. For information regarding permission, write to Scholastic Inc., 524 Broadway, New York, NY 10012.

Editors: Lois Bridges and Gloria Pipkin

Production: Amy Rowe

Cover designer: Brian LaRossa

Interior designer: Sydney Wright

Copy editor: Chris Borris

ISBN-13: 978-0-545-05891-9
ISBN-10: 0-545-05891-0

Copyright © 2009 by Maryann Manning, Gayle Morrison, and Deborah Camp

All rights reserved. Published by Scholastic Inc.
Printed in the U.S.A.
1 2 3 4 5 6 7 8 9 10   23   12 11 10 09 08 09

Contents

Acknowledgments

If we thanked all the people in our lives who have helped us, our list would be longer than this text, so we will just point out a few. Lois Bridges is our "shero" because she placed her faith in us to write a book supporting teachers. Her cheery e-mails and phone calls empowered us as we wrote. We also thank Margie Ross for her photographic abilities, and Emily Treadwell, Kyoko Osaki, Tsuguhiko Kato, Pat Nix, and Gay Johnson for assisting with manuscript preparation and technical details.

Deborah thanks her teacher friends who have shared their successes, struggles, and thoughts about literacy practices. She is also indebted to her husband and children, who have encouraged her through one project after another.

Gayle thanks her many professional friends, colleagues, and acquaintances who are constantly asking her "how" and "why." She thanks her family members, especially her husband, because they keep her balanced and focused on what is really important.

Maryann thanks her University of Alabama at Birmingham colleagues, who challenge her thinking and support her outlandish notions. Her life is more fun because of her daughter, Marilee, and little Tori, who loves her Meme.

Foreword

Whether you are brand-new to the teaching profession or a veteran with many successful years in the classroom, it's easy to feel overwhelmed these days. With each new program, professional development activity, or mandate passed down through the system, we find ourselves swimming in questions, searching for the life preserver of common sense. *How do I possibly fit it all in? What can I let go of in order to layer in and address the new expectations? How can I do this without compromising my own philosophy about teaching and learning?*

Maryann, Gayle, and Deborah have been there, too. But over the years they have come to understand that questions and concerns are less overwhelming when viewed through a shared and well-focused lens. They understand that new recommendations, new programs, and new ideas do not mean you must abandon your own professional knowledge or your current practice. They also understand that it would be foolish to add new teaching strategies haphazardly, without thought—to end up with a day of bits and pieces that don't make sense for children.

I have known Maryann, Gayle, and Deborah for two decades, and I trust their insights and professional judgments. These three supremely talented, long-experienced educators are grounded in a solid knowledge base and a well-defined constructivist philosophy. I know that they weigh each decision about teaching and learning against their knowledge and beliefs and never fail to stand up for children and teachers. Each, in her own role, exemplifies what we strive for in our profession.

Maryann has led both undergraduate and graduate students to discover what it means to teach from a thorough knowledge base. She has a distinguished career that includes not only teaching but also leadership in many professional organizations including the International Reading Association and National Council Teachers of English. Gayle is one of the finest teachers I have ever observed, and has lived her teaching life as an example of innovation, energy, and compassion. She spent much of her career working in schools with "at-risk" children who never knew that the world expected them to fail. Deborah has tirelessly supported schools and classrooms from the district level, with a consistent focus on constructivist teaching over many years.

As you'll discover when you enter the pages of this invigorating, hopeful book, the authors bring their years of experience and deep knowledge of language and literacy learning to thoughtful, responsive teaching, sharing their sincere belief in the right of every child to have the best instruction our profession can offer.

With Gayle, Maryann, and Deborah as your guides, you'll learn how to easily and effectively craft your own literacy block that will enable you to support your students with compassion and skill and make the most of every precious instructional moment. Perhaps the most important quality the authors convey is their commitment to human dignity and intellectual integrity.

In this resource, Maryann, Gayle, and Deborah offer you common sense, reaching out with the life preserver that just may be what you need to keep your classroom afloat. Brimming with abundant practical information shaped and refined by the authors' years of working with young children, this book will enable you to catch your breath, refocus your energy, and find your vision. Now swim like there's no tomorrow.

—Lester L. Laminack
Asheville, North Carolina

Introduction

This book was written for primary teachers who are developing the reading of each child, helping each child feel like a reader, sharing the very best literature with children, meeting the needs of every child in the classroom—and trying to maintain their sanity at the same time.

Because all three of us have been teachers for what seems forever, we know classrooms. We have "walked in your shoes," and no three people could have more respect for teachers. Before we begin this journey together, we want our readers to know a little bit about us.

Among the three of us, we have taught almost every grade and discipline, and we have had rural, urban, and suburban experiences. During our careers, we have been exposed to almost every reading program that has been published in the last few decades. You name the program, and one of us has either taught it or was in a school where it was being used.

Gayle is the career baby in the group—she has taught one year less than Deborah, who has 24 years of experience. Gayle's experience is different from that of the other two of us because she didn't experience a skills-oriented teacher education program and has never been forced to use a terrible program. She was the first National Board Certified teacher in the Birmingham Public Schools. She has had thousands of visitors to her inner-city classroom and shares her knowledge with teachers in workshops and at state, national, and international conferences such as National Council of Teachers of English and the International Reading Association. She is also an adjunct professor at the University of Alabama at Birmingham.

Maryann began her teaching in the crack of a two-page map of Nebraska and even taught for two years in a K–8 one-room schoolhouse like her grandmother did 60 years before her. She recounts that in that country school she had family grouping and spent more than one year with her students. It was family grouping because her 19 students came from seven families in the district. She spent her last five years in primary education in an urban fourth-grade classroom in the Omaha Public Schools. Even though she has been at the University of Alabama at Birmingham for more than 30 years, she is in and out of classrooms each week and spends her summers testing and teaching readers whose parents and teachers seek extra support for them. Maryann is currently on the board of directors of the International Reading Association and enjoys meeting teachers around the globe.

Deborah began her career as a special education teacher in the Jefferson County Schools in Alabama, followed by elementary classroom teaching in the Hoover City Schools there. In her last classroom years, she was as a middle school language arts teacher. Deborah was among the first 900 National Board Certified teachers in the nation. She now serves as the elementary curriculum director for the Hoover City Schools. Like Gayle, she speaks at National Council of Teachers of English and International Reading Association conferences and is an adjunct professor at the University of Alabama at Birmingham. She encourages teachers and administrators to seek what is best for children.

Why did we want to write a book on reading? For a number of years we have been trying to help teachers accomplish their goals. We have continued to refine our thinking, and many teachers tell us we have been helpful in meeting the literacy needs of all their students.

There are several challenges in the lives of all teachers who are trying to teach reading. Some of them include the high number of students we have, the range of student needs, the materials we have in our classroom, our school and our community, the degree of administrative support, and our ability to orchestrate a balanced literacy program. Most of us believe that to meet individual needs, we must have a combination of one-on-one, small-group, and large-group instruction. The situation is not unlike an orchestra: sometimes the flute plays a solo, but no one instrument dominates the entire composition in the making of music.

We have never met a teacher who is totally satisfied with his or her teaching of reading. Each year, Maryann would ask Gayle how she felt her reading instruction was going, and Gayle would recite so many improvements she thought she could make. Gayle would mention individual children who were not making the progress she was expecting, or she would share her reflections about changes she wanted to make. Even though Maryann thought Gayle was the best first-grade teacher she knew, Gayle was always critiquing her own instruction and setting new goals for herself.

For many years, Maryann wrote a reading and writing column for *Teaching K–8* and received daily e-mails from her readers. The most frequently cited concern that teachers shared was that they couldn't accomplish everything during their reading and writing blocks. Much of this book is dedicated to helping those teachers accomplish more of their goals each day. We cannot separate reading and writing, and much writing will be recommended, but this book is devoted to the teaching of reading.

Pulling together a classroom reading program doesn't sound like a big deal, but on a day-to-day basis, it isn't easy. Teachers often receive a different message from every professional authority they encounter. Whenever we heard new ideas from literacy authorities, we questioned our beliefs about teaching. Sometimes we threw out excellent practices because we weren't grounded in our own philosophy enough to withstand the critiques of others. Other times, we implemented a new practice without discarding anything, so we ended up with a jumbled conglomerate of activities that weren't coherent or cohesive. We just added and added because somebody said it was a good idea.

We realized that instead of adding the latest educational buzzword to our classroom practice, we needed to match each new idea with our beliefs. We also needed to have a structure that supported how we implemented our beliefs. These new understandings led to the development of our instructional program.

When we talk about literacy, teachers often remark that they recognize the influence of Lucy Calkins, Debbie Miller, Sharon Taberski, Donald Graves, Regie Routman, Bobbie Fisher, Linda Dorn, Don Holdaway, Brian Cambourne, Marie Clay, and other reading authorities we respect. It is no wonder that these authors come out in what we say and write because they have indeed shaped our thinking and our practice. Kenneth and Yetta Goodman and Frank Smith, along with some of their students, helped us understand the reading process. Because we are constructivists who have studied with Constance Kamii, we are also students of Emilia Ferreio, who has contributed to our understanding of the beginnings of literacy. Our philosophies are a composite of the thinking of so many authorities who continue to contribute to our growth through the years.

We hope, as you read this book, that you will compare your beliefs with ours and, after much reflection, consider incorporating some of our ideas into your teaching. We are still "green and growing," as they say down under, and have never tired of "talking shop" with teachers. Better ways to teach reading and writing consume our conversations. We even consider professional books to be as interesting as "beach novels."

When you complete this book, please don't stop with our words and suggestions. We know you are like us as we continue to read professionally, observe children carefully, learn from colleagues, reflect on our practices daily, and strive to improve the lives of the children and parents we serve.

Welcome to Gayle's Classroom

Welcome to Gayle's classroom, where children are immersed in literacy through independent reading, peer interaction, and intentional teaching. Her community is organized around rituals and routines that create an environment in which students thrive as readers and writers.

Community Gathering ～

Community in itself is more important to learning than any method or technique. When community exists, learning is strengthened—everyone is smarter, more ambitious, and productive. Well-formed ideas and intentions amount to little without a community to bring them to life.

—Ralph Peterson, *Life in a Crowded Place: Making a Learning Community* (1992)

Gayle reads the big book *Bella Lost Her Moo* by Judith Zorfass for the opening gathering. The children are engrossed in the story, so they can predict whom the cow will ask next for her moo.

Creating the Best Literacy Block Ever

All hands are up as students eagerly await an opportunity to share their connections to the read-aloud *Beetle Bop* by Denise Fleming. Gayle can easily observe the students who are using prior knowledge and information from the text and pictures to make connections.

Intentional Instruction ~

It has always been our job to teach directly and explicitly in response to students' needs—carefully demonstrating, specifically showing how, clearly explaining. Whatever we want our students to do well, we first have to show them how.

—Regie Routman, *Conversations: Strategies for Teaching, Learning, and Evaluating* (1999)

This literature discussion group is engaged in a conversation about the problem of the lost mittens in their book *Junie B. Jones Is Not a Crook* by Barbara Park. Judith thinks that Junie B. is a crook, while Leonid and Kathy believe somebody else stole the mittens because the author said she is not a crook.

Gayle conducts an individual student conference with Judith, who is having difficulty identifying the problem and solution of the story she has just read in her literature journal. Gayle is showing her how to revisit her book to validate her thinking.

Gayle conducts a reading conference during intentional instruction. She listens to Tori share her favorite part of a book before she asks her to retell the book orally. In her previous conference, Tori struggled to sequence the events of the story she had read.

Creating the Best Literacy Block Ever

Independent Engagement ∼

Kids need to read a lot if they are to become good readers. The evidence on this point is overwhelming. To ensure that all students read a lot, schools need to develop standards for expected volume of reading (and writing). The cornerstone of an effective school organizational plan is allocating sufficient time for lots of reading and writing.

—Richard Allington, *What Really Matters for Struggling Readers: Designing Research-Based Programs* (2005b)

James and Mark are engaged in independent reading of self-selected books. Each is in his own world, engrossed in different genres. James is reading a fiction book recommended by a classmate, and Mark is reading nonfiction for a research project.

Beth listens to one of her favorite reads on an iPod. When she finishes, she will read the book orally into the iPod, to be discussed at her next conference with Gayle. Beth is working on reading fluently to refine her comprehension.

Mary Beth enjoys reading and rereading the book she will conference on with Gayle tomorrow. She has read all of the books in the Magic Tree House series and is wondering about what she will read next.

James can't read enough books about sea life. He lived on an island in Southeast Asia when his father was in the military. He is a reluctant reader on many topics, but he enjoys and comprehends anything about the ocean, no matter the reading level.

Creating the Best Literacy Block Ever

Peer Instruction ~

I believe that the school is primarily a social institution. Education being a social process, the school is simply that form of community life in which all those agencies are concentrated that will be most effective in bringing the child to share in the inherited resources . . . and to use his own powers for social ends.

— John Dewey, "My Pedagogic Creed" (1998)

Jeremy and Robin compare the events between the book and in the movie adaptation of C. S. Lewis's *Chronicles of Narnia*. They are using a Venn diagram to demonstrate the similarities and differences between media and text.

Carmen, Tyler, and Brittney reread a passage in *Frog and Toad Are Friends* to resolve their differing interpretations.

Leonid and Tanisha and Brock and Olivia are deeply engrossed in investigating bats for their theme immersion. The pairs are in different stages of their research. Leonid and Tanisha are still gathering information, while Brock and Olivia are taking notes about what they have just read.

Kanesha, Mary Beth, and Leonid practice a Readers Theater skit they will present at the next day's community sharing. They are intent on reading with expression so the audience will enjoy their presentation.

Creating the Best Literacy Block Ever

Community Sharing ~

Life in a learning community is helped along by the interests, ideas, and support of others. Social life is not snuffed out; it is nurtured and used to advance learning in the best way possible. Caring and interest of others breathe purpose and life into learning.   —Ralph Peterson, *Life in a Crowded Place* (1992)

Kanesha shares some unfamiliar words with the class during the sharing. As Gayle looks at the list, she mentally notes that during intentional teaching she needs to work with Kanesha on inferring meaning of words using context clues.

Brittany is sharing some facts she learned about desert animals during her reading. One group of animals she read about was javelinas. Someone suggested that she read the fiction book *The Three Javelinas*.

Literacy Block Framework

Community Gathering Suggested time: up to 15 minutes

Focus lesson, read-aloud, think-aloud, shared reading, interactive writing, author studies

Intentional Instruction Suggested time: 30–45 minutes.
Activities in all columns occur simultaneously during workshop.

Intentional Instruction	Independent Engagement	Peer Interaction
Individual conferences (daily) ▪ Assessment (miscue analysis, running record) ▪ Oral reading ▪ Strategy/**concept check** ▪ Reading **response** Small-group instruction (as needed) ▪ Guided reading ▪ Shared reading ▪ Language experience ▪ Word study Rove the room (daily)	Independent reading of appropriate self-selected text (usually beyond emergent level) Literacy encounters with appropriate texts ▪ Listening ▪ Technology: computer, iPod ▪ Big books ▪ Word study Response journals Independent writing Fine-arts representations	Peer conferences Literature circles Readers Theater Plays (writing and/or performing) Technology book projects (podcasting) Buddy reading Written book reviews Book talks Word study Reciprocal teaching Book clubs Webbing Response groups for writers Book recommendations Buddy reading Book discussions

(Optional) Community Sharing Suggested time: up to 10 minutes

Examples of activities: author's chair, student's reading of short excerpt from book (e.g., favorite part), book recommendations, turn and talk; responses to questions and prompts such as *What did you learn about yourself as a reader or a writer?, What new facts/information/words, etc., did you encounter?*

· CHAPTER 1 ·

A Literacy Block Makes Your Reading/Writing World Go 'Round

A literacy block is a designated time during which students and teachers work together as a community to enhance reading and writing development and enjoyment. This block of time is very different from a skills-based classroom because ideally we design the curriculum based on the strengths and needs of our students rather than following a set curriculum. We are constantly assessing students to determine their strengths and identify strategies that need strengthening by reading quality literature.

Most of us find it difficult if not impossible to meet the needs of all students. Just as we want to do everything perfectly in our personal lives as a spouse, a parent, or a friend, we also want to be the perfect teacher. We want to improve the life of every child we teach, and if a child isn't functioning at an expected level, we want to find the magic bullet to solve the problem. We simply want to fulfill all unmet needs. We don't want to waste a minute. We want each child to like the read-aloud books, and we want to always plan interesting experiences.

The Literacy Block: Time and Logistics ~

There is no standard or optimum number of minutes for the reading block. Teachers tell us the length ranges from one hour to two hours, although some teachers have a literacy block that includes the writing workshop, which, of course, lengthens the block. We encourage the combination of the reading and writing blocks, but few teachers tell us they combine the two. We have known a few teachers who have incorporated both into an excellent literacy workshop, but it takes years to get to that point. Most of these teachers began with separate reading and writing blocks, which evolved into one seamless workshop.

The framework we are sharing with you can be expanded from 90 minutes to a longer experience. We would be cautious about decreasing the time, however, because students need adequate time to engage with text. If you have no choice but to work within a one-hour block, you can still implement many of our ideas.

As we will state in other parts of the book, we do not believe we have the perfect solution to every teacher's reading block questions, but our notions have helped many teachers. In the following pages, we explain the framework in detail. We hope this explanation helps you critique your current practices and explore new ideas.

We are not suggesting you abandon everything you are doing, because many of your practices will likely fit into the framework. The old saying "There is nothing new under the sun" is true much of the time in reading instruction. The important thing is that you reflect on your practice and continue to learn.

The Five Components of the Literacy Block ~

Whether you have a literature-based or commercial program, we recommend you build your reading block around five components. As a quick overview, here are the components and a short explanation of each. Then we address each one in turn and provide more detailed information.

Community Gathering

The opening component creates the mood for the block that follows. The oral reading of a poem or other short text, a shared reading of a big book, or a whole group focus lesson builds a community where literacy thrives.

Intentional Instruction

This component comprises the majority of your time spent during the reading block. You are busy conducting shared reading sessions, supportive reading sessions, focus lessons with a small group, or individual student reading conferences.

Independent Engagement

This component occurs simultaneously with intentional instruction. After all, what are the rest of the children doing while you are engaged in intentional instruction with individuals or small groups? Students are reading independently for lengthy periods of time. Although students may be engaged in reading-related activities such as responding to reading in journals, they must spend the majority of this time reading to make optimal gains in their reading development.

Peer Interaction

Along with independent engagement, this component also occurs simultaneously with intentional instruction. During this time, students are working together in pairs, triads, or small groups. Their interactive literacy activities may include book discussions, technology projects, art projects, or reading games that highlight a focus strategy.

Community Sharing

This conclusion of the reading block provides students an opportunity to share with one another such experiences as their passion for a particular book or excerpts from their journals. The time allotted for this component is brief.

A Closer Look at Each Component ~

Community Gathering

The community gathering is a daily occurrence that brings the classroom community together to begin the reading block. The suggested time for this component of the block is up to 15 minutes. The time will vary according to the experiences we plan for this component. Also, we can't determine in advance the amount of discussion that will follow a piece of literature. We can't always predict what will evoke the passions of students. A picture book that we choose for one reason may fall flat or become the impetus for a theme immersion. On other days, the students may express so much interest about a topic that we have to stop the discussion and continue it later. Spontaneity is a factor that you don't want to discount. There should always be some degree of flexibility built into the time frame because of the unpredictable nature of children's notions. On the other hand, we feel it is important to watch the clock carefully, as this component can easily extend past 15 minutes and consequently decrease the amount of time children have to interact individually with texts, not to mention the time we have to work with children individually or in small groups.

be a form of money and it must be Italian, because the book takes place in Italy. I used what we call the context of the sentence and all the ways in which written language is constructed to figure out the meaning of this word."

Teacher as Co-Learner

We also share with our students that we are co-learners within the classroom community. When we make statements such as the ones below, we send a message to students that we are intellectually curious and that we learn from a variety of sources and people.

- You taught me something when you talked about the different new dinosaurs. I knew most of them, but the lambeosaurus was new to me.

- Just like you, I add new words to my vocabulary every day. Many books that I have read have at least one new word for me.

- I'm not sure how to pronounce Caribbean. I've heard it pronounced a couple of different ways, and I'm frankly not sure which one is correct. Maybe we can find this out together.

- I want to remember how this book began because I can use that technique in my own writing.

- Together we can learn more about wind energy. We should all be on the lookout for newspaper and magazine articles and maybe books on the topic.

Setting the Stage for Literature Extensions

Often we want to begin a literature happening that will be extended during the peer interaction time or independent reading time. After reading a piece of literature, we can ask pairs or triads of children to follow by developing a puppet show based on what we read. We can ask them to rewrite a scene from a read-aloud with a peer. Many of our peer interaction activities can come from literature that was first read during the gathering.

Focus Lessons

We prefer the term *focus lesson* to *mini-lesson*. The *mini* prefix has created some misconceptions about the importance and intentionality of these experiences. A mini-lesson has been misinterpreted by some educators as a brief mentioning of a skill or strategy with little follow-up, akin to a scattering of fairy dust across the classroom with the teacher's hope and a prayer that the instruction "sticks" to all students. The term *focus* implies a more serious and intentional approach to reading instruction.

A focus lesson is a short period of time during which you deliver important information to your students to guide them in their literacy development. You are likely to do most of the talking during this time. You want to impart this important knowledge in the shortest period of time possible while thoroughly but succinctly delivering your message. These short lessons allow you to devote the majority of your reading block time to independent student reading, conferring with individuals, working with small groups of students, and providing opportunities for students to learn from one another.

Focus lessons can be divided into seven different categories. The listing below includes examples in each category.

- Reading block procedures: how to carry through the block from start to finish

- Strategies: cognitive processes readers use to process text

- Rote literacy skills: social knowledge such as learning the alphabet, connecting the conventions of print, or mastering book-handling skills

- Literary elements: narrative structures such as setting, characters, and plot, as well as nonfiction text structures such as chronology, cause and effect, and description

- The writer's craft: figurative language the author uses such as similes and metaphors, and writing techniques like repetition, sentence length, and organization

- Self-assessment: students' reflections on reading process, reading progress, and reading dispositions; retrospective miscue analysis, which is described in Chapters 4 and 5, also fits into this category

- Socialization skills: knowledge and skills necessary to work together successfully with the teacher and others during the reading block

Procedure Focus Lessons

Focus lessons at the beginning of the school year will fall primarily into this category. This "front-loading" of information provides children with the understanding of how things are done during the reading block. Once children practice and internalize the routines, they become more self-directed, you have more time to spend with individuals and small groups, and you maximize learning. Sometimes you might feel that you aren't teaching anything, but you are laying the groundwork so the teaching of content and process can occur.

Here are some examples of procedure focus lessons:

■ What is expected of students during each component of the reading block, e.g., "During the community gathering, you will sit quietly on the floor and listen to me. Once our gathering is completed, you will find your reading folder and book and return to your table unless you are reading with me or working with a partner."

■ Where students are to keep materials such as books, reading folders, and project supplies

■ How the books are organized in the classroom

■ How to check books in and out of the classroom library

■ How to select appropriate books

■ How to sign up for literacy centers, conferences, peer experiences, or community sharing events

Strategy Focus Lessons

A strategy is an action learners take to help literacy development occur. Examples of strategy focus lessons include:

■ "Chunking" part of a word to determine pronunciation

■ Using context to determine the meaning of an unfamiliar word

■ Using picture cues to determine the meaning of words and text

■ Asking self, "Does this make sense to me?"

■ Asking self, "Does this sound like language to me?"

■ Using comprehension strategies such as predicting, using prior knowledge, retelling, visualizing, asking questions, synthesizing, summarizing, inferring, and determining important information

■ Using fix-up strategies such as rereading and slowing reading pace

■ Using knowledge of narrative and nonfiction text structure to comprehend text

Rote Literacy Skills Focus Lessons

According to Jean Piaget (1971), one form of knowledge that children acquire is social knowledge, or knowledge that is communicated within one's culture. In other words, this is information that someone tells us, and this form of communication is the easiest way for children to learn this knowledge. Examples of focus lessons in this category include:

- The letters of the alphabet
- The sounds of letters
- The difference between consonants and vowels
- Graphophonic knowledge such as blends, digraphs, and vowel patterns
- Concepts of print
- Book-handling skills
- Structural analysis skills such as prefixes, suffixes, and root words
- The definition of words used in a lean rather than rich context
- Antonyms, synonyms, and homonyms

Literary Elements Focus Lessons

Text is organized in certain patterns. For example, most fiction contains a setting, a main character, a problem for the main character to solve or a goal to be reached, and then a resolution to the problem or an attainment of the goal. Nonfiction, on the other hand, is not that predictable. Informational books and materials are written using different text structures. Knowledge of these patterns and structures helps children to better comprehend text, either fiction or nonfiction. Examples of focus lessons in this category include:

- Fiction elements: setting, major character, minor characters, problem/goal, plot line, resolution
- Genres
- Nonfiction text features: table of contents, glossary, captions, diagrams, boldface words
- Nonfiction text structures: description, cause and effect, problem and solution, chronology, compare and contrast

The Writer's Craft Focus Lessons

Primary children are not too young to start understanding the reading and writing connection. When we help children notice the way an author turns a phrase or organizes a text, we are planting seeds that will facilitate the replication of these techniques in their own writing pieces. They also discover the beauty of language, which can enhance reading pleasure. Examples of writer's craft focus lessons include:

- Simile, metaphor, onomatopoeia
- Precise nouns and verbs
- Size of text and type of font
- Patterns such as repetitions or contrasts such as "fortunately/unfortunately"

Self-Assessment Focus Lessons

Even primary students need to pause and reflect on their learning processes, yet this ability does not come easily. Therefore, these focus lesson topics are useful:

- Daily reflections: What did I learn today? How well did I read my new book?
- Weekly reflections: What have I learned to do in reading this week?
- Retrospective miscue analysis (explained on p. 140 in Chapter 4)
- Demonstration for assembling a reading portfolio
- Goal setting

Socialization Skills Focus Lessons

Life in a crowded classroom isn't always easy. Students benefit when you take the time for these focus lessons:

- Turn and talk
- Think–pair–share
- Guidelines for partner reading
- Instructions for beginning, sustaining, and concluding a literature circle or a book club
- Discussion etiquette
- Procedures for orderly sharing of materials
- Respectful responses to others' viewpoints
- Peer conferences
- Taking turns

De-Emphasize Competition

How we spend the time during this component should be a combination of setting the stage for the reading block, promoting pleasure with literacy, and yes, teaching intentionally the various aspects of literacy. We must do all of this, however, without having literacy winners or losers. This means when visitors enter the classroom, they won't find contests or special treats for the best readers or charts identifying who has read the most pages or who has read the most difficult text. The negative messages these exercises send to the underachiever cannot be measured but will have far-ranging effects.

Intentional Instruction

In terms of purposeful instruction, this component of the reading block requires the most planning but can also be the most rewarding time of your day. You are up close and personal with the children in your classroom—listening to them read, asking questions, facilitating a small-group discussion, or delivering a focus lesson, among various other events.

Teacher and Student Roles

The bulk of the reading block is spent with students in small groups or individually. Some of the students will be working directly with you, while others are engaged in independent reading or peer interactions. Our intentional teaching is based on individual assessments that have determined the needs of the students. In Chapter 8, we provide detailed suggestions for assessment tools and practices.

Because the needs and interests of our children change from day to day, no two days in the classroom look the same. Sometimes we will have a conference with the same student two days in a row, but we won't necessarily meet with the same small groups of students day after day. Students' needs and interests dictate our every move as we try to reach as many as possible.

Minimize Interruptions From Students

Children must come to understand early in the school year that your time with individual students or small groups must be considered sacred and that no interruptions are to occur unless there is an emergency. One technique that helps is to designate a child to be a class helper during this period. It shouldn't be the same child each day, but make sure someone is always available to help others. Also, ask children to try to figure out words by themselves and to decide whether it is important to the meaning of the story to know the word. Ask students to use the words around the important unknown word as well as the picture. Students can also write words on a sticky note for further discussion with you or other students.

Between conferences and small-group sessions, get up from your chair and "rove the room," a term we borrowed from teachers in New Zealand. Make a quick sweep by all children working independently or together. Monitor to make sure everyone is engaged, and provide brief assistance if needed. Then get back to the other students, preparing for your intentional teaching as quickly as possible.

Talk With Students, and Then Talk Some More

We can't emphasize enough how important student talk is during your intentional teaching time with them. When students talk about what they are reading, they are deepening their understanding of the text. Talking is a critical conduit into comprehension. During individual conferences and small-group instruction, discuss texts with children to help them analyze and think critically. Even kindergartners who have listened to a story will think deeply as they discuss their own personal meanings. The same logic they employ when they discuss texts will be used when they are comprehending texts independently.

As Students Travel Their Reading Paths

Although the structure of this component will look very similar from one early childhood grade to the other, the nature of the instruction will look different. As students progress though the grades, texts become more sophisticated and classroom discussions become more insightful. Children are also able to work independently for longer periods of time. Obviously, we would expect more emphasis on comprehension than on word work in third grade than in kindergarten. Chapters 2 through 5 will provide grade-specific explanations for your role during this component.

Independent Engagement

We are totally committed to the value of independent reading, and we want children to select their own reading throughout the school day. The champion of independent reading is Richard Allington (2008), who speaks and writes about the importance of children reading texts for extended periods of time. Allington is to reading engagement what Stephen Krashen (2004) is to the importance of the availability of good children's literature and libraries.

What Are Students Reading?

The first answer is excellent children's literature from your classroom, school, or public library and maybe from the child's personal collection. Texts that students read during this time should be self-selected from appropriate texts for that particular student. We aren't opposed to asking students to sometimes select from several tubs of books or one bookshelf that contains leveled texts for some of their reading. Please notice that we aren't saying that all texts in your library room should be leveled. Interest in a book takes priority over the level of the text, although we certainly want students to be really reading and not just holding and "fake-reading" books. We are not suggesting that if Johnny selects *War and Peace* and can't understand anything he should hang on to the book for weeks. What we are saying is that we are opposed to the over-leveling that has occurred in some classrooms across the country. There are times during shared reading, supportive reading, and some independent reading that we want to make certain that books are on an appropriate level for the children and that the levels were predetermined by assessment. We do, however, want to make sure that we don't stifle interest in reading by telling a child that he or she can't read a particular book.

Maryann now feels ashamed that she taught children the five-finger method of knowing whether a book was too hard. She hates to admit it, but she actually told children that if they came to five words they didn't know on a page, then the book was too hard. She made no allowances for the number of words on the page and most especially whether the reader was making sense of the text. She now knows that an interested reader can make meaning even when he or she doesn't know five or more words on a page. She wishes she had said to students, "Don't continue reading a book that isn't making sense." This also pertains to the "just right" book method.

Representing Knowledge

This time can also be spent by children representing their reading knowledge through a variety of methods. One of the most common examples is a reading response journal. Other vehicles can be art and dramatization as well as technology projects. These representation options will be discussed in the grade-specific chapters that follow. One caveat we offer is to monitor closely how much time students are spending in response activities in relation to actual silent reading time. Silent reading should far outweigh any response activity. Voluminous reading is critical to reading development.

Peer Interaction

During intentional teaching with small groups or individuals and independent reading time, some students may be engaged in interactive work. An essential aspect of the reading block is peers working together in pairs or in triads.

Reading Is a Social Act

Students can learn much from each other. Reading and listening are ways students gain new information, and speaking and writing are how they share their new learning. Through student-to-student interaction combined with teacher questioning, learners move to higher levels in their thinking. It is through the exchange of points of view that students often change their ideas; therefore, it is essential that there are times during the day when students talk to one another about substantial ideas. Students also need to exchange different points of view to become objective in their thinking. Having students discuss points of view also creates schema for future reference when needed.

Sometimes when we talk to teachers about the exchange of ideas and we use the term *arguing*, someone will say, "Oh, you don't mean arguing." Our response is, "Yes, we do mean arguing." We want our students to be passionate about the views they hold and to verbalize them to peers and teachers. The word *argue* conjures up different emotions, and we certainly don't mean throwing things or shouting. We mean dialogues and interchanges like the following:

> Marsha: "I think we see all the islands there are in the world on our map. I don't think there are any islands other than the ones we see."
> Louisa: "My uncle flew back from Mexico City to New Orleans and he said there were islands everywhere. Some were little ones and others were pretty big. None of them were shown on the map."
>
> This second-grade class was divided on whether there were lots of little islands or only the ones on the world map. They talked to parents and read books. Finally, they asked Louisa's pilot uncle who flies international routes to visit the class and to talk to them. He told the students that there were indeed lots of islands that don't show up on the maps in social studies books. He brought an aviation map in which all land masses were shown. He discussed how ship captains also had maps that indicated every island, and also told the class that sometimes new islands appear or disappear because of earthquakes. Now, whenever the students look at a map of water,

they will know they are looking at one type of map. Social interaction and new information helped the students move to a higher level of thinking.

- Another example of building new knowledge through social interaction was when Jonathon distributed samples of mixed nuts left over from a PTA function. The class had been reading about almond trees growing in California. They sorted and identified the different nuts and plotted on a chart where some thought each nut grew, in the ground or on a tree. These conversations led to research on what is a nut, where nuts grow, and how a seed is different from a nut.

    Students argued over whether all macadamia nuts come from Hawaii, since most of the packages in their stores were labeled with the word *Hawaii*. They argued about whether cashews grow like peanuts since they look similar. They found it hard to believe when they saw pictures of a cashew growing on the end of what appeared to be a fruit, and they also learned there are many countries near the equator where cashews grow. As they asked questions of adults and other children, read books, and used the computer, they changed their ideas about nuts and where they grow.

- Three first graders were discussing whether firefighters always sleep at the fire station or if they ever go home. Catherine was adamant that firefighters always sleep at the station, because she had seen beds there during a kindergarten field trip to a new fire station in the community. Jerold said, "No, they don't always sleep there because Richard, my neighbor, comes home in a big red pickup truck and sleeps at home some nights." Talking to their parents and friends, reading books, and interviewing firemen resulted in the class discovering firefighters don't just sleep at the station.

In Chapters 2 through 5 are other suggestions with regard to peer interaction. Some of these experiences include Readers Theater productions and technology projects.

Community Sharing

There is no exact time period that the sharing should last, but the range is usually between five and eight minutes. This short closing to the reading block wraps up the session with a warm feeling; however, there are reasons that go beyond affective purposes. First, let us say that there is no one right way to conduct community sharing. We have observed, however, a number of different styles for sharing:

- Spontaneous

- Invited

- Planned

- A combination of the three styles on different days

Often the sharing is a blending of discussions of different texts, sharing of products related to book extensions, and discoveries students have made about reading and writing processes, such as the results of retrospective miscue. "What I learned today about myself as a reader" often is a part of the conversation.

Some excellent teachers we know have children gather and then say to them something like "Who has something they would like to present to the class?" or "You have all been very busy today doing some marvelous things. I would like some of you who are willing to share the essence of your discussions with other class members." This spontaneous sharing can present rich results.

Sometimes we notice students engaged in experiences that we want them to share with the entire class. We invite them to share either that day or on a future day. An example we saw was a pair of third graders who had both watched the video of Chris Van Allsburg's *The Polar Express*. They had watched the video twice and reread the book so they could discuss places where the video was different from the book. They also shared how the visual images they imagined were different from the video version. Other children who had seen the movie joined in the discussion.

Sometimes teachers will have a planned rotating schedule of children who are responsible for sharing. Sometimes they choose from a list of children who haven't presented during a given week or they ask children to sign up. One day a small group that was planning the gatherings for the week had a schedule that included everyone in the class. On the Thursday before the week began, the students went around the room asking if anyone was writing a play, had a choral reading prepared, had a mural in the works, or had anything else they were prepared to present. The group then slotted the different presentations, figured out who wasn't in any of the groups, and asked those individuals if they would read a poem or give a short book review. Before the week began, there was a complete schedule of the gathering. We don't recommend that every week be scheduled this way, but it is an option that works for some teachers. Also, you may display charts around the room on which students have posted questions or vocabulary about texts they are reading that will be discussed.

Getting Started ~

Establish Routines

Whenever you institute a new format, it takes time for you and your students to adjust to the organization. Twenty-plus human beings working within the confines of a classroom is challenging. Although we believe that fostering autonomy should be the aim of education, we know that certain routines are necessary for you to meet the needs of so many students within a given time frame. Something as simple as when and how often you can interrupt the teacher during the reading workshop is important. Like you, we value the importance of involving children in making rules. Gayle had a "gripe basket" where students deposited complaints while she was working with other students and didn't want to be disturbed. Chapter 6 includes an explanation of rituals and routines to establish in your classroom.

With explanation and practice, kindergartners and older primary children have no difficulty understanding what they are supposed to do during the block. Some explanations may include "We are all together during this time" and "I'm with a small group of you while everyone works independently, except for Joshua, Reagan, and Roderick, who are working together on recording their poem for the listening center." Kindergarten teachers often use color codes to show rotations throughout the reading block.

Organize Your Classroom

Your classroom organization and arrangement have a lot to do with successful implementation of a reading block. In Chapter 6 we discuss the physical arrangement of classrooms. No two classrooms should be alike, because configuration, furnishings, and needs are different. Just as we exercise our individual tastes in decorating our personal spaces, we also share ourselves through our classroom space; however, several general needs should be considered:

- Spaces for meetings
- A sense of student ownership of the classroom achieved through the display of individual and group products
- Easy access to materials
- Sufficient amount of text in the room to support choice in independent reading

Understand the Importance of Intention, Independence, and Interaction

Chapters 2 through 5 provide explanations and activities for all components of the reading block for the different primary grades. You will discover suggestions for the intentional teaching of reading strategies, independent student reading and experiences, and peer interaction. Each of these components contribute to successful reading development for young children.

In Conclusion ∽

Our model of a literacy block contains five components: a community gathering, intentional instruction, independent engagement, peer interaction, and a closing community sharing. Throughout the literacy block, students are engaged in rich experiences within a safe and warm learning family.

Kindergarten Literacy Block

Community Gathering Suggested time: up to 15 minutes

- Reading aloud short texts
- Shared reading of enlarged texts
- Focus lessons
- Interactive writing
- Author studies
- Dictation
- Vocabulary study

Intentional Instruction Suggested time: 30–45 minutes

Activities in all columns occur simultaneously during workshop.

Teacher/student Instruction	Independent Engagement	Peer Interaction
- Discussion of texts - Think-alouds - Reading assessments - Reading conferences - Guided reading - Supportive reading - Focus lessons - Rove the room	- Independent reading of appropriate self-selected text (usually beyond emergent level) - Book logs - Reading response journals - Creating word logs - Independent research - Technology projects - Listening stations - Word work - Fine-arts representations	- Sharing dramatizations - Graphic organizers - Technology projects - Word work - Reading big books together - Partner reading - Fine-arts representations

(Optional) Community Sharing Suggested time: up to 10 minutes

- Rereading a big book
- Student reading of selected passages
- Role-playing/dramatizations
- Discussion of texts and/or reading processes

CHAPTER 2

The Kindergarten Literacy Block

It's 9:00 Monday morning and Kim starts a recording by Dr. Jean Feldman, which signals her kindergartners to move to the rug for the 15-minute community gathering. When they arrive, they begin singing along with the song "Tutti Ta Ta" and making hand gestures for the words they are singing. When the song finishes, the children sit and wait for the community gathering to begin. The rituals and routines of the classroom are so ingrained in these kindergartners' minds that they know exactly what to expect from their teacher.

Kim and the children start reading the nursery rhymes from last week. She has written the nursery rhymes on charts for shared reading. Together, Kim and the children read the first rhyme, "Little Jack Horner." Kim then asks, "Who heard some rhyming words in that poem?" Children raise their hands, anxiously wanting to show their knowledge. Jemisha states that *Horner* and *corner* rhyme, and Andrew volunteers that *plum* and *thumb* rhyme. Next, Kim reviews a nursery rhyme they had previously read, and she observes that most of the students demonstrated understanding of the pairs of rhyming words.

Next they read the poem "Peas Porridge Hot," and Kim asks, "What sound do *peas* and *porridge* start with?" Almost all of the children give her the /p/ sound. She continues, "What are some more words that start with that sound?" The children immediately give examples, letting her know that with the exception of two students, they have an understanding of that particular consonant sound.

Finally, they read the last nursery rhyme, "Jack and Jill," together. Kim asks the group, "What is this poem talking about?" Kenisha replies, "This boy and girl go up a hill and get some water." Kim then asks, "Where do you think it takes place?" Houston answers, "Well, I think it was outside on top of this mountain." Several children correct Houston by stating, "No, it's not a mountain. It's a hill. A mountain is much bigger." Kim continues the discussion by asking, "Why do you think Jack and Jill were getting a pail of water?" The children immediately supply answers that let her know that they can use prior knowledge to answer this last question. She feels satisfied about the children's reading development over the past week.

Following this shared reading experience, Kim begins her read-aloud with the book *Click, Clack, Moo: Cows That Type* by Doreen Cronin by asking some questions to activate their content knowledge. "Who do you think some of the characters will be in this book?" Kim asks the children. Jeremy looks at the cover of the book and says, "Well, I see some cows and I see a duck and a chicken."

Allison states, "The title has the word *cows* in it, so I think it's going to be about cows, too, but they can't type. They don't have fingers!"

"Why do you think the author put the words *click, clack,* and *moo* in the title?" Kim continues.

Elvira exclaims, "Cows moo, but they don't click and clack! What does click and clack mean, anyway?"

Kim replies, "Well, let's look at the cover of the book to see if it will help us answer your question."

"Miss Kim, what is that thing the cows are looking at?" asks Elvira.

Kim replies, "What do you think it is?"

Kids reply, "We don't know. We've never seen that thing before."

Kim continues, "The word *type* is in the title. What does the word *type* mean?"

Angelica cries, "Oh, my daddy types on a computer, but it doesn't look like that thing! What is it?"

Kim answers, "It's called a typewriter, but we don't use those anymore. When we go to the computer lab, we will look up some pictures of typewriters. Ask your parents if they have a typewriter at home or have ever used one. Using the title and the pictures, tell me what you think the book will be about."

Kim walks over to the whiteboard and tells the students that she will record their predictions, and after they read the book they will revisit their predictions to see if they were correct.

James raises his hand and says, "Well, I think the cows are scared of that thing. Look at their eyes. I think they found it and don't know what it is."

Tiffany states, "I think the cows are going to start typing because in the title it says that cows type and he's got his foot up over that thing and the duck is holding some paper for him."

After Kim writes their predictions on the whiteboard, she says, "Let's read the book and see if we can get some answers for all these questions."

Kim begins her read-aloud, pausing during the reading to continue to build on the strategies, prediction, and the use of prior knowledge used during their grand conversations about the nursery rhyme "Jack and Jill." On the first page she reads, "Farmer Brown has a problem. His cows like to type. All day long he hears click, clack, moo. Click, clack, moo. Clickety, clack, moo." Kim thinks aloud, "Hmm. I think that answers one of our questions about what *click clack* means. I'm going to read the page again and listen carefully to see if our question is answered. That's what good readers do. They reread to find the answers to their questions."

Molly raises her hand after the rereading. "I know what *click clack* means. It's when that cow puts down his foot on that thing. It makes a noise that says 'click clack' and then he moos."

Kim continues in this same manner, looking for the answers to their questions and focusing on picture cues and student dialogue to bring meaning to the text for the students. When they finish the read-aloud, she rereads their predictions and asks if any of them were correct.

Elvira raises her hand and says, "Yes, the one about typing is right because the cows did type."

Kim tells them that this book is in the listening center so they can listen to the story a second time. Afterward, they have the opportunity to write about their favorite character in the book or to write a letter to Farmer Brown.

Next, Kim reviews the "Reading Encounters" chart with the class to make sure that each child knows what to do. By using three 20-minute rotations, Kim sees three different groups of children for intentional instruction. Suzy and Henry walk over to the chart, on which the teacher has purposely chosen the centers they will engage in that particular day. Suzy sees that she will go to the focus encounter, where she will meet with the teacher and work on a strategy or concept that she needs. This focus center lesson is determined through assessment data and teacher observations. Suzy goes over to the cubbies and finds the basket with her name on it. The basket contains books and games that will be used during the focus center. She carries it to the table in the center of the room, where she will meet with the teacher and Kenisha, Houston, and Elvira to work on hearing medial sounds in words. Henry walks to the reading center, where he will engage with the nursery rhymes the children have read in their whole-group gathering. He will read the nursery rhymes and then re-create the nursery rhyme puzzles with Tiffany, James, Allison, and Jessica. Other children check the chart, find the necessary materials, and travel to their literacy encounter location. After this first 20-minute segment of reading encounters, the bell chimes and the students move to their second rotation. The bell chime at the end of each rotation signals the students to move to their next encounter. These encounter routines are established at the beginning of the year and remain constant throughout the year.

During the second rotation, Kim meets with another small group of children in the focus center for intentional teaching. As mentioned previously, this intentional instruction is guided by assessment data, including teacher observation. In this second focus lesson, Kim and the children begin a building-words activity. The children explore the –og, –ot, and –ug word families with Kim. She reads a short poem. They then begin a second reading of the poem, and Kim asks different students to raise their hands when they hear a word that ends with one of those word chunks. The student then circles that word on the chart. Finally, the children use magnetic letters and boards to make words using these rimes.

While Kim meets with children for a focus lesson, the other children work together in pairs, triads, or groups of four. During this time, the children read books on the BookFlix Web site on the computer, listen to stories on iPods, downloaded from United Streaming, partner-read simple alphabet books, and complete nursery rhyme word puzzles—all rich experiences to enhance listening and reading comprehension. As the kindergartners begin reading connected text, the focus groups become more of a reading workshop. The teacher will use a conference form (Resource 2-16, page 86) and an instructional text progression form to document conferences and update needs and growth in student learning.

Toward the end of intentional instruction and during the children's independent practice, Kim walks around the room checking on the other groups of students and making sure everyone is engaged. As she observes students practicing reading tasks and reading texts, she makes notes on her recording sheet. These notes help inform her instruction for the next day and bring to her attention those encounters that are not engaging students and those that are not purposeful. After the third rotation, the bell chimes and the students move to the rug for a community gathering to discuss what took place in the literacy encounters that day.

The Block in Kindergarten ∼

Now that you have had a glimpse of a kindergarten classroom, we will discuss the daily reading block and help you organize your time. Each class of kindergarten students is different. The nature of the block may vary to meet the needs of your students. A majority of our classroom time will be spent on supportive strategies and providing a balanced diet of literacy experiences for emergent readers.

If you haven't read Margaret Mooney's *Reading To, With, and By Children* (1990) please put it on your "must-read" list. This text helps us understand the necessity of balance—reading aloud, reading with students during shared and guided reading, and providing opportunities for students to read independently.

Kindergarten students enter our classrooms at different reading levels ranging from pre-emergent and emergent stages to the beginning stage and occasionally to the independent stage. At the beginning of the kindergarten year, we help children learn routines and begin to know the children's unique personalities.

The kindergarten block looks different from other grades, but we contend the reading block should not be "letter of the week," a common practice in some kindergarten classrooms. It is our observation that many children come to kindergarten with much knowledge about letters through exposure to environmental print. McDonald's taught them *M*, and Kellogg's cereal taught them *K*. We don't want children to wait until the 26th week of the year to be able to use all the letters they either already know or those they need immediately to express ideas.

The community gathering and sharing times of the kindergarten reading block are the same in grades 1 through 3. Because most children can't read on their own at the beginning of the year, the independent component does not exist unless there are some children who come into kindergarten reading. The peer interaction component consists primarily of games, computer activities, listening, and "reading" big books and poems. The intentional component is a time of the block when the teacher focuses on student needs.

The Literacy Encounters charts have 20-minute rotations (see Resources 2-1 and 2-2). Each rotation has two sections: intentional literacy encounters and interactive literacy encounters. The teacher sees three different groups of children in intentional instruction.

You may be surprised that we don't recommend that a form of interactive writing be a part of the reading block. We believe there is no better beginning literacy practice for kindergartners than daily

See Resource 2-1, Literacy Encounters With Two Rotations, p. 71.

See Resource 2-2, Literacy Encounters With Three Rotations, p. 72.

news, but we suggest you implement it at a different time of the day. Children love to start the morning sharing ideas through daily news but we prefer to conduct this at another time because daily news can consume the entire time of the gathering each day. Again, we wholeheartedly support daily news because children learn so much about written language during this time. Many concepts and conventions of print and letter–sound relationships can be successfully taught as you think aloud as a writer and demonstrate what writers do.

Because most kindergartners aren't reading independently, it is necessary for us to organize the block with a heavy emphasis on intentional teaching and peer interaction.

Resource 2-1: *Literacy Encounters With Two Rotations*

Community Gathering

At the beginning of the year, we spend time during the gathering establishing rituals, routines, and procedures. These rituals and routines not only help your reading block run smoothly but they also help you build community.

We will discuss several activities appropriate for the gathering; however, we feel that demonstrating your own literacy to your kindergartners is one of the most effective ways to help them develop as readers. Even those students who have had frequent literacy experiences in the home and during preschool will benefit from seeing you share your own literacy process. Students who have had few literacy demonstrations will be mesmerized by the ease with which you read and write. Children who have had daily read-aloud experiences in the home will still benefit from you thinking aloud as a reader and writer.

We have chosen the following reading practices for the gathering because they are the ones we have used successfully with an entire class. We suggest that you provide a variety of these activities over the course of the year. We also remind you to be cognizant of the clock. The gathering is intended to be engaging and informative but brief. We have all experienced the temptation to linger over our favorite book or poem or conclude a shared reading with an exciting topic, but the bulk of the reading block needs to involve students practicing literacy tasks with you, with small groups and independently, in order to develop as readers.

Read-Alouds

The read-aloud you may choose to conduct at the beginning of the reading block is just one of several read-alouds you will provide during the day. We know kindergarten teachers who read six times each day, but the episodes are spread over the entire six and a half hours. New Zealand educators tell us that children need to hear 1,000 books, including repeated read-alouds of favorite books, before teachers begin formal instruction in reading (Tate, 2005).

This gathering time can be used to read many of the marvelous picture books that take no longer than five minutes, even allowing time for looking at the illustrations. You can also read poems, nursery rhymes, riddles on transparencies, charts, or big books. These texts can also be used later for shared reading. After reading the text aloud, ask your students to conduct a short oral retelling of the text. These retellings are valuable because they send a clear message that it is important to make meaning from text.

Thinking aloud about text is one of the most helpful strategies we can use when children are beginning to read. The idea of "How did you figure that out?" helps emergent readers who are struggling both with decoding and understanding the text. It is important to help them understand that what we read sounds like oral language. It is important that they understand that when it is nonsensical, they can reread and try to think about what they are having

■ Resource 2-2: *Literacy Encounters With Three Rotations*

difficulty understanding in the text.

The texts we choose for use in the reading block should be selected to meet the developmental and instructional needs of our students. These read-alouds help our students begin to understand the reading process and also learn about texts themselves, such as how a fiction book follows a predictable pattern of a main character overcoming a problem or reaching a goal. Although not the purpose of this specific read-aloud time, the incidental building of content knowledge is always an added benefit.

For a list of some of Gayle's favorite kindergarten books for read-alouds and focus lessons, please see page 69.

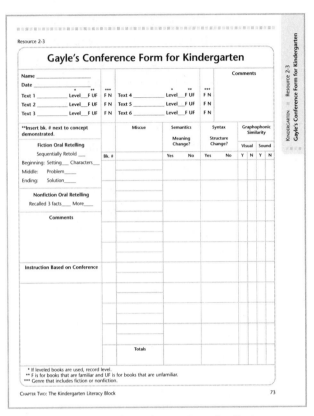

Resource 2-3: *Gayle's Conference Form for Kindergarten*

Shared Reading of Enlarged Texts

So much can be taught through the shared reading strategy. In fact, many children can learn to read from shared reading alone. We define shared reading as an instructional practice in which we provide enlarged text for children to observe while we read the text aloud. We move our finger or pointer under each line as we read aloud to direct children's attention to the corresponding text.

We can't talk about shared reading without mentioning Don Holdaway, an Australian educator who studied American research concerning the identification of early readers. He found that children who had been read to on the laps of family members were usually early readers. Holdaway set about to reproduce the lap-reading experience in the classroom with a whole class, and thus the shared reading strategy was born (1979). Shared reading is the perfect strategy for the kindergarten gathering because children are fully supported as they learn to read. If some of the children can already read, they read along with the other children. None of the children are required to read alone without your support and that of the other children.

Shared reading demonstrates everything that happens in the reading process. Through masking or covering certain letters or words with easily removable sticky tape we can emphasize graphophonic features and other cueing systems. For example, if our focus lesson is on recognizing the sight words *go*, *the*, and *to*, we can have students come up and place a piece of highlight tape on those words in the shared reading book or poem.

We can help students develop the ability to predict what will happen next by discussing pictures and text.

Shared reading is an incredibly useful strategy to support emergent readers. We hope you will read Bobbi Fisher and Emily Fisher Medvic's (2000) book *Perspectives on Shared Reading* and *Read It Again!* by Brenda Parkes (2000). Also, the chapter in *The Foundations of Literacy* by Don Holdaway (1979) is a seminal piece of writing about how to conduct shared reading sessions.

Some of Gayle's favorite big books are listed on page 70.

Resource 2-4: *Gayle's Strategies Conference Form for Kindergarten*

Focus Lessons

Focus lessons are very appropriate for kindergartners because by their very nature they must be brief. A focus lesson is just another name for a mini-lesson, but we prefer the term *focus lesson* because the word *focus* indicates that we are teaching purposefully those strategies that meet our learners where they are in their reading development. We define focus lessons as short periods of time lasting from three to seven minutes during which we introduce or review an important concept, skill, or strategy. Topics for these focus lessons can range from comprehension strategies to graphophonic knowledge, depending on curriculum and student needs.

An example of a kindergarten focus lesson is using picture clues to predict what is happening in a book. For example, after reading *No, David!* by David Shannon, we focus on each picture with the children and encourage them to study the clues contained in the illustrations to figure out why David keeps getting into trouble. The author developed this delightful tale from a book he remembered writing when he was five years old. On each page, he writes of a different action he is not supposed to be doing, such as tracking mud into the house.

We ask the students questions like "Why is David in the corner?" "Why is his mother mad?" and "How does David feel by the end of the book?"

Focus lessons are also discussed in the intentional teaching component of this chapter because they are effective with individuals, pairs, and triads, and with groups of five or six. The important thing to remember when teaching kindergartners is that the content of the focus lesson should be something students are ready to learn and is important to know for reading development. Most focus lessons on reading and writing strategies are repeated many times throughout the year because more is demanded of students as texts become more difficult.

Reading strategy books that have been helpful to us include *Reading With Meaning* by Debbie Miller (2002), *The Primary Comprehension Toolkit: Grades K–2* by Stephanie Harvey and Anne Goudvis (2008), and Developmental Studies Center's *Making Meaning* (2006).

See Resource 2-3, Gayle's Conference Form for Kindergarten, p. 73.

See Resource 2-4, Gayle's Strategies Conference Form for Kindergarten, p. 74.

Refer to Gayle's reading conference forms (Resources 2-3 and 2-4) for a list of strategies that can guide your focus lessons.

Interactive Writing

"Sharing the pen" is another phrase used to describe children and teachers engaged in thinking about writing and reading together. In this strategy, the children and teacher take turns writing letters and words. Interactive writing differs from daily news. The teacher acts as scribe for the children, doing all the writing in order to provide a demonstration of how to translate words to print.

The most important aspect of interactive writing is the constant support that students receive as they learn about written text. A large whiteboard, a big piece of chart paper, or an overhead projector and a marker are all we need along with an idea for a text. The idea for the text is interesting because it is primarily student-generated. For example, the antics of the two classroom gerbils can be the topic of a hundred different short texts. The topic for the paragraph can also come from us. We might ask the children to help us write about a recent field trip to view a play.

The emphasis is on the communication of ideas and constructing knowledge about phonemes, letters, words, sentences, and paragraphs to strengthen reading development. The reading and writing connection is never as obvious to us as during this strategy because we are helping our students become literate through both processes. We ask the students questions such as "What sound do you hear?" "What letter do you think comes first in *lamp*?" "Do you hear two or three sounds in *cup*?"

In kindergarten, conventional spelling should not be stressed. We believe children should write what they hear without the pressure of trying to spell words conventionally. Much of the time, what is written during interactive writing is not published and never leaves the classroom. If a letter is being composed to be sent to someone out of the classroom, at the very end of the drafting process we should edit the piece for mechanics, including conventional spelling. We also believe it is important to never "put down" invented spelling, but rather to say something like "Because we are sending our letter to the principal, we will make it like 'big people' spelling." Many teachers we know call themselves the "room editor" and say to their students, "I'm the oldest person in the classroom and I've been writing a long time, so I'm the editor." As we mentioned earlier, daily news is a great interactive strategy, but we prefer that it be conducted at other times during the day. The reading block is too full.

A book we recommend on interactive writing for the primary grades is *Dancing With a Pen*, published by the New Zealand Staff Ministry of Education (1992). Maryann's friend Ro Griffith was instrumental in the writing of this most informative book. We know you will find this book an invaluable resource on primary writing.

Author Studies

We suggest brief author studies for the gathering and reserving in-depth author studies for other times of the day. After we have read several works by one author, we will conduct a study of that author/illustrator/poet.

For example, after reading aloud a couple of works written and illustrated by Lois Ehlert, the creator of *Chicka Chicka Boom Boom* and *In My World*, we would share other books she has illustrated. Some of her other books are *Pie in the Sky*, *Leaf Man*, *Cuckoo Cucù*, and *Wag a Tail*. We would spend a few minutes with the children looking at her illustrations, comparing the differences and similarities among her books and discussing the different media she used for the illustrations.

We would then read a short biography of Ehlert and find pictures of her studios in Chicago and Maine. There are Web sites devoted to this important author-illustrator, including www.rif.org/art/illustrators/ehlert.mspx. We might then write her to tell her how much we love her work, excusing her from writing us back but instead asking her to use her time to illustrate more books for us to read.

Dictation

In dictation the teacher dictates words or short sentences for children to write. We like to use individual whiteboards for dictation, but clipboards and paper also work well. We highly recommend that kindergarten students write down a dictated sentence at least once a week. Observing how children write a dictated sentence can reveal much about graphophonic growth. Children who are comfortable sharing what they have written and who discuss their invented spellings with the class can help other students understand the graphophonic system.

Vocabulary Study

Kindergartners learn new words every day through incidental exposure, but we can also increase their vocabulary through deliberate actions. Studying vocabulary together as a community can be enjoyable in short spurts with useful words. We recommend having word study during the gathering segment for a few minutes at least once a week. The words can come from current read-aloud books and content-area texts. Not all unknown words are worth knowing, so we want to choose words that will help students understand what they read and express themselves orally and in writing. Having students act out words also helps them gain a lasting understanding.

Intentional Instruction

Intentional instruction refers to the bulk of time during the block when we work with individual children and small groups. In the beginning, the instruction generally takes the form of games that focus on a needed concept while engaging the students in the learning process. After a month of school, we begin to acquire a good feel of where our students are in their evolution toward literacy. We have an initial understanding of their graphophonic knowledge, their concepts of print, and their interest in learning to read.

In kindergarten, the intentional teaching primarily occurs during literacy encounters and reading conferences. During this time, we engage students in many different learning experiences that can confine us to a table or specific area of the room, so we like to informally roam the room at least once during this time. Not only is this a good break for us, but we learn a lot about our students when we roam. We can also conduct incidental teaching that is perfectly timed for a student who wants or needs our gentle support.

The students we work with and the number of students we work with every day changes throughout the year. When we write about small groups, we don't mean the old-fashioned three-group rotation; we mean flexible groups, not rigid groups based only on ability. We sometimes base our groups on the need for a strategy or common interests of a few children.

Our teaching during this phase addresses student needs we have uncovered through the phonological awareness/phonics assessment (see Resources 2-5, 2-6, 2-7, 2-8, and 2-9). We believe that intentional teaching should center around whole texts and not minute, isolated, meaningless parts. We use real children's literature, observing students' interests, maximizing the reading and writing connection, and supporting students every step of the way. A large part of practicing and applying concepts in emergent reading takes places when children write and play literacy games.

See Resource 2-5, Phonological Awareness Pretest: Level 1, p. 75.

See Resource 2-6, Phonological Awareness Pretest: Level 2, p. 76.

See Resource 2-7, Phonological Awareness Pretest: Level 3, p. 77.

See Resource 2-8, Phonics Pretest: Levels 1, 2, 3, p. 78.

See Resource 2-9, Phonics Pretest: Levels 4, 5, 6, p. 79.

Discussion of Texts

Not all kindergartners can read the text being discussed in the classroom; however, most students can talk about what has been read to them and contemplate the meaning of wordless books. Yet some students at this age can read. Our friend Emily read all of her birthday cards as she opened them on her fourth birthday and has continued to blossom as a learner. During the reading block, we may have a small group of readers anxious and able to discuss what they have read, and that group will grow as the year goes on.

Conducting retellings is a good way to begin a kindergarten book discussion. One child can begin, and then another student can chime in with other events or details. Our goal during any discussion is to help students increase their understanding and to use the strategies they have learned to build meaning in future texts. The questions that we ask shouldn't be canned ones, although many are the same from one text to another. "What can you tell me about the characters in the story?" is a good question for most fiction. Asking about the problem and solution is usually appropriate for fictional texts. The questions we ask in nonfiction are not quite as predictable, and the best question is often open-ended, such as "What did you learn from this book about (the topic)?" Great questions such as "What do you think?" and "Why do you think that?" always get the children to think deeply about what they have read. Gayle's questioning bookmark is a great reference for teachers developing questioning skills (Resource 2-10).

Although we have not really addressed mandated materials, many of you have commercial materials that you are expected to use for reading instruction. Our hope is that your required materials are composed of rich children's literature. That way you can modify the way you use them and not have children think that reading isn't a joyful experience.

See Resource 2-10, Questions for Developing Deeper Thinking bookmark, p. 80.

Resource 2-5

KINDERGARTEN ■ Resource 2-5 ■ Phonological Awareness Pretest: Level 1

Phonological Awareness Pretest

Name _____ Teacher _____ Date _____

Level 1

1. Awareness of Gross Differences
Read example: The cat can climb up the tree. Model putting down a marker for each word heard.
Read aloud each sentence, repeat slowly, and ask student to put down a marker for each word heard.

   1. I have three dogs.   _____

   2. I love to eat cake   _____

   3. I am five.   _____
                                       /3

2. Awareness of Rhyme
Read example: loose, cat, goose Ask the student to tell you the rhyming words.
Read the following words, repeat slowly, and ask the student to tell you the ones that rhyme.

   1. mat, dog, rat   _____

   2. moon, spoon, fly   _____

   3. money, cake, bunny   _____
                                       /3

3. Segmentation of Words Into Syllables
Read example: baby, model how to clap out syllables.
Read the following words and ask the student to clap out the syllables for each.

   1. dog   _____

   2. happy   _____

   3. bathtub   _____
                                       /3

Comments: 3/3 Secure   2/3 Developing   1/3–0/3 Needs Additional Time

CHAPTER TWO: The Kindergarten Literacy Block   75

■ Resource 2-5: *Phonological Awareness Pretest: Level 1*

Reading Conferences

Most kindergarten students will not be ready for reading conferences at the beginning of the year. We begin with intentional literacy encounters (focus lessons based on instructional needs), keeping anecdotal records, and gradually incorporate literature response journals and reading conferences for many students. (See the developmental progression class chart in Resource 2-11.) Please remember when you use this chart that there is no linear progression because we know that each child's literacy experiences influence his or her early reading development. This progression does give you a focus for instruction, along with what you know about your students.

See Resource 2-11, Developmental Progression Chart, p. 81.

See Resource 2-11, Developmental Progression Chart, p. 81.

Resource 2-10

KINDERGARTEN ■ Resource 2-10
Questions for Developing Deeper Thinking

Questions for Developing Deeper Thinking

KNOWLEDGE—Identifying and recalling information. Who, What, When, Where, How _____ ?
Describe _____

COMPREHENSION—Organizing and selecting facts and ideas
Retell _____ in your own words.
What is the main idea? _____

APPLICATION—Using facts, rules, and concepts
How is _____ an example of _____ ?
How is _____ related to _____ ?
Why is _____ significant?

ANALYSIS—Separating the whole into smaller parts
What are the parts or features of _____ ?
Classify _____ according to _____ .
How does _____ compare/contrast with _____ ?
What evidence can you present for _____ ?

SYNTHESIS—Combining ideas to form a new whole
What would you predict/infer from _____ ?
What ideas can you add to _____ ?
How would you create/design a new _____ ?
What might happen if you combine _____ with _____ ?
What solutions would you suggest for _____

EVALUATION—Developing opinions, judgments, or decisions
Do you agree that _____ ?
What do you think about _____ ?
What is the most important _____ ?
Prioritize _____ according to _____ .
How would you decide about _____ ?
What criteria would you use to assess _____ ?

Questions for Developing Deeper Thinking

KNOWLEDGE—Identifying and recalling information. Who, What, When, Where, How _____ ?
Describe _____

COMPREHENSION—Organizing and selecting facts and ideas
Retell _____ in your own words.
What is the main idea? _____

APPLICATION—Using facts, rules, and concepts
How is _____ an example of _____ ?
How is _____ related to _____ ?
Why is _____ significant?

ANALYSIS—Separating the whole into smaller parts
What are the parts or features of _____ ?
Classify _____ according to _____ .
How does _____ compare/contrast with _____ ?
What evidence can you present for _____ ?

SYNTHESIS—Combining ideas to form a new whole
What would you predict/infer from _____ ?
What ideas can you add to _____ ?
How would you create/design a new _____ ?
What might happen if you combine _____ with _____ ?
What solutions would you suggest for _____

EVALUATION—Developing opinions, judgments, or decisions
Do you agree that _____ ?
What do you think about _____ ?
What is the most important _____ ?
Prioritize _____ according to _____ .
How would you decide about _____ ?
What criteria would you use to assess _____ ?

80

The Literacy Block

■ Resource 2-10: *Questions for Developing Deeper Thinking bookmark*

We know that as soon as students understand sound–symbol correspondence, remember some basic sight words, and are able to use picture clues, they are ready for instructional reading.

Individual reading conferences are five-to-ten-minute periods in which you talk to a student about a familiar text. Conferences can be conducted with any student who can read a book. If you are thinking, "I can't do that every day," you are right. But you may be able to conduct one a week or maybe even two a week by assigning a specific day for each student. An individual conference is one way to meet the needs of the "Emilys" in the classroom who can read several levels ahead of their peers and want to be challenged in their reading.

You can ask the student to read aloud a favorite paragraph, talk about a character if appropriate, and talk about other story elements. A short oral summary of what was read since the last conference is often a good idea. Previewing the student's reading journal offers a glimpse of what the reader was thinking before, during, and after the reading of the book. This information can inform instruction.

During the conference with the child, it is important to record the book that is being read and any additional information that would inform instruction. Gayle's conference forms (see Resources 2-3 and 2-4) allow her to make note of miscues, meaning interferences, sentence structure interferences strategy application. Each of these cueing systems informs her instruction for each student. By noting miscues she can determine if the miscue is graphophonic, structural, or semantic. A book that has good ideas about all aspects of reading, but especially conferences is *Reading Essentials* by Regie Routman (2003).

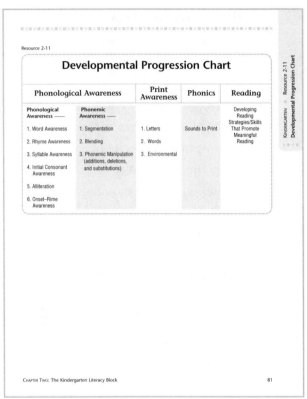

Resource 2-11: *Developmental Progression Chart*

Shared Reading

We touched on this strategy briefly in the gathering because shared reading is an excellent strategy for large and small groups. We use either a big book or another type of enlarged text, such as songs or poetry. In kindergarten, every child will profit from this strategy because it allows children who are readers to read along with the text, and children at the pre-emergent stage can learn much about the relationship between speech and print. Beginning readers can read the text several times until they are fluent with it.

Shared reading done in small groups for intentional teaching is enjoyable and has many advantages because with fewer students each one can contribute more to the discussion and grow in his or her reading development. Each student can make more predictions, and we can focus our comments to support each child. Although we emphasize shared reading in kindergarten and first grade, we think there are times in all grades when this strategy has value for teaching reading.

Guided Reading

When students have one-to-one correspondence, which is an understanding that each spoken word matches a word in print, and can accurately identify 90 to 95 percent of the words on a running record, they are ready to transition to reading independently. Although they still participate in shared reading in the gathering, they will profit from more intentional teaching as they continue their growth as readers.

For many children, guided reading provides a structure for this intentional teaching. There are some excellent books regarding recommended procedures of guided reading that have been developed by Irene Fountas and Gay Su Pinnell (1996, 1999, 2005), the gurus of guided reading, have written the definitive books on the subject.

Resource 2-12: *Phonological Awareness Assessments: Kindergarten*

Guided reading has much in common with shared reading. Both employ many of the same actions, except in guided reading, six or fewer students work on more difficult text. Also, instead of using big books or other enlarged texts, each student in the group reads from an age-appropriate children's trade book. Numerous sources provide reading levels of children's books, both online and in print. *The Fountas and Pinnell Leveled Book List K–8* (2006) contains reading levels for more than 18,000 popular books. For finding reading levels online, we recommend the Scholastic Teacher Book Wizard (bookwizard.scholastic.com/tbw) and the Reading Recovery Council of North America (www.readingrecovery.org/rrcna/membership/books.asp).

In a guided reading lesson for kindergartners, students take a picture walk through the illustrations in the book and predict what the book is about. Together, we conduct a choral reading of each page of the text. As the book progresses, and if we feel the children can read the book alone, we gradually diminish our participation so we only hear the children's voices. Throughout the book, we pause and ask the children to predict what will happen next and we observe how they use oral language to provide them with syntactic clues. We strengthen their sound–symbol correspondences as we provide on-the-spot assistance with using graphophonic cues to read unfamiliar words. Repeated guided teaching with increasingly more difficult text often helps students become independent in their reading.

Focus Lessons

Based on our observations, individual assessments, and conferences, we determine areas that a child needs to develop or strengthen, such as letter–sound relationships, conventions of print, and comprehension strategies. In kindergarten, these lessons take place during the focus center.

The intentional teaching that we do with pre-emergent readers is derived from Gayle's phonological awareness/ phonics assessment (see Resources 2-5 to 2-9 on pages 75–79). Each student is assessed three times a year to inform instruction. The results for the class are color-coded (Resources 2-12 and 2-13 on pages 82 and 83), and focus lessons occur during intentional instruction. The color red on the class chart indicates the need for additional intentional teaching. We have included a blank form for you to modify for you to meet your intentional teaching needs (Resources 2-14 and 2-15 on pages 84 and 85).

Resource 2-13

Summary of Phonics Assessment
Kindergarten

Teacher _____

S–Secure   D–Developing   N–Needs Improvement

Name / DATE January	Level One (Letter Recognition)	Level Two (Letter–Sound Correspondence)	Level Three (Int. Con. Awareness)	Level Four (Word Study Blending)	Level Five (Word Study Segmenting)	Level Six (Word Reading)
	S	S	S	S	S	S
	S	S	S	S	S	S
	D	D	D	N	N	N
	S	S	S	D	D	N
	S	S	D	D	N	N
	S	S	S	D	D	N
	S	S	S	D	D	N
	S	D	D	N	N	N
	S	S	S	S	S	S
	S	S	S	D	D	N
	S	S	D	N	N	N
	S	S	S	S	D	S
	S	S	S	S	S	S
	S	S	S	S	D	D
	S	S	D	D	N	N
	S	S	D	N	N	N
	S	S	S	D	D	D
	S	S	S	D	N	N

Chapter Two: The Kindergarten Literacy Block   83

KINDERGARTEN ■ Resource 2-13
Summary of Phonics Assessment: Kindergarten

Resource 2-13: *Summary of Phonics Assessment: Kindergarten*

See Resource 2-12, Phonological Awareness Assessments: Kindergarten, p. 82.

See Resource 2-13, Summary of Phonics Assessment: Kindergarten, p. 83.

See Resource 2-14, Phonological Awareness Assessments: Kindergarten (blank), p. 84.

See Resource 2-15, Phonics Assessment Summary (blank), p. 85.

Writing, interacting with peers, and playing games show evidence of your young reader's level of understanding. We identify a small group of students who have similar needs and create a focus group. If we have more than six children, we add another focus group because children need the attention smaller groups provide. It is our view that we are more effective when we employ the reading–writing connection whenever possible and that using good literature in our focus lessons enables us to do that. We do not need elaborate materials—most of the time a whiteboard and marker, puppets, picture cards, games, or a piece of rebus text is all we need. For a group of kindergartners having problems with identifying rhyming words, the lesson would be to sort picture cards by matching pictures that rhyme.

Resource 2-14: *Phonological Awareness Assessments: Kindergarten (blank)*

Independent Engagement

The purpose of the reading block is to further each student's reading development. To do this, we must dedicate time for students to read independently. Most kindergartners do not come to school in September reading independently, although a wide range of levels is typical. As the year progresses, more and more children tend to move from emergent to beginning readers. The more exposure children have had to preschool and home read-alouds, the sooner they will make the shift from beginning to independent readers.

If you have to use a commercial core program, we hope it employs good children's literature that can be used in flexible ways. Many teachers we know use only parts of the program and still continue with a rich reading curriculum based on quality children's books.

Whenever students are reading independently, the notion of self-monitoring must be at the center of whatever we say, the questions we ask, and our demonstrations. Our focus on comprehension ("Does that make sense?") must be present from the beginning of kindergarten and not a year or two down the road.

Challenges of Self-Selection

We wish that all children could self-select texts, but that isn't always possible. Many classroom and school libraries simply lack enough books at different levels. There are other obstacles to self-selection, which we will discuss below.

1. Children choose books that are not appropriate. When given choices, many kindergartners will select a book based on the pictures without considering the difficulty of the text. We provide students with baskets, tubs, or shelves filled with the kind of predictable texts that pre-emergent readers respond to.

2. The leveling of text is not an exact science. Text gradient systems that we have used include the Reading Recovery Council's book list, *The Fountas and Pinnell Leveled Book List, K–8*, and Scholastic Teacher Book Wizard. Books are classified by level according to several variables, including vocabulary, sentence length, concept load, and the way the text is laid out on the pages. A critical attribute that even the best text gradient cannot provide, however, is the level of a child's content knowledge related to the topic of a particular book. This prior knowledge or lack thereof may allow a child to read above or below a level determined through assessments. While there is no perfect system in existence, we believe the use of leveling systems is helpful in providing a starting point for matching readers to appropriate texts. We suggest a flexible approach, however,

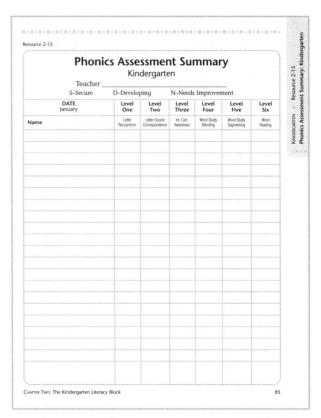

Resource 2-15: *Phonics Assessment Summary (blank)*

and caution others to avoid a rigid adherence to using leveled text. Maryann's article, "On the Level," further explains our approach (2006).

3. Availability of books is limited by money and space. No teacher or school can keep a library stocked with every book that students find interesting. Even if we had all the money in the world to buy books, none of us would have the space to store them. Also, despite a recent explosion in the publication of nonfiction texts in the last few years, there are still topics on which few or no books have been written.

In the absence of a robust classroom or school library, an alternative would be for students to reread the texts or books that have been used for shared or supportive reading. Below we discuss some other things that students can do independently.

Resource 2-16

Text Progression Form

Date		Name of Text	Genre and Level *		Unfamiliar (benchmark for next level) ***
Book Received	Conferenced		Fiction	Nonfiction	

Student Name _____
* If books are leveled, the level can be inserted.
*** Unfamiliar book that is new to reader

86   Creating the Best Literacy Block Ever

■ Resource 2-16: *Text Progression Form*

Book Logs

In their literature response journals, children can document the title of each book read during the block. Kindergartners begin their journals when they are in Level A books. Gayle uses a text progression form for recording books read by the students during conferences (Resource 2-16). Teachers keep track of this and all forms related to reading conferences in a reading notebook. This way the conference forms are easily accessible for parent conferences and teacher meetings (see Resources 2-3 and 2-4).

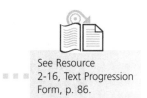

See Resource 2-16, Text Progression Form, p. 86.

Literature Response Journals

Writing in journals during and after reading has many benefits. In kindergarten, this writing takes place during intentional instruction. The reading–writing connection strengthens letter–sound relationships whenever the child writes. Because the child responds to some part of the story or has a personal reaction to the text, journals help with reading comprehension. Gayle has structured kindergarten responses in a gradual-release style that taps into students' strengths at each reading level. Kindergartners need to interact with text no matter where they are in their reading development. Students who are capable of what Fountas & Pinnell call "developmental reading" in their leveled text A–B (1999) show their understanding by drawing a picture of their favorite part of a text and retelling the story to the teacher during their reading conference (Resource 2-17). Next, the shift moves from visual to written responses. Students who are reading in Fountas and Pinnell leveled text C respond to the text by using the predicting strategy and recognizing unfamiliar words (Resource 2-18). They also write about what the book reminds them of. In level C nonfiction, they list five facts they learned (Resource 2-19). At levels D, E, and above in fiction text, we want students to make connections to the text as well as recognize the accuracy of their predictions (Resource 2-20). At this level in nonfiction, we still want them to list five facts they learned from their text (Resource 2-21). Additionally during this level, we begin "Growing as a Reader" pages to focus on curriculum standards. These blank pages at the back of the journal are where we record

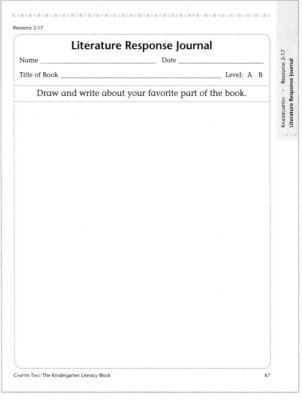

Resource 2-17

Literature Response Journal

Name _____ Date _____

Title of Book _____ Level: A B

Draw and write about your favorite part of the book.

KINDERGARTEN ■ Resource 2-17
Literature Response Journal

CHAPTER TWO: The Kindergarten Literacy Block   87

■ Resource 2-17: *Literature Response Journal*

See Resource 2-17, Literature Response Journal, p. 87.

See Resource 2-18, Reading Journals: Fiction Level C, p. 88.

See Resource 2-19, Reading Journals: Nonfiction Level C, p. 89.

See Resource 2-20, Reading Journals: Fiction Level D–E, p. 90.

See Resource 2-21, Reading Journals: Nonfiction Level D–E, p. 91.

an appropriate skill for the student to work on. For example, say we want a student to locate and record words in texts that have the *–an* chunk. Because the *–an* rime was a recent focus lesson, the child's ability to complete the "Growing as a Reader" assignment will show how well he or she can apply the skill when they read. There is an example of "Growing as a Reader" in Chapter 3, Figure 3.2. Gayle's bookmarks for kindergarten (Resource 2-22) contain the same information as their journal pages and serve as a visual aid to remind students of what to write in their journals. The kindergarten reading journal guidelines (Resource 2-23) come into play as the children move away from needing a form to support their thinking as they read.

See Resource 2-22, Getting to Know My Book bookmark, p. 92.

See Resource 2-23, Kindergarten Reading Journal Guidelines, p. 93.

Creating Word Logs

Literature response journals provide a place for children to record unfamiliar or interesting words. These include words they can't pronounce and words whose meaning is unknown. It is important that students write the page numbers so they can refer back to the word and read it in context when conferencing with the teacher. This contextual rereading gives the teacher an opportunity to help the student develop "fix-up" strategies for the next time an unfamiliar word crops up.

Independent Research

Yes, kindergartners can research. They may not be able to read the texts for the research, but the texts can be read to them or they might listen to a recording of it. To begin the process, they just need a question to be answered. The resulting "report" may be a combination of visual representations and words. Children can dictate to the teacher what information from their search they want others to read and learn about. For example, a group of kindergartners wanted to learn more about bees, so Gayle found several videos for them to watch and several books on tape to listen to. After listening and viewing the information about bees, they made a list (using very rough, invented spelling) of all of the things they learned. They dictated the facts to Gayle and then she put one fact per page for the students to illustrate. Once the pages were bound, they became an important addition to her nonfiction library. Figure 2.2 is an example of a kindergarten research project.

Peer Interaction

Independent reading is vital for reading development, but social interaction is necessary for improving reading comprehension. When groups of children replay games that were introduced in intentional instruction, they exchange their points of view. This is how we build new knowledge and move to higher levels of thinking. We conduct many discussions with children, but they need numerous opportunities to share their viewpoints with peers when the teacher is engaged with other students. Therefore, the more peer discussions, the more learning that will take place.

Some peer interaction activities help students build fluency, increase interest in reading and writing, and improve comprehension by expressing new knowledge. Examples are Readers Theater or dramatizations, graphic organizers, and technology projects. These interactions can take place during reading centers, which are a part of literacy encounters. If you have a group of precocious readers in your classroom, you can read Chapter 3 for ideas.

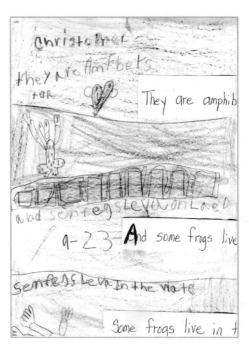

■ Figure 2.2: *Kindergarten research project*

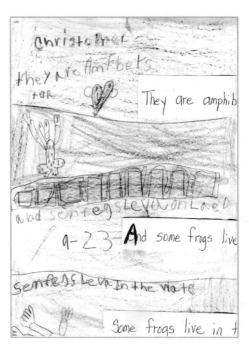

■ Resource 2-19: *Reading Journals: Nonfiction Level C*

Dramatizations

Kindergartners love to act out stories based on a big book, a chapter in a book that was read aloud, or just a scene from a book. Fiction is generally a better source than nonfiction for dramatization. Kindergartners who read independently can plan a presentation and ask other students to join in acting out a book or scene. The value of dramatizing isn't just the pleasure it brings children. Acting out the ideas deepens their understanding of the text because of the experience of being the character. No costumes are necessary, and a few simple props are all that is needed.

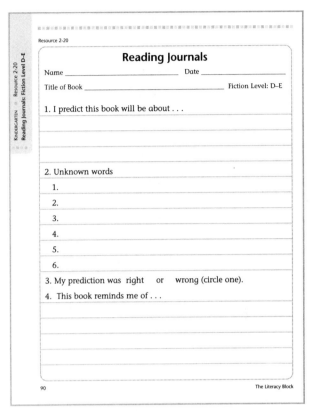

■ Resource 2-20: *Reading Journals: Fiction Level D–E*

Graphic Organizers

These are simply tools to help organize understandings about a text into a logical format. One of the most popular graphic organizers is the Venn diagram. For example, one circle represents unique attributes of one character, the other circle signifies unique attributes of the other character, and the overlapping area of the circles shows shared attributes.

Technology Projects

Kindergartners use the computer to practice reading strategies and to listen to books read during their reading centers. Bookflix (teacher.scholastic.com/products/bookflixfreetrial/index.htm) offers a variety of good literature for students to choose from. They also can illustrate their favorite part of a book by using a program like Kidpix (www.kidpix.com). The class can illustrate a different part of a story and make a PowerPoint presentation to share with parents and other classes. Kindergartners can also have tech buddies, who help them create slide presentations and other projects.

Community Sharing

The last few minutes of the workshop are spent in a large-group gathering to celebrate reading. Much community building goes on as we laugh and sometimes cry together over texts. Because not all kindergartners can read, at the beginning of the year we lead most of the reading. For example, we might reread a big book from a previous shared reading session. As the year goes on and more and more students can read, we ask students for suggestions of passages in books they find interesting and would like to have reread.

Students may also role-play a story they practiced earlier. Other days can be devoted to book talks, during which students share their thoughts about what they have read. Sometimes we begin the gathering with a question and ask the students to contribute to the discussion. Your greatest challenge may be encouraging shy children to share, while making more vocal children aware that others need to be heard. Some questions we have found to elicit interesting responses include the following:

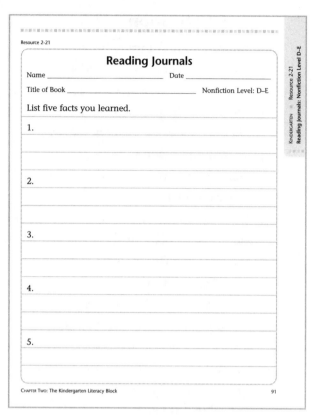

Resource 2-21: *Reading Journals: Nonfiction Level D–E*

- ■ "Who is the funniest character in any book you have heard or read?"

- ■ "What is the funniest animal in a book that you have heard?"

- ■ "What is the best book you ever heard read aloud?"

- ■ "If you were a book illustrator, who would you most like to be like?"

- ■ "What have you learned about reading today?"

The following are some presentation ideas that students can share during the closing derived from either independent engagement or interaction with peers.

Artistic Sharing

ABC book

Illustrations

Costumes of characters

Block constructions of scenes

Story sequence cards

Drama

Beast tales

Chanting nursery rhymes

Flannel-board stories

Readers Theater

Role-playing

Jokes

Plays

Storytelling

Puppet plays

Skits

Riddles

Literary Style

Parallel big book

Lists of facts

Speech Forms

Favorite story or character
    speeches

Demonstrations

Oral reports

Symbolic Presentations

Cartoons

Charts

Diagrams

Graphs

Maps

Three-Dimensional Art

Constructions

Dioramas

Sculptures

Shadow boxes

Technology

PowerPoint

Kidpix

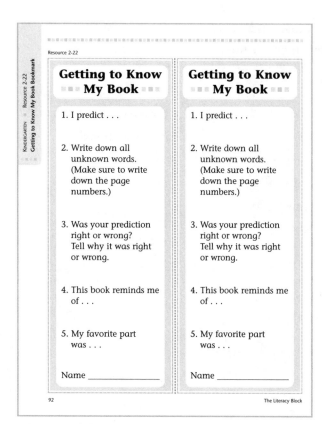

Resource 2-22: *Getting to Know My Book bookmark*

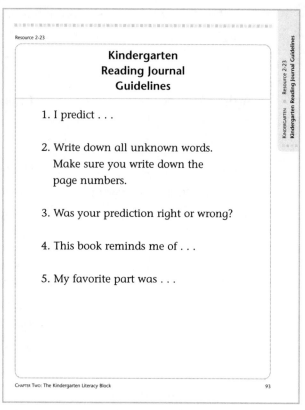

Resource 2-23: *Kindergarten Reading Journal Guidelines*

In Conclusion ～

The format of the kindergarten reading block is designed for you to model the reading process so students can practice reading as they interact with peers and apply strategies independently in developing comprehension of texts. Kindergarten is like no other grade because most of the children enter at an emergent level. They can interact with text, though, because they gain meaning from the illustrations. Almost all learning takes place through intentional teaching and peer interaction, which means the bulk of your time is spent with the whole class and small groups. As the year goes on, children move to beginning reading, and eventually some become independent.

Some of Gayle's favorite books for kindergarten read-alouds and focus lessons include:

Archambault, J. (2004). *Boom Chicka Rock*

Bang, M. (1999). *When Sophie Gets Angry—Really, Really Angry . . .*

Beaumont, K. (2008). *Who Ate All the Cookie Dough?*

Carle, E. (2007). *"Slowly, Slowly, Slowly," Said the Sloth*

Cooper, H. (2006). *Delicious: A Pumpkin Soup Story*

Cowley, J. (2003). *Mrs. Wishy-Washy's Farm*

Cronin, D. (2000). *Click, Clack, Moo: Cows That Type*

Cronin, D. (2005). *Click, Clack, Quackity-Quack*

Cronin, D. (2006). *Click, Clack, Splish, Splash*

Dewdney, A. (2007). *Llama Llama Mad at Mama*

DiPucchio, K. (2004). *Bed Hogs*

DiPucchio, K. (2005). *What's the Magic Word?*

Emberley, E. (1992). *Go Away, Big Green Monster!*

Fleming, D. (1991). *In the Tall, Tall Grass*

Fleming, D. (1992). *Count*

Fleming, D. (1993). *In the Small, Small Pond*

Fleming, D. (1994). *Barnyard Banter*

Fleming, D. (2002). *Alphabet Under Construction*

Jorgensen, G. (1992). *Crocodile Beat*

MacLennan, C. (2007). *Chicky Chicky Chook Chook*

Martin, B. (2001). *Rock It, Sock It, Number Line*

Numeroff, L. (2004). *Beatrice Doesn't Want To*

Root, P. (2006). *Looking for a Moose*

Saltzberg, B. (2007). *Cornelius P. Mud, Are You Ready for School?*

Shields, C. D. (1997). *Saturday Night at the Dinosaur Stomp*

Sullivan, E. (2006). *The Night Before Big School*

Wheeler, L. (2004). *Bubble Gum, Bubble Gum*

Williams, S. (2001). *Dinnertime!*

Wood, A. (2003). *Alphabet Mystery*

Wood, A. (2006). *Alphabet Rescue*

Yolen, J. (2000). *Off We Go!*

Some of Gayle's favorite big books include:

Allen, P. (1996). *Who Sank the Boat?*

Bond, F. (2000). *If You Take a Mouse to the Movies*

Brett, J. (1999). *The Hat*

Ehlert, L. (1991). *Red Leaf, Yellow Leaf*

Fox, M. (1988). *Hattie and the Fox*

Gardner, B. (1986). *Have You Ever Seen? An ABC Book*

Hutchins, P. (1991). *Good-Night, Owl!*

Hutchins, P. (1993). *Titch*

Raffi. (1993). *Everything Grows*

Titherington, J. (1986). *Pumpkin Pumpkin*

Williams, S. (1989). *I Went Walking*

Creating the Best Literacy Block Ever © 2009 by Maryann Manning, Gayle Morrison, and Deborah Camp: Scholastic Professional

Literacy Encounters With Two Rotations

Teacher _____ Date _____

First Rotation: Time _____
Focus of Reading Instruction

Intentional Instruction	Activity/Game	Friends Who Need This Center
1.		
2.		
3.		
4.		
5.		

Second Rotation: Time _____
Focus of Reading Instruction

Intentional Instruction	Activity/Game	Friends Who Need This Center
1.		
2.		
3.		
4.		
5.		

Literacy Encounters With Three Rotations

Teacher _____ Week of _____

| Rotations | Intentional Literacy Encounter | | | Interactive Literacy Encounter |
	Skill	Activity/Game	Friends	
First	1.			1.
				2.
				3.
	2.			4.
				5.
Second	1.			1.
				2.
				3.
	2.			4.
				5.
Third	1.			1.
				2.
				3.
	2.			4.
				5.

Creating the Best Literacy Block Ever © 2009 by Maryann Manning, Gayle Morrison, and Deborah Camp: Scholastic Professional

Gayle's Conference Form for Kindergarten

Name _____			Comments			
Date _____						

Name _____

Date _____

	* **	***		* **	***	Comments
Text 1 _____ Level___F UF		F N	Text 4 _____ Level___F UF		F N	
Text 2 _____ Level___F UF		F N	Text 5 _____ Level___F UF		F N	
Text 3 _____ Level___F UF		F N	Text 6 _____ Level___F UF		F N	

**Insert bk. # next to concept demonstrated.	Miscue	Semantics Meaning Change?		Syntax Structure Change?		Graphophonic Similarity			
						Visual		Sound	
Fiction Oral Retelling Sequentially Retold ___ Beginning: Setting___ Characters___ Middle: Problem_____ Ending: Solution_____	Bk. #	Yes	No	Yes	No	Y	N	Y	N
Nonfiction Oral Retelling Recalled 3 facts____ More____									
Comments									
Instruction Based on Conference									
	Totals								

* If leveled books are used, record level.
** F is for books that are familiar and UF is for books that are unfamiliar.
*** Genre that includes fiction or nonfiction.

Creating the Best Literacy Block Ever © 2009 by Maryann Manning, Gayle Morrison, and Deborah Camp: Scholastic Professional

Gayle's Strategies Conference Form for Kindergarten

Name _____

Date _____

	*	**	***			*	**	***
Text 1 _____ Level___ F UF			F N	Text 4 _____ Level___ F UF				F N
Text 2 _____ Level___ F UF			F N	Text 5 _____ Level___ F UF				F N
Text 3 _____ Level___ F UF			F N	Text 6 _____ Level___ F UF				F N

Comments

**Insert bk. # next to concept demonstrated.

Fiction Oral Retelling

Demonstrates:

1. Sequential Retelling ___
   Beginning: Setting__ Characters__
   Middle: Problem_____
   Ending: Solution_____
2. Making Connections/Using Prior Knowledge_____
3. Visualizing_____
4. Questioning Skills _____
5. Informally Making Inferences__

Nonfiction Oral Retelling

Recalled 3 facts____ More____

Comments

Instruction Based on Conference

	Miscue	Semantics Meaning Change?		Syntax Structure Change?		Graphophonic Similarity			
						Visual		Sound	
Bk. #		Yes	No	Yes	No	Y	N	Y	N
Totals									

 * If leveled books are used, record level.
 ** F is for books that are familiar and UF is for books that are unfamiliar.
 *** Genre that includes fiction or nonfiction.

Creating the Best Literacy Block Ever © 2009 by Maryann Manning, Gayle Morrison, and Deborah Camp: Scholastic Professional

Phonological Awareness Pretest

Name _____ Teacher _____ Date _____

Level 1

1. Awareness of Gross Differences
Read example: The cat can climb up the tree. **Model putting down a marker for each word heard.**
Read aloud each sentence, repeat slowly, and ask student to put down a marker for each word heard.

    1. I have three dogs.   _____

    2. I love to eat cake   _____

    3. I am five.   _____

         /3

2. Awareness of Rhyme
Read example: loose, cat, goose **Ask the student to tell you the rhyming words.**
Read the following words, repeat slowly, and ask the student to tell you the ones that rhyme.

    1. mat, dog, rat   _____

    2. moon, spoon, fly   _____

    3. money, cake, bunny   _____

         /3

3. Segmentation of Words Into Syllables
Read example: baby, **model how to clap out syllables.**
Read the following words and ask the student to clap out the syllables for each.

    1. dog   _____

    2. happy   _____

    3. bathtub   _____

         /3

Comments: 3/3 Secure   2/3 Developing   1/3–0/3 Needs Additional Time

Creating the Best Literacy Block Ever © 2009 by Maryann Manning, Gayle Morrison, and Deborah Camp: Scholastic Professional

KINDERGARTEN ■ Resource 2-6
Phonological Awareness Pretest: Level 2

Phonological Awareness Pretest

Name _____ Teacher _____ Date _____

Level 2

1. Awareness of Initial and Final Consonant Segments

Example: cat, mouse, canary **Ask the student to repeat the three words and tell you the two that begin with the same sound. Example:** rat, car, mat **Ask the student to repeat the three words and tell you the two that end with the same sound.**

Read aloud each group of words, then ask the student to repeat the words and tell you the two words in each group that begin or end with the same sound.

1. frog, sun, sail (beg.)   _____
2. ball, fall, play (end)   _____
3. goat, duck, goose (beg.)   _____
                                        /3

2. Alliteration

Example: fox, fan, funny **Ask the student to tell you the first sound heard.**

Read the following words, then ask the student to repeat the words and tell you the first sound heard in each group.

1. sand, sun, sock   _____
2. moon, mushy, mud   _____
3. pan, pet, puppy   _____
                                        /3

3. Awareness of Onset and Rime

Example: "I'm going to say some words and I want you to give me another word that ends the same way as these words." hop, pop, _____

Read the following words and ask the student to think of another word that ends the same way.

1. tell, bell, _____   _____
2. mat, cat, _____   _____
3. say, day, _____   _____
                                        /3

Comments: **3/3 Secure**   **2/3 Developing**   **1/3–0/3 Needs Additional Time**

Creating the Best Literacy Block Ever © 2009 by Maryann Manning, Gayle Morrison, and Deborah Camp: Scholastic Professional

Resource 2-7

Phonological Awareness Pretest

Name _____ Teacher _____ Date _____

Level 3

1. Awareness of Phonemic Segmentation

Example: Ask the student to tell you the sounds heard in cat. If the student is unable to do this, model for him/her: /c/ /a/ /t/

Read aloud each word, then ask the student to tell you the sounds heard in each word.

1. sun
2. wag
3. cheek

_____
_____
_____
/3

2. Awareness of Blending Phonemes and Syllables

Example: "I'm thinking of a word that names an animal. It is a /d/ /og/. What is the word?" (dog)

Segment the following words, then ask the student to tell you the word.

1. /f/ /all/
2. /b/ /u/ /s/
3. /t/ /op/

_____
_____
_____
/3

3. Awareness of Phonemic Manipulation

Example: "What word do we have if we change the /d/ in *dog* to /l/?"

Listen carefully to the directions I give you for each word.

1. "What word do we have if we change the /r/ in *rain* to /p/?"
2. "What word do we have if we add /k/ to *row*?"
3. "What word do we have if we take away the first sound in *bat*?"

_____
_____
_____
/3

Comments: 3/3 Secure   2/3 Developing   1/3–0/3 Needs Additional Time

Creating the Best Literacy Block Ever © 2009 by Maryann Manning, Gayle Morrison, and Deborah Camp: Scholastic Professional

KINDERGARTEN ■ Resource 2-8
Phonics Pretest: Levels 1, 2, 3

Phonics Pretest

Name _____ Teacher _____ Date _____

Levels 1, 2, and 3

1. Letter Recognition
Use the Marie Clay Alphabet Recognition Task.

    1. 53–54 letters   _____ 3 _____
    2. 50–52 letters   _____ 2 _____
    3. Below 50   _____ 1 _____

2. Letter–Sound Correspondence
Give the Sentence Dictation.

    1. 33/35–30/35   _____ 3 _____
    2. 19/35–32/35   _____ 2 _____
    3. Below 19/35   _____ 1 _____

3. Onset and Rime
Example: Write the word *dog* on the back of the dictation sheet. Say the word, /d/ /og/. Underline the onset and the rime. Underneath the word *dog* write the word *log*. Voice how both words have the same rime, /og/. Tell the student he/she is going to do some now.

Write the following rimes on the paper and ask him/her to make two words by adding an onset to each. Have them read the words.

    1. __ot   __ot   _____
    2. __ug   __ug   _____
    3. __at   __at   _____

Comments: 3/3 Secure   2/3 Developing   1/3–0/3 Needs Additional Time

Creating the Best Literacy Block Ever © 2009 by Maryann Manning, Gayle Morrison, and Deborah Camp: Scholastic Professional

Creating the Best Literacy Block Ever © 2009 by Maryann Manning, Gayle Morrison, and Deborah Camp: Scholastic Professional

Phonics Pretest

Name _____ Teacher _____ Date _____

Levels 4, 5, and 6

4. Word Study—Blending (Letter Sounds)

Example: Using magnetic letters, make the words *cat, dog, cup,* and *ten*. Demonstrate *cat* by blending letter sounds to pronounce *cat*.

1. _____
2. _____
3. _____

_____
_____
_____
/3

5. Word Study—Segmenting (Make-a-Word)

Example: Using picture cards of 3-letter words, students will segment the letter sounds to spell the word.

1. _____
2. _____
3. _____

_____
_____
_____
/3

6. Clay Word Reading—Lists A, B, and C

1. 42–45
2. 25–41
3. Below 25

_____ 3 _____
_____ 3 _____
_____ 3 _____

Comments: 3/3 Secure   2/3 Developing   1/3–0/3 Needs Additional Time

Questions for Developing Deeper Thinking ■■■

KNOWLEDGE—Identifying and recalling information. Who, What, When, Where,
How _____?
Describe _____

COMPREHENSION—Organizing and selecting facts and ideas
Retell _____ in your own words.
What is the main idea? _____

APPLICATION—Using facts, rules, and concepts
How is _____ an example of _____?
How is _____ related to _____?
Why is _____ significant?

ANALYSIS—Separating the whole into smaller parts
What are the parts or features of _____?
Classify _____ according to _____.
How does _____ compare/contrast with _____?
What evidence can you present for _____?

SYNTHESIS—Combining ideas to form a new whole
What would you predict/infer from _____?
What ideas can you add to _____?
How would you create/design a new _____?
What might happen if you combine _____ with _____?
What solutions would you suggest for _____

EVALUATION—Developing opinions, judgments, or decisions
Do you agree that _____?
What do you think about _____?
What is the most important _____?
Prioritize _____ according to _____.
How would you decide about _____?
What criteria would you use to assess _____?

Questions for Developing Deeper Thinking ■■■

KNOWLEDGE—Identifying and recalling information. Who, What, When, Where,
How _____?
Describe _____

COMPREHENSION—Organizing and selecting facts and ideas
Retell _____ in your own words.
What is the main idea? _____

APPLICATION—Using facts, rules, and concepts
How is _____ an example of _____?
How is _____ related to _____?
Why is _____ significant?

ANALYSIS—Separating the whole into smaller parts
What are the parts or features of _____?
Classify _____ according to _____.
How does _____ compare/contrast with _____?
What evidence can you present for _____?

SYNTHESIS—Combining ideas to form a new whole
What would you predict/infer from _____?
What ideas can you add to _____?
How would you create/design a new _____?
What might happen if you combine _____ with _____?
What solutions would you suggest for _____

EVALUATION—Developing opinions, judgments, or decisions
Do you agree that _____?
What do you think about _____?
What is the most important _____?
Prioritize _____ according to _____.
How would you decide about _____?
What criteria would you use to assess _____?

Creating the Best Literacy Block Ever © 2009 by Maryann Manning, Gayle Morrison, and Deborah Camp: Scholastic Professional

Developmental Progression Chart

Phonological Awareness		Print Awareness	Phonics	Reading
Phonological Awareness ------ 1. Word Awareness 2. Rhyme Awareness 3. Syllable Awareness 4. Initial Consonant Awareness 5. Alliteration 6. Onset–Rime Awareness	**Phonemic Awareness -----** 1. Segmentation 2. Blending 3. Phonemic Manipulation (additions, deletions, and substitutions)	1. Letters 2. Words 3. Environmental	Sounds to Print	Developing Reading Strategies/Skills That Promote Meaningful Reading

Creating the Best Literacy Block Ever © 2009 by Maryann Manning, Gayle Morrison, and Deborah Camp: Scholastic Professional

Phonological Awareness Assessments
Kindergarten

Teacher _____

S–Secure   D–Developing   N–Needs Improvement

Date	Level One			Level Two			Level Three		
Name	Word Awareness	Rhyme Awareness	Syllable Awareness	Int. Con. Awareness	Alliteration	Onset–Rime Awareness	Seg.	Blend	Manip.
	N	N	N	N	N	N	N	N	N
	N	N	N	N	N	N	N	N	N
	N	N	N	N	N	N	N	N	N
	D	N	N	N	N	N	N	N	N
	N	N	N	N	N	N	N	N	N
	S	S	S	N	S	N	N	S	N
	S	N	N	N	N	N	N	N	N
	S	S	S	N	S	N	N	N	N
	S	S	S	N	N	S	D	S	D
	N	N	N	N	N	N	N	N	N
	N	N	N	N	N	N	N	N	N
	S	S	D	D	S	S	N	S	N
	S	N	N	N	N	N	N	N	N
	S	S	D	S	S	S	D	S	N
	N	N	N	N	N	N	N	N	N
	D	N	S	N	N	N	N	N	N
	S	N	D	N	N	N	N	N	N
	S	S	S	N	N	N	N	N	N

Creating the Best Literacy Block Ever © 2009 by Maryann Manning, Gayle Morrison, and Deborah Camp: Scholastic Professional

Summary of Phonics Assessment
Kindergarten

Teacher _____

S–Secure   D–Developing   N–Needs Improvement

DATE January	Level One	Level Two	Level Three	Level Four	Level Five	Level Six
Name	Letter Recognition	Letter–Sound Correspondence	Int. Con. Awareness	Word Study Blending	Word Study Segmenting	Word Reading
	S	S	S	S	S	S
	S	S	S	S	S	S
	D	D	D	N	N	N
	S	S	S	D	D	N
	S	S	D	D	N	N
	S	S	S	D	D	N
	S	S	S	D	D	N
	S	D	D	N	N	N
	S	S	S	S	S	S
	S	S	S	D	D	N
	S	S	D	N	N	N
	S	S	S	S	D	S
	S	S	S	S	S	S
	S	S	S	S	D	D
	S	S	D	D	N	N
	S	S	D	N	N	N
	S	S	S	D	D	D
	S	S	S	D	N	N

Creating the Best Literacy Block Ever © 2009 by Maryann Manning, Gayle Morrison, and Deborah Camp: Scholastic Professional

Phonological Awareness Assessments
Kindergarten

Teacher _____

S–Secure   D–Developing   N–Needs Improvement

Date	Level One			Level Two			Level Three		
Name	Word Awareness	Rhyme Awareness	Syllable Awareness	Int. Con. Awareness	Alliteration	Onset–Rime Awareness	Seg.	Blend	Manip.

Creating the Best Literacy Block Ever © 2009 by Maryann Manning, Gayle Morrison, and Deborah Camp: Scholastic Professional

Phonics Assessment Summary
Kindergarten

Teacher _____

S–Secure   D–Developing   N–Needs Improvement

DATE January	Level One	Level Two	Level Three	Level Four	Level Five	Level Six
Name	Letter Recognition	Letter-Sound Correspondence	Int. Con. Awareness	Word Study Blending	Word Study Segmenting	Word Reading

Creating the Best Literacy Block Ever © 2009 by Maryann Manning, Gayle Morrison, and Deborah Camp: Scholastic Professional

KINDERGARTEN ▪ Resource 2-16

Text Progression Form

Text Progression Form

Date		Name of Text	Genre and Level *		Unfamiliar (benchmark for next level) ***
Book Received	Conferenced		Fiction	Nonfiction	

Student Name _____

* If books are leveled, the level can be inserted.

*** Unfamiliar book that is new to reader

The Literacy Block

Creating the Best Literacy Block Ever © 2009 by Maryann Manning, Gayle Morrison, and Deborah Camp: Scholastic Professional

Literature Response Journal

Name _____ Date _____

Title of Book _____ Level: A   B

Draw and write about your favorite part of the book.

Creating the Best Literacy Block Ever © 2009 by Maryann Manning, Gayle Morrison, and Deborah Camp: Scholastic Professional

KINDERGARTEN ■ Resource 2-18
Reading Journals: Fiction Level C

Reading Journals

Name _____ Date _____

Title of Book _____ Fiction Level: C

1. I think this book will be about . . .

2. List unknown words.

1.

2.

3.

4.

5.

6.

This book reminds me of . . .

Creating the Best Literacy Block Ever © 2009 by Maryann Manning, Gayle Morrison, and Deborah Camp: Scholastic Professional

Reading Journals

Name _____ Date _____

Title of Book _____ Nonfiction Level: C

List five facts you learned.

1.

2.

3.

4.

5.

Creating the Best Literacy Block Ever © 2009 by Maryann Manning, Gayle Morrison, and Deborah Camp: Scholastic Professional

KINDERGARTEN ■ Resource 2-20
Reading Journals: Fiction Level D–E

Reading Journals

Name _____ Date _____

Title of Book _____ Fiction Level: D–E

1. I predict this book will be about . . .

2. Unknown words

1.

2.

3.

4.

5.

6.

3. My prediction was right   or   wrong (circle one).

4. This book reminds me of . . .

Creating the Best Literacy Block Ever © 2009 by Maryann Manning, Gayle Morrison, and Deborah Camp: Scholastic Professional

Reading Journals

Name _____ Date _____

Title of Book _____ Nonfiction Level: D–E

List five facts you learned.

1. _____

_____

2. _____

_____

_____

3. _____

_____

_____

4. _____

_____

_____

5. _____

_____

_____

Creating the Best Literacy Block Ever © 2009 by Maryann Manning, Gayle Morrison, and Deborah Camp: Scholastic Professional

KINDERGARTEN   Resource 2-21
Reading Journals: Nonfiction Level D–E

Getting to Know My Book

1. I predict . . .

2. Write down all unknown words. (Make sure to write down the page numbers.)

3. Was your prediction right or wrong? Tell why it was right or wrong.

4. This book reminds me of . . .

5. My favorite part was . . .

Name _____

Getting to Know My Book

1. I predict . . .

2. Write down all unknown words. (Make sure to write down the page numbers.)

3. Was your prediction right or wrong? Tell why it was right or wrong.

4. This book reminds me of . . .

5. My favorite part was . . .

Name _____

Creating the Best Literacy Block Ever © 2009 by Maryann Manning, Gayle Morrison, and Deborah Camp: Scholastic Professional

Creating the Best Literacy Block Ever © 2009 by Maryann Manning, Gayle Morrison, and Deborah Camp: Scholastic Professional

Kindergarten
Reading Journal
Guidelines

1. I predict . . .

2. Write down all unknown words. Make sure you write down the page numbers.

3. Was your prediction right or wrong?

4. This book reminds me of . . .

5. My favorite part was . . .

First-Grade Literacy Block

Community Gathering Suggested time: up to 15 minutes

- Read-aloud short texts
- Shared reading of enlarged texts
- Focus lessons
- Interactive writing
- Author studies
- Dictation
- Vocabulary study

Intentional Instruction Suggested time: 30–45 minutes.
Activities in all columns occur simultaneously during workshop.

Teacher/student interactions	Independent engagement	Peer interactions
■ Discussion of texts ■ Think-alouds ■ Reading assessments ■ Reading conferences ■ Guided reading ■ Supportive reading ■ Focus lessons ■ Meeting with literature circles ■ Rove the room	■ Independent reading of appropriate self-selected text (usually beyond emergent level) ■ Preparing for literature circles ■ Book logs ■ Reading response journals ■ Creating words logs ■ Independent research ■ Technology projects ■ Listening stations ■ Word work ■ Sketch books/sketch to stretch ■ Fine-arts representations	■ Literature circles ■ Readers Theater ■ Sharing dramatizations ■ Graphic organizers ■ Technology projects ■ Word work ■ Reading big books together ■ Partner reading ■ Fine-arts representations

(Optional) Community Sharing Suggested time: up to 10 minutes

- Rereading a big book
- Student reading of selected passages
- Role-playing/dramatizations
- Discussion of texts or reading processes

CHAPTER 3

First-Grade Literacy Block

It's 9:00 Monday morning as Rachel rings a bell for the 15-minute community gathering to begin. As the children settle down, Rachel places a question chart on the easel. The chart displays questions generated last Friday during the block, to be discussed in today's community gathering:

- How do I know what the problem of the story is?
- How do I know who the main character is?
- What if the story takes place in different places? Can a story have more than one setting?

These questions will be addressed during focus lessons for the next few days.

Rachel reads the questions every Friday afternoon and plans her focus lessons for the next week. Today she tells the students they are going to talk about story problems. She reads aloud the book *Mouse Cleaning* by Rose-Marie Provencher. When she finishes, Rachel asks the students to turn and talk with a partner about the problem of the story. After a few minutes, she asks for volunteers to share what they thought the problem was in the story.

Victoria and Rebecca are the first to raise their hands to share.

"We think the problem is there's a mouse in their house," says Victoria.

Rachel records this answer on a chart.

Henry says, "We think the problem is that she needs to get the spring cleaning done."

Rachel records that answer on the chart and asks, "Any other suggestions?"

Ashcon says, "We thought the problem was she had a hole in her house where the mouse came in."

Rachel records this final thought on the chart, leaving tracks of the students' thinking. She then rereads the story and asks the students to turn and talk with their partner to see if they still agree with their first thought. Some change their minds, agreeing with others, leaving three possible problems for the story. Rachel tells them that this book, along with the chart, will be in the listening center. Students will listen to the book again, focusing on what they think the problem is, and then write their names on the chart next to the problem they choose. Rachel tells them that the next day they will discuss their thoughts and determine the problem in the book.

Next, their focus during independent reading, along with bookmark assignments, will be to determine the problem in the fiction books they are independently reading and document the problem in their literature response journals. The children have 30 to 45 minutes for independent reading. During this time, they read books that are instructionally appropriate, based on beginning-of-the-year assessments, ongoing assessments, and weekly conferences. The instructional levels are monitored and benchmarked during weekly conferences to make sure students are reading in appropriate texts and growing in their reading development.

During the reading block, students are talking with peers, responding in their literature journals, conferencing with Rachel, and posting questions on the question board, which Rachel reads at the end of each day and uses to direct instruction and focus lessons. Each student has a conference day during which he or she reads and discusses books with Rachel. During the conference, the teacher uses a conference form and the instructional text progression form to document growth over time. She administers a miscue analysis, writes anecdotal notes for future instruction, and talks with students about books they have read. The information she gathers helps her determine their level of comprehension.

At the sound of a bell, the students return to the rug for the community sharing of their reading successes and questions for the day. It is now time for lunch. When the class returns, the students will have a read-aloud followed by a discussion on the focus for the day, in this case: identifying the problem in the read-aloud story.

The Block in First Grade ∼

Some first graders can read text independently, while many are still emerging as readers. In either case, many first graders may not be ready to read independently for a long period of time. If many of your students are independent readers, Chapter 2 offers suggestions for best practices.

Just as in kindergarten, the literacy block shouldn't be a "letter of the week" study or a phonics boot camp, complete with the worksheets from the long-distant past when we actually believed that paper-and-pencil practice was a good way to improve reading. We now know that real reading of appropriate text is what improves reading. Phonological awareness/phonics assessments are appropriate for readers who enter at the emergent level (see Resources 2-5 to 2-9 on pages 75–79). These assessments guide instruction for these students during the independent reading component.

The literacy block is devoted exclusively to helping students develop as readers, although other activities throughout the day also contribute to reading improvement. During content-area reading, students increase their content knowledge as they use their semantic, syntactic, graphophonic, and pragmatic cueing systems. When children write during content studies, they strengthen their graphophonic knowledge.

Community Gathering

The community gathering provides an opportunity for us to demonstrate reading and writing processes for our students and to think aloud as a literate person. Some first graders, even after a year in kindergarten, have few role models for literacy, and we can serve in that role during the year. When we think aloud as a reader and writer, children hear the thought processes we use as we construct meaning.

Daily news is a form of shared writing and is an excellent way to open the school day, but we do not recommend that you use it during your community gathering experience because it takes away from the reading block focus. For many years, Gayle had daily news as part of her daily opening activities, which occurred outside of the reading block. Daily news provides children experience with the written model of communication, and this activity is one of the best opportunities to teach phonics skills.

Read-Alouds

Reading carefully selected children's literature during the gathering is just one of several times our students hear good texts; the gathering read-aloud is just one part of our literacy program. All literature we share throughout the day has a special attribute that meets the curriculum and the needs of our students.

We read short picture books with the same teaching focus, such as rhyming words. We might choose a relatively new series like *Skippyjon Jones* by Judy Schachner, which contains short songs and rhymes within the texts, or we can use poems, an effective way to share beautiful or vivid language that stirs the imagination and fosters visualization. Poems and songs can be written on charts or transparencies, or placed on Elmos, so they can be revisited throughout the year. Gayle always makes sure all students have copies of the shared poems to place in their poetry binders to read and reread with family and peers.

To help students develop as readers who seek meaning from text, we ask them to orally retell the story of the text, talk about the setting, walk through the story sequence, and contemplate the main character's problem and the solution to that problem.

Gayle has a world map on the wall behind her community gathering space. The students place the title of the book on the map where they think the story took place. Students use clues from the text to infer where it could have happened. The map helps students remember setting and gives them a place to visit when they are in doubt about a setting. Locating places on the map also teaches social studies skills within the context of reading. See page 120 for a list of some of Gayle's favorite books for first-grade read-alouds and focus lessons.

Shared Reading of Enlarged Texts

The shared reading strategy offers endless opportunities for student learning. Don Holdaway (1979) contributed a special gift to primary children and teachers when he studied American research concerning early readers. He found that children who had been read to on the laps of family members were usually the most precocious readers. Holdaway's idea was to duplicate the lap-reading experience in a classroom, and through this idea the shared reading strategy was created.

In a first-grade gathering, especially at the beginning of the year, there is no better strategy than shared reading. Bobbie Fisher and Emily Fisher Medvic's *Perspectives on Shared Reading: Planning and Practice* (2000) is a must for early primary teachers.

When a majority of the children are emergent, whole-group shared reading is ideal because no child is asked to read without support. An example of a shared reading session follows.

The children are seated on the carpet waiting for the teacher to share the big-book version of *The Enormous Watermelon* by Brenda Parkes. As the teacher moves toward the easel, she can hear the students predicting what they think the book is about.

Katelin says, "This is going to be about a watermelon. I have read this book before."

Taylor observes, "They are trying to pull it off the vine, but they can't. I think they are going to have to get a saw and cut the vine."

Nora says, "No, they are going to get everybody to help them and then it is going to come off."

As the teacher hears the predictions, she writes them on a chart close by. After she has recorded five predictions, she turns to the class and says, "You have been doing what good readers do before they read a book. They make predictions. They use what they know and take a guess as to what the book may be about. Now let's read the book and see if any of our predictions are correct."

She reads the title of the book and tells the children she wants them to listen to her read the book first and then to read along with her. By the time she reaches the end of the book, hands are up everywhere, letting her know that one of the predictions was correct. She asks the class to reread the book with her. Together they read the book again, with the teacher's voice fading in and out, asking about the strategies children are using to figure out some of the words on their own. At the end of the shared reading, everyone wants to reread the book, but the teacher tells them they will revisit the book the next day. They validate their predictions and everyone leaves the gathering feeling like a reader. For a list of some of Gayle's favorite books for shared reading, please see page 120. Note that any enlarged text can be used for shared reading.

Focus Lessons

We prefer the term focus lesson rather than mini-lesson because it is more self-explanatory: we intensely focus on one skill or strategy during this time. A focus lesson is brief. It's five to ten minutes during which we first share with students the purpose of the lesson, give examples of the focus topic, and often demonstrate by thinking aloud. The student can then practice the focus lesson topic in the peer interaction and independent engagement components of the block.

constantly rereading what is being written. You are saying things like "What sounds do you hear?" "What letter do you think comes first in *truck*?" "Do you hear two or three sounds in *phone*?"

The topic can come from us or our students. If you are writing about an experience, it needs to be something familiar to the entire class. Animals, class field trips, and family happenings are usually good topics. Gayle has pets in her room that create countless stories. The escaping turtle Domino was always a popular topic. At least three times a year, the students put Wanted posters around the school for the missing reptile. Gayle even used one of Domino's infamous escapes to teach making inferences.

In first grade, the stress should not be on using conventional spelling. Worrying about spelling can stunt children's imaginations. Young children should write what they hear without the pressure of trying to spell words conventionally. What is written during interactive writing is not usually published and never leaves the classroom. Our policy is that any written pieces that do leave the classroom and head home should be transcribed into conventional spelling and mechanics. You can say, "Because we are sending our letter to Mrs. Evans, we will make it like big people spell." The teacher acts as the editor of those pieces in order to gain insight into what the students can do, and use this information to guide the instruction.

A book on interactive writing that we recommend for the primary grades is *Dancing with the Pen* published by the New Zealand Staff Ministry of Education (1992). Maryann's friend Ro Griffith was instrumental in the writing of this most informative book.

Gayle's Conference Form for First Grade

Name _____

Date _____

Comments

Text 1 _____ Level__ F UF F N Text 4 _____ Level__ F UF F N
Text 2 _____ Level__ F UF F N Text 5 _____ Level__ F UF F N
Text 3 _____ Level__ F UF F N Text 6 _____ Level__ F UF F N

**Insert bk. # next to concept demonstrated.

Fiction Oral Retelling

Sequentially Retold ___

Beginning: Setting___ Characters___

Middle: Problem_____

Ending: Solution_____

Nonfiction Oral Retelling

Recalled 5 facts____ More____

Comments

Instruction Based on Conference

Totals

* If leveled books are used, record level.
** F is for books that are familiar and UF is for books that are unfamiliar.
*** Genre that includes fiction or nonfiction.

122   Creating the Best Literacy Block Ever

Resource 3-2: *Gayle's Conference Form for First Grade*

Author Studies

We aren't suggesting an in-depth author study here because there isn't enough time during the block. Those can be done at other times during the day. What we recommend is more of a mini/author or illustrator study after you have read several works and you want to draw attention to a particular author, illustrator, or poet.

Our daily read-aloud often focuses on a particular author, helping students note likenesses between the various books in setting, problem, solution, or characters.

We might read *In the Tall, Tall Grass* and *The Cow Who Clucked*, both written and illustrated by Denise Fleming. We also share copies of other Fleming books, such as *Time to Sleep* and *Mama Cat Has Three Kittens*. We look at her illustrations and compare the differences and similarities among books. We might ask the students "What media has she used?" and "What picture is your favorite in the book?"

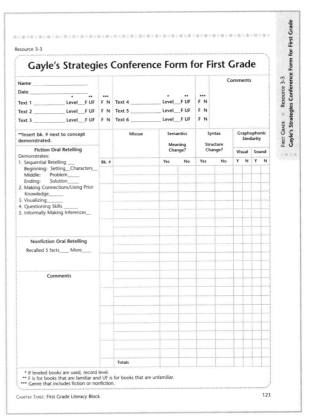

Resource 3-3: *Gayle's Strategies Conference Form for First Grade*

During literacy centers, students might then read a short biography of Fleming on the Internet and find information about her painting style. The students sometimes write to an author such as Fleming to tell her how much they enjoy her books. They ask the author not to write back but to keep busy writing and illustrating wonderful books for them to enjoy.

Dictation

We like to use individual whiteboards for dictation because they can be used for many literacy tasks, such as writing an answer to a question and then discussing the different words that appear in our answer. We recommend that first-grade students write down a dictated sentence at least once a week. Observing how students write a dictated sentence can reveal much about graphophonic growth. Children who are comfortable sharing what they have written can help other students understand the graphophonic system. The reading and writing connection helps strengthen literacy growth as well.

Vocabulary Study

Studying vocabulary together as a community can be enjoyable if it is done in short spurts. Not all unknown words are worth using time to learn, so we want to choose words that will help children understand what they are reading as well as express themselves in both speech and writing. We also want them to know there are words they can't figure out through phonics; if they haven't heard the word pronounced, they may not be able to say it correctly.

Having students act out words also helps them gain a better understanding. A book that Gayle uses to introduce students to acting out vocabulary is *Miss Alaineus: A Vocabulary Disaster* by Debra Frasier. Vocabulary study during the community gathering helps students learn how to chunk words by finding base words and determining meaning before endings are added.

Gayle has an "interesting words" chart tablet where ongoing word lists from read-alouds are recorded. For example, *Johnny Appleseed* by Steven Kellogg introduced the word *boisterous*, which was noted and recorded. The children remembered the storyline, and when they wanted to use an "interesting" word that meant loud and noisy, they took this word from the chart.

A picture of the cover of each read-aloud was included on the left-hand side of the chart, with the interesting words from the books written on the right-hand side. Granted, the students often can't read these complex words, but once they identify the book cover they can recall the interesting words. Use of a word is the first step to that word becoming a part of the child's vocabulary. Children's literature is a great resource for teaching vocabulary.

Think-Alouds

When we read aloud, we want to share our thinking processes so our students can hear our thoughts as we interact with the text. It is during this time that we share our love for reading and our excitement for literature and other texts. It is never too early to share these think-aloud experiences with children. You will often hear them copy your thought processes when they are reading their own books.

In first grade, we want children to make connections based on their prior knowledge. For example, as Gayle reads *Trevor's Wiggly Wobbly Tooth* by Lester Laminack, she pauses and says, "This reminds me of the time I had a loose tooth and I had to constantly wiggle it until it came out. I can understand why Trevor is having a difficult time."

Intentional Instruction

We spend the bulk of our time working with individuals and small groups. If your first grade is like most, you probably have a diverse span of literacy levels. You're likely to have children who can read chapter books sitting beside children who are reading at the emergent level and just beginning to understand sound–symbol relationships. Through informal and formal assessments, including observations, we learn much about our students' reading development, their interests, and what needs to be taught.

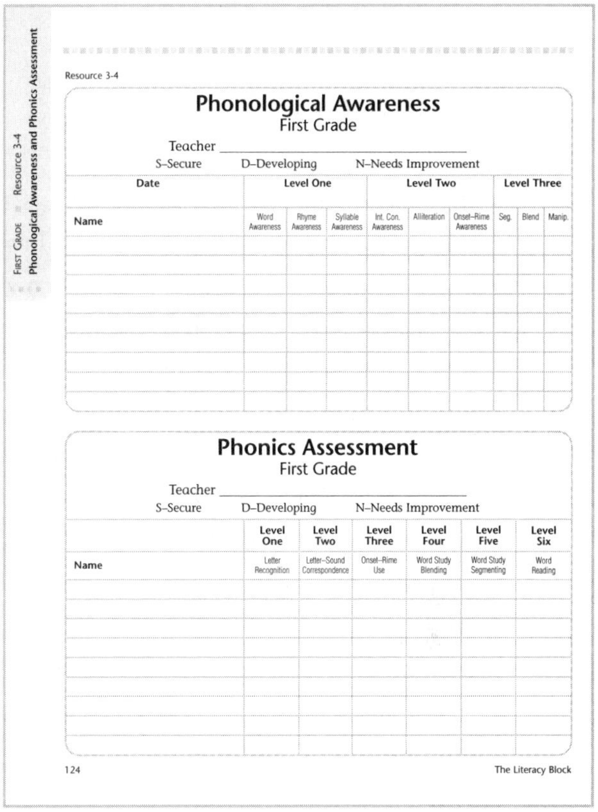

What will we teach and to whom will we teach it? As the teacher, we have so many choices, and we're not always happy with our own decisions. Most teachers we know punish themselves for not accomplishing as much as they plan. It is important to set realistic goals, but leave enough time to roam the room. Roaming allows you to learn more about your students and interact with them via incidental teaching.

Each day as we work with groups and individuals, the composition of these groups varies. In the mid-twentieth century, three-group reading programs prevailed. Maryann remembers that the only changes ever made to the groups came as the result of a child moving out of the school zone. Today we know that groups will change often as we look at individual needs and interests. As we plan curriculum, we study both our assessments and our knowledge of individual students and their needs, gleaned from observation, instruction, and interaction. During this time, we want to use the best children's literature we can find as we support literacy growth. Refer to Resources 2-5 through 2-9 on pages 75–79 for Gayle's assessments that guide intentional teaching. Resource 3-4 shows phonological awareness and

See Resource 3-4, Phonological Awareness and Phonics Assessment, p. 124.

Resource 3-4 sidebar:

Resource 3-4

Phonological Awareness
First Grade

Teacher _____

S–Secure   D–Developing   N–Needs Improvement

Date		Level One			Level Two		Level Three		
Name	Word Awareness	Rhyme Awareness	Syllable Awareness	Int. Con. Awareness	Alliteration	Onset–Rime Awareness	Seg.	Blend	Manip.

Phonics Assessment
First Grade

Teacher _____

S–Secure   D–Developing   N–Needs Improvement

Name	Level One	Level Two	Level Three	Level Four	Level Five	Level Six
	Letter Recognition	Letter–Sound Correspondence	Onset–Rime Use	Word Study Blending	Word Study Segmenting	Word Reading

124   The Literacy Block

Resource 3-4: *Phonological Awareness and Phonics Assessment* phonics assessment summary forms to guide your intentional teaching.

Discussion of Texts

All first graders can discuss either what they have heard read aloud to them or text they have read themselves. Many first graders can read connected texts but are unable to read words in isolation. These students should discuss with you and their peers the meanings they have constructed.

You may be required to use a mandated text, and our hope is that the one your school or district uses contains quality children's literature. Because the canned questions contained in the teacher's guide may not be meaningful to your students, we encourage you to ask your own questions. The best question to ask often depends upon the last response made by the students. Gayle has a questioning bookmark (Resource 2-10) that will help you develop questions for critical thinking.

Retellings are an excellent way to begin a book discussion. As different students contribute to the discussion, each contribution can trigger other students' memories of other events and details. We often choose to follow a retelling by asking readers to summarize the text, a task that utilizes more complex comprehension ability. Our purpose in a discussion of any text is generally the same: We want our students to construct as much meaning as possible. We also want them to use the strategies they develop with other texts. Debbie Miller's (2002) *Reading With Meaning* provides excellent strategies. We find that the notion of relating text to self, text to text, and text to world is understandable to first graders.

Not all first graders know that reading is supposed to make sense. Some may know how to pronounce all the words without being able to construct meaning from the text. When we think aloud, we demonstrate our own thought processes and then help our students try the same strategies to construct meaning from print. Talking about how we found a clue in a picture or in the text and how we made a connection with our content knowledge helps readers. In addition, talking about how we substituted a word for an unknown word and how we changed our minds because it didn't sound like language that made sense is also helpful.

Reading Conferences

Individual reading conferences are short meetings with a child, usually five to ten minutes, when we discuss books the child has read or is reading. At the beginning of the year, some of your students will not be reading independently. (See the kindergarten chapter for strategies to use with emergent readers.) As the year goes on, the number of students who can read text independently will grow. Those who are reading need to meet the teacher in a conference at least once or twice a week. Although it's often challenging to find the time for the conferences, they are especially important because they enable us to learn how a child is constructing meaning from the text. Conducting conferences also encourages children to read independently because they will want to meet an individual goal before the next conference.

During the conference we may ask the child to read a paragraph or so aloud, summarize what has been read, talk about characters, and discuss other story elements. As teachers, we feel we never have enough time to sit and enjoy the child and book as much as we would like to, but these weekly conferences are nonnegotiable if our goal is to develop readers. We record the name of the books read since the last conference on a progression form (Resource 2-16), which is kept in the teacher's reading conference notebook.

See Resource 2-16, Text Progression Form, p. 86.

We use two different conference forms to document oral reading. On the first one (see Resource 3-2 on page 122), we record miscues and responses to story elements, facts the student learned, and the instructional implications gleaned from the conference. On the second form (see Resource 3-3 on page 123), we also make note of the use of comprehension strategies. Regie Routman's *Reading Essentials* (2003) has many other excellent suggestions for conferences.

Shared Reading

This enjoyable literacy strategy is advantageous for both the whole-group community gathering and small groups during intentional teaching. For children who are still emergent readers in first grade, we can support them as they strengthen their knowledge of alphabetic principles and the mechanics of written language. Big books, other types of enlarged text, and multiple copies of texts offer many opportunities to discuss the relationship between the print and the illustrations. Some students benefit from rereading a big book introduced during community gathering if they weren't ready for the literacy element at the time we presented it.

Guided Reading

Students who have one-to-one correspondence of the spoken and written word and have 90 to 95 percent accuracy on a running record are ready to advance to forms of reading that foster independence. This does not mean they will not benefit from additional shared reading, which remains appropriate for the literacy block throughout the primary grades.

There are many similarities between guided reading and shared reading. Many of the strategies are the same, except guided reading is intended for a group of six or fewer students. The form of the text changes, and instead of enlarged texts, each child has an individual copy of a children's trade book. The texts for guided reading are at the appropriate level for the students. We recommend Scholastic's Teacher Book Wizard (bookwizard.scholastic.com/), which indexes and gives reading levels for thousands of children's books, and *The Fountas and Pinnell Leveled Book List K–8* (2006). This is not to say that the leveling sources know the content knowledge of our students, but authors of the leveled text gradient have studied the vocabulary, length of sentences, and complexity of ideas in the texts. The books are arranged from simple to more complex so students can be presented with more challenging texts.

As we mentioned, many of the same questions we ask during shared reading are also appropriate during guided reading. For example, we may ask students to look at illustrations through a picture walk to aid in prediction, or we may ask students if their responses sound like language and make sense. During these lessons, we continue to strengthen sound–symbol correspondences if that is still a challenge. With repeated guided reading using increasingly difficult text, students make the leap to becoming independent readers.

Focus Lessons

Focus lessons are an effective way to support emergent readers. Informal assessments such as Gayle's phonemic awareness and phonological assessment and observations made during conferences inform us as to which students need help with a particular strategy. The color-coded summary sheet (Resource 3-5) serves as a guide in developing intentional teaching. Conducting short focus groups with no more than five students is an effective way of supporting readers as they become proficient in their use of a particular reading strategy. We try to always use quality children's literature and to draw on the power of the reading–writing connection.

See Resource 3-5, Summary of Phonological Awareness and Summary of Phonics Assessment, p. 125.

We teachers often think there is a reading authority out there with such brilliant ideas that if we could only find them, our students would master every strategy. More often than not, however, our own ideas, including something as simple as employing a think-aloud with a short text, are even more effective.

Literature Discussion Groups

Some readers may be surprised that we are including literature discussion groups for first grade, but Gayle frequently uses them for precocious first-grade readers. Although not many students are in literature discussion groups at the beginning of the year, as the year progresses, more and more children want to participate. We are not suggesting that rigid roles or rules must be followed; instead, these students simply read chapter books and meet with Gayle at least twice a week for discussion. It is during these short meetings that Gayle clears up misconceptions or reteaches a strategy that will increase comprehension. Literature discussion groups will be discussed in more depth in the Peer Interaction section of the chapter.

Resource 3-5

Summary of Phonological Awareness
First Grade

Teacher _____

S–Secure D–Developing N–Needs Improvement

Name / Date	Level One			Level Two			Level Three		
	Word Awareness	Rhyme Awareness	Syllable Awareness	Int. Con. Awareness	Alliteration	Onset–Rime Awareness	Seg.	Blend	Manip.
	S	S	S	S	S	S	S	S	N
	N	D	S	S	S	S	S	S	N
	S	S	S	N	N	S	S	S	N
	S	S	D	S	D	N	S	S	D
	S	N	D	N	S	N	N	D	N
	S	S	S	S	D	S	D	D	D
	S	S	N	S	S	S	S	S	N
	D	S	S	N	D	N	N	S	N
	S	S	D	N	S	D	N	S	N

Summary of Phonics Assessment
First Grade

Teacher _____

S–Secure D–Developing N–Needs Improvement

Name	Level One	Level Two	Level Three	Level Four	Level Five	Level Six
	Letter Recognition	Letter–Sound Correspondence	Onset–Rime Use	Word Study Blending	Word Study Segmenting	Word Reading
	S	D	D	S	D	N
	S	D	N	N	S	D
	S	D	N	N	N	N
	S	N	N	D	D	D
	N	N	N	D	N	N
	D	D	N	N	N	N
	S	D	D	S	N	N
	S	N	N	N	N	N
	D	N	N	N	N	N

Resource 3-5: *Summary of Phonological Awareness and Summary of Phonics Assessment*

Independent Engagement

During this time, students read appropriate text that will further their reading development. Having students monitor their own reading processes and select appropriate texts helps them to become mature, independent readers. You may be required to use a commercial text; if so, we hope that it includes quality children's literature. We think it is a good idea for students to keep a list of the books they read independently. If students are responding in a literature reading journal, writing the name of the book before the entry serves this purpose.

Students have an opportunity to apply a strategy that was introduced during a focus lesson by making entries in the "Growing as a Reader" pages in the back of their reading journals (see Figure 3.2 on page 100). For example, if our focus lesson was on the blend *st-*, we add a page in the back of each student's journal for documenting at least two words from the text they are reading independently that contain the blend. This recording shows us that the student understands the blend and can recognize its use in print.

We are reminded of an old phrase that Goodman, Watson, and Burke (1996) use to describe our involvement in encouraging students to read independently: "You can lead a horse to water but you can't make him drink." Reading is a cognitive process that each human does alone. We can "season the water" to tempt children to read, but students must connect individually with texts that are special to them. Parents also provide the conditions that support their children and engage them as readers at home.

Challenges of Self-Selection

We wish that all children could self-select a majority of their texts, but that isn't always possible. In the section that follows, we address some of the challenges.

1. Children choose books that are not appropriate. We like the way in which Jobe and Dayton-Sakari (2002) use the story of the three bears when thinking about leveling books. The story of baby bear tasting porridge has relevance for this discussion. When baby bear was eating, he didn't want his porridge too hot (i.e., too difficult, with students not understanding what they're reading), but neither did he want the porridge too cold (too easy, offering no challenge). He wants his porridge *just right* (at the right level of difficulty, so the students can understand what they read at the same time they continue to be challenged to make meaning).

2. Leveling of text is not an exact science. Some educators are rigid about the use of leveled books. We appreciate the available text gradient systems because we believe they help us quickly approximate a book's level. We especially like these three: 1) Scholastic's online Teacher Book Wizard (**bookwizard.scholastic. com/tbw**), 2) the Reading Recovery Council of North America's online database (available by subscription at **www.readingrecovery.org/rrcna/membership/books 2.asp**), and 3) *The Fountas and Pinnell Leveled Book List K–8* (2006). All systems use several text characteristics that include vocabulary, sentence length, concept load, and textual features. We hold a psycholinguistic theory of reading; we are convinced that each reader needs to possess the content knowledge necessary to construct meaning, and this consideration is left out of the leveling systems. Children who have grown up on an island will have a deeper understanding of texts about water than children who grew up in the Midwest without easy access to large bodies of water. Content knowledge must be considered when looking at levels. Maryann's article in *Teaching PreK–8*, "On the Level," which discusses the overuse of leveling, is easily accessible online in the magazine's archives at www.teachingk-8.com.

3. Availability of books is limited by money and space. There are only so many books that can be stored in classrooms and school libraries. Although we want to possess the books that are interesting to children, we cannot anticipate the interests of all the children who will be in our classrooms. Fortunately, more and more nonfiction books are being published each year, but there are still topics that lack books at different levels.

Below are a few of the activities in which students can participate as they are engaged in reading appropriate texts.

Literature Response Groups

We are not suggesting that all your students will be engaged in literature discussion groups all year, but you may have some children who can participate. As the year progresses, you will have more and more who will join them. The students silently read the chapters or sections of the book they have decided to read before the next discussion group. We suggest you ask them to keep a list of words they can't pronounce or don't know the meaning of, along with the page number. The bookmarks guide comprehension and understanding of story elements during these discussions. These entries can be made in their literature response journals and discussed with the groups.

Literature Response Journals

We especially like literature reading response journals because they provide students an opportunity to summarize in writing what they have read and/or respond personally to the text (making text-to-self, text-to-text, or text-to-world connections). Gayle's student bookmarks and Thinking About My Book form (Resource 3-6 and 3-7) help to guide students' thinking and writing. The actual journal can be a bound blank book or something as simple as paper stapled together with a construction paper cover. An example of a journal entry is shown in Figure 3.3.

See Resource 3-6, My Reading Responses book-mark, p. 126.

See Resource 3-7, Thinking About My Book, p. 127.

At the back of students' literature response journals are the "Growing as a Reader" pages, in which students apply strategies they learn in focus lessons. Gayle usually folds down a page toward the end of the journal noting the beginning of these pages.

Creating Word Logs

Students record interesting words in their literature response journals. When children are reading independently, they need to make lists of words they can't pronounce, words they don't know the meaning of, and words that are used in interesting ways. It is especially important to have children record page numbers so they can go back and read the word in context when conferencing with you. These entries show us that they are consciously aware of breakdowns in meaning while reading.

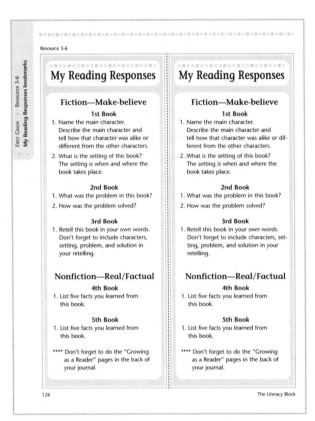

■ Resource 3-6: *My Reading Responses bookmarks*

Some teachers we know don't use journal entries but have children write interesting words on sticky notes. Other teachers just use narrow strips of paper. The reason we prefer literature response journals is that sticky notes can fall out and strips of paper are easy to lose. A record of words recorded over time in a journal can help us assess the type of words that are troublesome for students and can provide us a glimpse of words they consider interesting.

Writing Book Critiques

Children have very definite opinions about books, and they should be encouraged to express them. To scaffold their efforts, have students choose three or four questions from those listed below and use them as a guide as they write a critique.

■ Did you like the book?

■ What are the reasons for your answer?

- What parts of the book did you find interesting?
- Did the book have any lessons for people?
- Would you recommend that others read the book? Why or why not?

Although writing critiques is a valuable experience in making reading–writing connections, children should not be expected to critique every book they read. When students write critiques, you can discuss their responses during the community sharing.

Independent Research

First graders are fully capable of doing research on topics that interest them. Children first need a guiding question, which can result from any area of the curriculum. The question can be related to science, social studies, or another discipline, a book that was read aloud or a television show. We recommend that you demonstrate to your students how to conduct research. Isolate a question and then read and view your information while taking notes on the overhead or on chart paper. Write your report in front of the children so you demystify the process and give them a concrete sequence of steps to refer to during the process.

Gayle demonstrates the steps in the research process for the whole class during a theme immersion (a unit of study that focuses on a particular topic or theme). The children break into small "research teams" around chosen topics of study and follow the same steps. Each member of the research team takes notes by reading, viewing, and listening to texts. Members of the team then compile their notes into one list capturing their most important ideas from their note-taking. In general, a research project follows these steps:

Resource 3-7

Thinking About My Book

Name _____ Date _____

Title _____

Setting _____

Characters _____
_____

Problem _____
_____
_____

What Happened in the Beginning _____
_____
_____

What Happened in the Middle _____
_____
_____

What Happened at the End _____
_____
_____

How the Problem Was Solved _____
_____

- Resource 3-7: *Thinking About My Book*

1. Put together text sets of materials on the research topic, including picture books, nonfiction magazines, newspapers, and primary source documents such as handwritten letters, photo albums, and diaries.

2. Gather information by reading, viewing, and listening to texts; each member of the team takes notes.

3. Compile notes from each team member into one comprehensive document.

4. Arrange for a content conference with a peer (discuss the notes and determine what's most important to emphasize).

5. Arrange for a content conference with the teacher.

6. Edit information.

7. Participate in an editing conference with a peer.

8. Participate in an editing conference with the teacher.

9. Write a draft book.

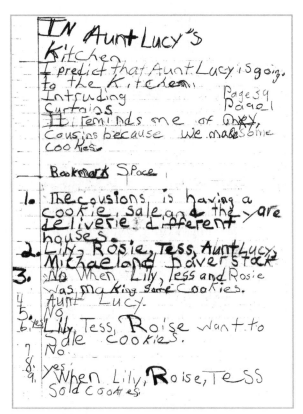

■ Figure 3.3: *Sample of first-grade journal entry*

Gayle then takes the draft book and publishes it in a format for the students to illustrate. These books become part of the nonfiction library in the classroom as well as the school library. One year, Gayle's class published 57 books. An example of a research page is shown in Figure 3.4. See also RealeBooks.com for ideas about publishing online.

The students use the steps while independently researching topics of choice during the reading block. The steps are also displayed on a bulletin board for reference as students research topics throughout the day.

Peer Interaction

Independent reading should receive the most attention during the reading block, but time must also be devoted to social interaction among peers. Discussion is

The Literacy Block

essential during the reading block because without exchanging points of view, children may never reach high levels of thinking. Literature response groups, graphic organizers, and research work together to foster critical thinking and promote comprehension, which results in learning.

Not all interaction is for the purpose of promoting analytical thinking. Some group experiences focus on particular reading skills. For example, to improve reading flow, students participate in Readers Theater and read poems together. Artistic representations and technology projects offer ways for our students to express the knowledge they build during their reading.

Many other learning experiences also involve pairs or triads of students. You may have some favorites that we haven't included. The following sections describe a few of our favorite peer interaction engagements.

The Brooklyn Bridge is the oldest and most popular bridge in New York City.

1.

Fig. 3.4: *Sample of first-grade research*

Literature Discussion Groups

Not all first graders are ready to participate in literature discussion groups, but some are. When a few children seem ready to pace themselves through a book together, let them choose a book from titles you have multiple copies of that are appropriate for these particular readers. During the first few literature discussion groups, sit with the students and demonstrate questioning and discussion skills. You may be thinking that we should have told you that the students should follow different roles, but at the primary level, our goal is to develop comprehension through discussion. We especially like the book *Grand Conversations: Literature Groups in Action* by Ralph Peterson and Maryann Eeds (1990) for its description of the value of classroom discussions. (A 2007 updated edition of this best-selling classic, with new booklists, is available from Scholastic.)

Readers Theater

A favorite strategy of our students is the reading of plays, poems, and texts prepared for Readers Theater. This activity is more appropriate for children who have moved beyond the emergent reading level and can read text that is less repetitive and predictable.

We've seen an explosion of published texts available for use in this way, since many authorities recommend Readers Theater as a way to develop oral reading flow. Students may also choose favorite books and write scripts to perform.

There are no hard and fast rules for preparing Readers Theater passages. Students need text that isn't too difficult, although it may contain unknown words that can be decoded and understood in the process of practicing. Students can help as they practice the text. In preparation for Readers Theater and to improve reading flow, students can listen to prerecorded works in the listening center or on their iPods by authors such as Robert Munsch. We also especially like *It's Show Time: Poetry From the Page to the Stage* by Allan Wolf (1993) as a source of poems already scripted for choral reading. The author has the poems organized by level based on difficulty. Some of the level 1 scripted poems for several voices that work well for first graders are "Mice" by Rose Fyleman, "The Little Turtle" by Vachel Lindsay, and "My Dog" by Marchette Chute.

Other Readers Theater scripts can be found on the Internet at Aaron Shepherd's Readers Theater Page, www.aaronshep.com/rt/index.html. Although most of these free scripts are more appropriate for older students, there are two scripts we like for first grade. They are "Help!, Hilary!, Help!" about a little girl whose mother experiences a series of misadventures, and "Which Shoes Do You Choose?" in which young Katie can't make up her mind about which shoes to buy.

Some additional resources for Readers Theater scripts are *Readers Theatre for Beginning Readers* (1993) and *Multicultural Folktales: Readers Theatre for Elementary Students* (2006) by Suzanne I. Barchers. The scripts in these two books are organized by grade level and contain many stories familiar to first graders, such as "The Three Little Pigs" and "The Three Billy Goats Gruff." We also like Reading A–Z's Reader's Theater Web site (www.readinga-z.com), which has scripts that are leveled for difficulty and teaching tips for using them.

Of course, when we began our teaching careers there were no commercial Readers Theater scripts to purchase, so we made our own from the books we noticed our children enjoyed revisiting. Some teachers like to buy two or three copies of a single text and highlight the different parts for Reader one in the first copy, the parts for Reader two in the second copy, and so forth.

Graphic Organizers

There are many ways to extend the thinking of young children, but using graphic organizers is especially helpful in increasing logical thought processes. The Venn diagram is a popular tool for helping children analyze similarities and differences, temporal relationships, and number of occurrences. A visual comparison of two stories is developed by writing all the unique aspects of a story in one circle and those of another story in another circle, with all the commonalities of the stories in the overlapping section of the two circles. On a story vine, the student identifies story elements such as characters, setting, problem, and solution of a book that he or she has just read. The student writes the story elements on leaves along the vine, retelling the story along the way.

Any visual representation of different attributes, from a time line depicting the events in the story in chronological order to a bar graph illustrating facts in a nonfiction text, would be considered a graphic organizer. Different types of graphic organizers naturally fit the content of fiction and nonfiction. We have found that it is best to highlight a maximum of three graphic organizers. The students quickly become familiar with the format, and their focus will then shift from how to complete the graphic organizers to how the organizers support comprehension.

Literature discussion groups can also use graphic organizers to demonstrate an understanding of their text. When Gayle had a group reading a book that had been made into a movie everyone in the group had seen, she suggested they complete a Venn diagram on similarities, differences, and commonalities in the story as it was told in different media.

Dramatizations

Short periods of time spent acting out a story can be a pleasurable way to think deeply about a story. Small groups of students can reread a text and improvise ways to express the meaning. Our students are rarely bored when they are engaged in dramatic play. Oral language develops as children portray different parts of a story. Don't forget this choice because drama has so many benefits, including improving reading flow.

Acting out stories is fun and increases comprehension because a child must understand the characters' actions and dialogue. There are no rules with drama: costumes aren't necessary and props can be as simple as a piece of paper with a word written on it. The stories can be from read-alouds, literature response journals, and books students have read independently. Usually, fiction is the best source for text, but some nonfiction can be adapted. One scene is usually enough for a reenactment. Some favorites for first graders are the Frog and Toad series and the Carl books; the latter are wordless picture books so dramatization is dependent upon students creating meaningful dialogue.

Technology Projects

The Web has greatly increased the amount of text we have in our classrooms. Schools can obtain site licenses for every classroom to have access to a wide variety of virtual libraries. Examples of these sites are Readinga-z.com (www.reading a-z.com/) and Bookflix (teacher.scholastic.com/products/bookflixfreetrial).

Our students can retell the stories they read through PowerPoint presentations and Kidspiration software. There are many Web sites, such as StudyDog (www.studydog.com/), where children can practice their reading strategies and skills.

Community Sharing

The last few minutes of each workshop are usually devoted to a whole-group gathering to celebrate reading. The reason we say usually is that some days everyone is so busy that we don't all come together. Some teachers we know have three gatherings each week, and others have one every day because of the psychological benefits to the community of enjoying reading together.

We know the benefits of gathering. The three of us belong to a book club that meets once a month. There are approximately 12 in the group, and we not only enjoy reading books but we also gain much pleasure giving our opinions about them. We often have surprisingly different perceptions, and seldom do we all agree on what a given chapter means. But we gain much from hearing others' opinions.

There is no correct format for community sharing within the classroom; some days a group will perform a play. The next day there may be a popcorn-style sharing (spontaneous, with no order of response) of favorite books. Some teachers we know have a sign-up sheet where students schedule a dramatization or a Readers Theater production. Some teachers ask students to bring passages and illustrations to the gathering to share. The following questions can evoke interesting responses:

- What is the name of a book that you would take as a gift to a birthday party for a girl? For a boy?

- Who is your favorite character from all the books you have read or that have been read to you?

- What is the most beautiful (or funniest) illustration you have ever seen in a book?

We have used the following ideas for presentations during the community gathering:

Artistic
ABC book
Illustrations
Costumes of characters
Character mobiles
Book posters

Drama
Readers Theater
Improvisations
Monologues
Plays
Puppet plays
Skits
Storytelling

Literary-Style Sharing
Parallel big book
Dictionary
Sharing journals
Lists of facts
Raps

Speech Forms
Demonstrations
Oral reports

Symbolic Presentations
Cartoons
Graphs

Three-Dimensional Art
Constructions
Diorama
Sculptures
Shadow boxes

Technology
Kidpix
Virtual tour of setting
Author/illustrator studies
Web site viewing
Podcasting
RealeBooks

In Conclusion ∼

Most students in first grade are readers who have gone beyond the emergent level. They are developing greater comprehension of text as they mature as silent readers and independent writers. Our literacy block at this level moves more smoothly among the components as students shift from a measure of dependence to more autonomy.

Some of Gayle's favorite books for first-grade read-alouds and focus lessons include:

Bruce, L. (1999). *Fran's flower*

Curtis, J. L. (1993). *When I was little: A four-year-old's memoir of her youth*

Ehlert, L. (2004). *Pie in the sky*

Ehlert, L. (2007). *Wag a tail*

Falconer, I. (2000). *Olivia*

Falconer, I. (2001). *Olivia saves the circus*

Falconer, I. (2003). *Olivia… and the missing toy*

Falconer, I. (2006). *Olivia forms a band*

Fleming, C. (2002). *Muncha! Muncha! Muncha!*

Fleming, C. (2007). *Tippy-tippy-tippy, hide!*

Fleming, D. (1997). *Time to sleep*

Fleming, D. (2001). *Pumpkin eye*

Fleming, D. (2006). *The cow who clucked*

Fox, M. (1994). *Tough Boris*

Fox, M. (1998). *Boo to a goose*

Henkes, K. (2000). *Wemberly worried*

Jarman, J. (2007). *Class two at the zoo*

Jeffers, O. (2006). *The incredible book eating boy*

Ketteman, H. (2000). *Armadillo tattletale*

Laminack, L. (1998). *Trevor's wiggly-wobbly tooth*

Lester, H. (1999). *Hooway for Wodney wat*

Lyon, G. (1999). *Book*

Meddaugh, S. (1997). *Cinderella's rat*

Mitton, T. (2002). *Down by the cool of the pool*

O'Malley, K. (2000). *Bud*

Penn, A. (2007). *A kiss goodbye*

Prince, J. (2006). *I saw an ant on the railroad track*

Provencher, R. (2001). *Mouse cleaning*

Root, P. (2003). *One duck stuck*

Root, P. (2001). *Rattletrap car*

Schachner, J. (2003). *Skippyjon Jones*

Shannon, D. (2002). *Duck on a bike*

Shannon, D. (2004). *Alice the fairy*

Trapani, I. (2000). *Shoo fly*

Some of Gayle's favorite books for shared reading include:

Carle, E. (1977). *The grouchy ladybug*

Carle, E. (1987). *The tiny seed*

Cowley, J. (1999). *When I was young*

Gretz, S. (1991). *Frog in the middle*

Hutchins, P. (1974). *The wind blew*

Numeroff, L. (1998). *If you give a mouse a cookie*

Parkes, B., & Smith, J. (1986). *The enormous watermelon*

Redhead, J. S. (1988). *The big block of chocolate*

Zorfass, J. (2000). *Bella lost her moo*

FIRST GRADE ■ Resource 3-1
Gayle's Phonics Progression Chart for First Grade

Gayle's Phonics and Reading Progression Chart for First Grade
Suggestions for Emphasizing Meaning and Phonics Throughout the Year

Grading Period (May Vary)	Phonics and Reading Focuses	Date of Intentional Instruction (whole group and small group)	Date of Practice (literacy centers, peer interactions)	Ongoing Independent Application Until Secure (e.g., reading journals)
1	Short Vowel Rimes—2 letters			
	Long Vowel Rimes –ake, –ate, –ame, –ice, –ide, –oke, –ore, –ine			
	Making Predictions/Validating			
	Making Connections			
2	Compound Words			
	Consonant l Blends –bl, –fl, –sl, –cl, –gl			
	Consonant r Blends –br, –cr, –fr, –gr, –pr, –dr, –tr			
	Consonant s Blends –st, –sc, –sk, –sp, –sn, –str, –sm			
	R-Controlled –ar, –ir, –er, –ur			
	Base Words and Inflected Endings –ed, –ing, –est, –er			
	Characters of Story			
	Setting of Story			
3	Vowel Digraphs –ea, –ei, –ey, –ie, –au, –aw, –oo			
	Short Vowel Rimes—3 letters ack, ell, est, ick, ill, ock, ump, uck, unk			
	Consonant Digraphs –sh, –ch, –th, –wh, –ph			
	Story Beginning/Middle/End			
	Story Sequence			
	Details			
	Problem/Solution			
4	–Contractions—n't, 'm, 'll, 's, 've, 're			
	–Diphthongs –ow, –ou, –oi, –oy			
	–Synonyms			
	–Antonyms			
	–Homonyms			
	–Multiple-Meaning Words			
	–Main Idea			
	–Visualizing			
	–Cause–Effect			
	–Drawing Conclusions			

Creating the Best Literacy Block Ever © 2009 by Maryann Manning, Gayle Morrison, and Deborah Camp: Scholastic Professional

Gayle's Conference Form for First Grade

Name _____

Date _____

	*	**	***			*	**	***
Text 1 _____ Level___	F	UF	F N	Text 4 _____ Level___		F	UF	F N
Text 2 _____ Level___	F	UF	F N	Text 5 _____ Level___		F	UF	F N
Text 3 _____ Level___	F	UF	F N	Text 6 _____ Level___		F	UF	F N

Comments

**Insert bk. # next to concept demonstrated.

Fiction Oral Retelling

Sequentially Retold ___

Beginning: Setting___ Characters___

Middle: Problem_____

Ending: Solution_____

Nonfiction Oral Retelling

Recalled 5 facts____ More____

Comments

Instruction Based on Conference

Bk. #	Miscue	Semantics Meaning Change?		Syntax Structure Change?		Graphophonic Similarity Visual		Sound	
		Yes	No	Yes	No	Y	N	Y	N
Totals									

 * If leveled books are used, record level.
 ** F is for books that are familiar and UF is for books that are unfamiliar.
 *** Genre that includes fiction or nonfiction.

Creating the Best Literacy Block Ever © 2009 by Maryann Manning, Gayle Morrison, and Deborah Camp: Scholastic Professional

Gayle's Strategies Conference Form for First Grade

Name _____

Date _____

		*	**	***			*	**	***
Text 1	_____ Level__	F	UF	F N	Text 4	_____ Level__	F	UF	F N
Text 2	_____ Level__	F	UF	F N	Text 5	_____ Level__	F	UF	F N
Text 3	_____ Level__	F	UF	F N	Text 6	_____ Level__	F	UF	F N

Comments

**Insert bk. # next to concept demonstrated.

Fiction Oral Retelling
Demonstrates:
1. Sequential Retelling ___
   Beginning: Setting__Characters__
   Middle: Problem_____
   Ending: Solution_____
2. Making Connections/Using Prior Knowledge_____
3. Visualizing_____
4. Questioning Skills _____
5. Informally Making Inferences__

Nonfiction Oral Retelling

Recalled 5 facts____ More____

Comments

Miscue	Semantics Meaning Change?		Syntax Structure Change?		Graphophonic Similarity			
					Visual		Sound	
Bk. #	Yes	No	Yes	No	Y	N	Y	N
Totals								

* If leveled books are used, record level.
** F is for books that are familiar and UF is for books that are unfamiliar.
*** Genre that includes fiction or nonfiction.

Creating the Best Literacy Block Ever © 2009 by Maryann Manning, Gayle Morrison, and Deborah Camp: Scholastic Professional

FIRST GRADE ■ Resource 3-6
My Reading Responses bookmarks

My Reading Responses

Fiction—Make-believe

1st Book

1. Name the main character. Describe the main character and tell how that character was alike or different from the other characters.

2. What is the setting of this book? The setting is when and where the book takes place.

2nd Book

1. What was the problem in this book?

2. How was the problem solved?

3rd Book

1. Retell this book in your own words. Don't forget to include characters, setting, problem, and solution in your retelling.

Nonfiction—Real/Factual

4th Book

1. List five facts you learned from this book.

5th Book

1. List five facts you learned from this book.

**** Don't forget to do the "Growing as a Reader" pages in the back of your journal.

My Reading Responses

Fiction—Make-believe

1st Book

1. Name the main character. Describe the main character and tell how that character was alike or different from the other characters.

2. What is the setting of this book? The setting is when and where the book takes place.

2nd Book

1. What was the problem in this book?

2. How was the problem solved?

3rd Book

1. Retell this book in your own words. Don't forget to include characters, setting, problem, and solution in your retelling.

Nonfiction—Real/Factual

4th Book

1. List five facts you learned from this book.

5th Book

1. List five facts you learned from this book.

**** Don't forget to do the "Growing as a Reader" pages in the back of your journal.

Creating the Best Literacy Block Ever © 2009 by Maryann Manning, Gayle Morrison, and Deborah Camp: Scholastic Professional

FIRST GRADE ▪ Resource 3-7
Thinking About My Book

Thinking About My Book

Name _____   Date _____

Title _____

Setting _____

Characters _____

_____

Problem _____

_____

_____

What Happened in the Beginning _____

_____

_____

What Happened in the Middle _____

_____

_____

What Happened at the End _____

_____

_____

How the Problem Was Solved _____

_____

Creating the Best Literacy Block Ever © 2009 by Maryann Manning, Gayle Morrison, and Deborah Camp: Scholastic Professional

Second-Grade Literacy Block

Community Gathering Suggested time: up to 15 minutes

- Read-aloud short texts
- Shared reading of enlarged texts
- Focus lessons
- Interactive writing
- Author studies
- Vocabulary study

Intentional Instruction Suggested time: 30–45 minutes.
Activities in all columns occur simultaneously during workshop.

Teacher/student interactions	Independent student engagement	Peer interactions
- Discussion of texts - Think-alouds - Reading assessments - Reading conferences - Shared reading - Supportive reading - Focus lessons - Meeting with literature circles - Rove the room	- Independent reading of appropriate self-selected text (usually beyond emergent level) - Prepare for literature circles - Book logs - Reading response journals - Interesting words logs - Writing book critiques - Independent research - Technology projects - Listening stations - Word work - Sketch books/sketch to stretch - Fine-arts representations	- Literature circles - Readers Theater - Sharing dramatizations - Graphic organizers - Technology projects - Word work - Reading big books together - Partner reading - Fine-arts representations

(Optional) Community Sharing Suggested time: up to 10 minutes

- Rereading a big book
- Student reading of selected passages
- Role-playing/dramatizations
- Discussion of texts or reading processes

CHAPTER 4

Second-Grade Literacy Block

It's 9:00, and Susan asks the students to move back to the carpet for the 15-minute reading block community gathering. The focus lesson for the day is visualizing, a strategy that improves reading comprehension. She reads *Rattletrap Car* by Phyllis Root and asks the students to visualize what the car looks like as she reads. She reads the book aloud without showing the students the pictures along the way. When she's done, she says that later on during literacy encounters in the reading center they will retell the story to a partner, draw a picture together of what the car looked like at the end of the story, and return the finished drawing to Susan. On Friday, after everyone has been to the reading center, all the pictures will be on display during the community gathering, and they will revisit the story and determine whose picture came closest to the author's story.

After the focus lesson, the students move with partners to an area in the room to read their instructional texts, talk about texts, and respond in their literature response journals for the next 45 to 60 minutes. In the journals, students will respond to bookmarks, teacher and student choice activities, and the "Growing as a Reader" skill pages. During this time, Susan is conferencing with students and roaming the room to observe students at work. Each student has a weekly conference in which Susan listens to him or her read, administers a miscue analysis, and discusses the books read to determine if the student is meaning making out of what he or she reads. Each book read is posted to an ongoing text progression form. All of this is documented on a conference form and put in the reading notebook where Susan keeps all conference data. Future instruction is determined by analysis of the conference form. During the last 15 minutes of the reading block, students gather back at the carpet ready to share successes and questions they might have had during their reading.

The Block in Second Grade ∿

Second graders read text at various levels, and most of your students have definite ideas about what they want to read. Many have discovered the enjoyment of reading and can read sophisticated plots and longer texts and understand complex characters. Others are still developing as readers and are reading several levels below their grade. For these students, refer to previous chapters for help in developing appropriate instruction.

Time spent at the beginning of the year establishing rituals and routines is a great investment. As the year goes on, independence increases and children grow in their literacy development. Although we want to establish rituals and routines, we also want to vary some of the content of the reading block to maintain students' interest. We've included strategies that we use in our classrooms, but this is not an exhaustive list.

Community Gathering

During this component of the reading block, literate adults and peers demonstrate and discuss their literacy. Modeling these discussions doesn't cease to be important in second grade. Hearing others thinking aloud as readers and writers can be helpful even to a very competent reader. The question "How did you figure that out?" when a student is thinking aloud not only flatters the student but also gives him or her an opportunity to further verbalize the strategies. Following are some suggestions for literacy experiences during this time.

Read-Alouds

The time we spend reading aloud helps us build a trusting community as we bond and form relationships through shared literature. The value of reading aloud is that the students hear rich literature that they cannot yet read independently. Often the text you read aloud will not be a book the students would choose to read themselves. Because you read it aloud and students enjoy it, you open up a new author or genre to them.

The reading block is not the only time we can read aloud. We might read a chapter book aloud at a designated time during the day, such as after physical education. You might read a nonfiction book aloud at times during social studies and share texts during the writing workshop. Second graders still need to hear lots of texts read aloud. The texts you choose for the reading block are short pieces of literature that have some special attributes that further the students' reading development. Many picture books can be used to teach particular skills within the context of a good story; for example, a great book for teaching adjectives is *Beetle Bop* by Denise Fleming. Poetry is an especially good genre for sharing because its concise language conjures up vivid visual images. Always be on the lookout for short texts and passages you can use during the community gathering that complement reading development. For a list of some of Gayle's favorite read-alouds for second grade, please see page 153.

Shared Reading

Shared reading is that time when you demonstrate the reading process with enlarged texts. Most second graders do not need the same level of support required in kindergarten and first grade; however, there are still occasions when shared reading is beneficial. Second graders can read along with you, and even those who may still be struggling can participate. This is a time when you can review all aspects of the reading process, including observation, punctuation, inflections, and contractions.

Some big books have text features that help with nonfiction reading. Songs and rhythmic verses on transparencies or charts or displayed by an Elmo can also be used as the enlarged text. During literacy encounters, students can reread these same texts. For a list of some of Gayle's favorite big books for second grade, please see page 153.

Focus Lessons

We define focus lessons as short periods of time, five to ten minutes, during which we tell students the purpose of the lesson, give examples of the focus topic, and demonstrate its use. The focus lesson is always aligned with the curriculum and addresses reading needs of the students. The focus lesson topic can then be practiced and applied in the peer interaction or independent engagement segments of the reading block.

An example of a second-grade focus lesson is differentiating between fact and fiction. We begin by reading aloud "Mice" by Rose Fyleman (2001).

Mice

I think mice are rather nice;
Their tails are long, their faces small;
They haven't any chins at all.
Their ears are pink, their teeth are white,
They run about the house at night;
They nibble things they shouldn't touch,
and no one seems to like them much,
but I think mice are rather nice.

We then read a description or definition of mice from an online or bound encyclopedia. The Columbia Electronic Encyclopedia says that *mouse* is "a name applied to numerous species of small rodents, often having soft gray or brown fur, long hairless tails, and large ears" (www.infoplease.com/ce6/sci/ A0834285. html). Then we ask, "Which of the two do you think is true, and which one is the poet's imagination?" Discussion follows, in which we talk about fiction and nonfiction texts that we have read. We make a list on chart paper of the ways that help us determine whether a text is true or real.

Focus lessons are important during the intentional segment because they are an effective way to support individuals, pairs, triads, and small groups of five or six children. For the community gathering, we use more general focus lessons than most students need. These lessons can be based on district and state standards. Gayle has developed a reading progression that uses her state and district standards to inform her focus lessons (Resource 4-1). As you know, reading and writing strategies become more complex as texts become more difficult, so focus lessons are taught over and over with more difficult text.

See Resource 4-1, Reading Progression Chart for Second Grade, p. 154.

The reading strategy lessons developed by Yetta Goodman, Dorothy Watson, and Carolyn Burke (2002) in *Reading Strategies: Focus on Comprehension* are excellent focus lessons. This wonderful resource includes over 40 lessons that support the development of the graphophonic, semantic, syntactic, and pragmatic cueing systems. Each lesson includes a rationale, the literacy experience, and the application of the strategy, and they are perfect for any size group of children. If the texts suggested in the lessons are too difficult or too easy, we substitute alternate texts.

Strategy books that have been helpful to us include *Reading With Meaning* by Debbie Miller (2002),

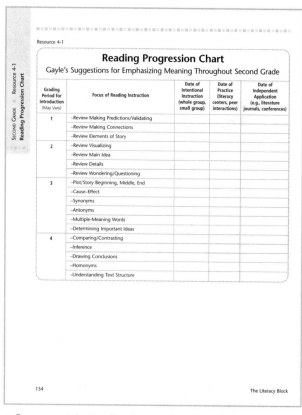

Resource 4-1

SECOND GRADE ■ Resource 4-1 Reading Progression Chart

Reading Progression Chart

Gayle's Suggestions for Emphasizing Meaning Throughout Second Grade

Grading Period for Introduction (May Vary)	Focus of Reading Instruction	Date of Intentional Instruction (whole group, small group)	Date of Practice (literacy centers, prs, peer interactions)	Date of Independent Application (e.g., literature journals, conferences)
1	–Review Making Predictions/Validating			
	–Review Making Connections			
	–Review Elements of Story			
2	–Review Visualizing			
	–Review Main Idea			
	–Review Details			
	–Review Wondering/Questioning			
3	–Plot/Story Beginning, Middle, End			
	–Cause–Effect			
	–Synonyms			
	–Antonyms			
	–Multiple-Meaning Words			
	–Determining Important Ideas			
4	–Comparing/Contrasting			
	–Inference			
	–Drawing Conclusions			
	–Homonyms			
	–Understanding Text Structure			

154

The Literacy Block

■ Resource 4-1: *Reading Progression Chart for Second Grade*

Developmental Studies Center's *Making Meaning* (2006), and *The Primary Comprehension Toolkit* by Stephanie Harvey and Anne Goudvis (2008).

Refer to Gayle's conference forms (Resources 4-2 and 4-3) for a list of strategies that can guide your focus lessons.

See Resource 4-2, Gayle's Reading Conference Form for Second Grade, p. 155.

See Resource 4-3, Gayle's Reading Strategies Conference Form for Second Grade, p. 156.

Interactive Writing

Interactive writing is another phrase used to describe how children and teachers engage in thinking about reading and writing together. The most important aspect of interactive writing is the constant support that students have as they learn more about written text. You'll need a large whiteboard, chart paper, or an overhead projector—plus a marker and an idea for a text. We prefer that our students generate the ideas because this promotes engagement in the writing experience.

Interactive writing utilizes the power of the reading–writing connection. The emphasis is on constructing knowledge about phonemes, letters, words, sentences, and paragraphs while communicating ideas. Many second graders don't need much phonics instruction, so their writing development proceeds rather quickly. Students can be the scribes, and topics can come from either students or the curriculum. Although we have said we prefer student-generated texts, the topic can come from you and curriculum requirements.

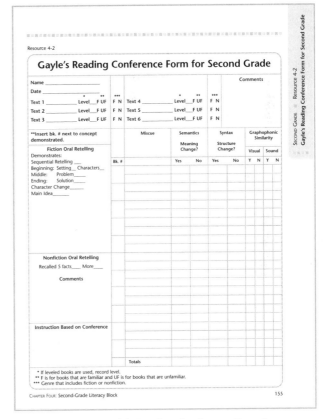

Resource 4-2: *Gayle's Reading Conference Form for Second Grade*

We discontinue interactive writing for the large group when the children show boredom. Many of them may have already learned the strategies we are emphasizing, so instead, we use interactive writing for small groups or individuals during intentional teaching.

Author Studies

Author studies are simply a time when we share details of an author's, illustrator's, or poet's life. Many authors have Web sites, which makes the sharing easy. Web sites we enjoy using include Denise Fleming's (www.denisefleming.com), Jan Brett's (www.janbrett.com), Mem Fox's (www.memfox.com), Robert Munsch's (www.robertmunsch.com), and Eric Carle's (www.eric-carle.com/home. html). The time allotted for community gathering doesn't allow for an in-depth author study, so we conduct mini-studies after we have read several of an author's works and want to draw attention to a familiar writer.

An author study of Pat Mora, for example, would include reading aloud some of her excellent books, including *Tomas and the Library Lady* and *Pablo's Tree*. We take a few minutes to look at the topics of her books and ask the children to identify differences and similarities among the books. We also share information from her Web site (www.patmora.com/) or the interesting biography *Pat Mora* by Hal Marcovitz, show pictures of her studio, and talk about our favorite books by her. We might also write to Ms. Mora, although we make it clear that we don't expect an answer from her—instead, we say that we want her to spend her time writing more books for us to read. In our letter, we tell her why the children like her work and ask her to please keep writing.

Vocabulary Study

Words intrigue our students, but many of them don't voluntarily engage in learning new words. We recommend having a few minutes of word study during the gathering segment at least once during the week. Further word study can occur as needed during the block on an individual or small-group basis.

Resource 4-3: *Gayle's Reading Strategies Conference Form for Second Grade*

Not all unknown words are worth taking time to discuss, especially those that are rarely used in reading or speaking. We choose words that will help students understand what they read and express themselves orally and in writing. Although most new words are learned through context, either as we read or as we listen to others speak, we encourage our students to substitute a word that makes sense when they can't figure out a word. We want them to know there are words that can't be determined through phonics, and if students haven't heard certain words pronounced, they may not be able to say them correctly. (An example would be *busy*.)

Gayle has her students list interesting words from the community sharing segment of the block on a classroom chart and in their reading journals. These words will inform future word study lessons. For example, in a sharing session, the posted word was *insecure*. The student knew the word *secure* but didn't understand *insecure*. This signals us to conduct a focus lesson on prefixes. Learning how to dissect words helps students create meaning.

One way to find new words is to ask students to collect sentences or even paragraphs that contain words they don't know. The words can come from read-aloud books, independently read books, and content-area texts. Posting interesting words in the literature response journals leaves permanent tracks for revisiting at any time, simply by asking the students to infer the word's meaning by using context clues.

Think-Alouds

Whenever we are sharing texts aloud, we are also sharing our own reading processes. When we read aloud books like *Bats at the Beach* by Brian Lies, we share our thinking when we come to places in the text that remind us of how our family prepares to go to the beach. We say things like "I wonder why they went at night. I wonder why they didn't have sandwiches to eat." Halfway through the book we might say, "I have the answer to my questions. Real bats come out at night, and they eat bugs, not sandwiches."

Intentional Instruction

Intentional instruction takes up the majority of the reading block. Second-grade readers represent a wide range of literacy levels. We have some students like Emily, who can read almost anything put in front of her, and then there are those who struggle to read a simple text. We have learned a lot about these students through our observations and informal assessments. We pack every minute during this time

children, reading conferences would be the one she would use. Regie Routman's *Reading Essentials* (2003) is also a good resource for ideas on conferences.

Shared Reading

Small groups of children can learn much about print conventions during shared reading with big books or other types of enlarged text. Revisiting familiar big books offers opportunities to aid comprehension, and rereading can help develop flow. The teacher usually leads by tracking words with a pointer, but students can also do the pointing. And if there are words that present problems for the students, the words can be highlighted and discussed. This is a great time to develop word study strategies.

Guided Reading

Guided reading is a way of helping our students become independent readers by encouraging them to focus on meaning rather than thinking about words in isolation. Guided reading often takes the place of the shared reading during intentional teaching because most students are becoming independent in their reading. Without question, one of the most effective strategies we can employ is supportive reading.

Most second graders possess all the sound–symbol knowledge they need, but they still have much to learn about the reading process. We are engaging in intentional teaching, but we are doing so within the context of good literature and demonstrations of the reading process. The most extensive work on guided reading that has been written for teachers is that of Irene Fountas and Gay Su Pinnell (1999). They have written multiple books on the topic that are very helpful.

Guided reading in second grade can take place with an individual or a small group of students (preferably no more than five). The texts are individual copies of children's leveled literature books that are on an appropriate level for the students.

Many different sources are available to assist teachers in determining reading levels for books; however, no list is completely accurate because of the differences in content knowledge our students bring to the texts. The books we use have been leveled based on several characteristics such as vocabulary, sentence length, and complexity of ideas. Leveled books are arranged from simple to more complex so students can be presented with texts that become progressively more challenging. Many different sources exist to help us determine reading levels. Scholastic's Teacher Book Wizard (bookwizard.scholastic.com/tbw) and *The Fountas and Pinnell*

Leveled Book List K–8 (2006) are excellent resources.

As we help students monitor their comprehension we keep the emphasis on meaning. We ask them: Did that make sense? Did it sound like language? As students experience supportive learning with increasingly more difficult text, they mature as independent readers.

Focus Lessons

Our informal assessments let us know which students have areas that need strengthening. Using short focus lessons with small groups of no more than six (four is the ideal number), we can accomplish much in strengthening these areas of need. We especially like the Developmental Studies Center's *Making Meaning* (2006), *Reading With Meaning* by Debbie Miller (2002), and *The Primary Comprehension Toolkit* (2008) by Stephanie Harvey and Anne Goudivs for help in planning focus lessons.

Strategy Lessons

Somewhat similar to focus lessons but not quite the same are the reading strategy lessons written by Yetta Goodman, Dorothy Watson, and Carolyn Burke (1996) in *Reading Strategies: Focus on Comprehension*. This brilliantly written book includes more than 40 lessons that develop all the cueing systems, and the semantic/pragmatic lessons are especially appropriate for this grade level. These lessons are complete with the rationale for the lesson, appropriate text, and the application of the strategy. If the text is too easy or too hard, you can easily find similar text at an appropriate level.

Literature Discussion Groups

You may be surprised to see discussion groups under intentional teaching, but we have a reason for this. Reading discussion groups involve small groups of students (no more than four) who choose a book at an appropriate level to read independently and then come together to talk about what they've read. Although the bulk of the time in discussion groups is devoted to students' interactions with their peers, we need to monitor by making daily observations of the groups. These observations allow us to clear up readers' misconceptions and introduce or reinforce strategies for maintaining comprehension.

You will have individual conferences with students about the book so you know how they are applying reading strategies. Also, during the conference you will want to make sure each student is advancing in reading development.

We meet with these groups for three purposes:

1. **To launch discussion groups.** We must participate in the first discussion group meeting of each book group to make sure all students have read the book and are prepared for a thoughtful discussion with their peers. We recommend starting with one group and launching it before meeting with a second group.

2. **To assess the reading discussion process.** From time to time, we sit in on discussion group meetings to determine if the students are all reading the book and participating in the discussions. As we stop by the group, we will want to acknowledge questions about meaning and vocabulary.

3. **To celebrate closure.** When a discussion group has finished a book, we schedule a few minutes during the community closing for the students to discuss why they did or didn't like the book and whether they recommend the book to others.

Retrospective Miscue Analysis

Retrospective miscue analysis is a useful strategy that helps readers become more aware of their own reading processes. If students are comfortable sharing their miscues with others, a small group of students can analyze their own miscues and those of peers. Ask students to divide into pairs and tape-record or record on an iPod each other's reading. After recording the text, they listen to each other's recording while reading along with the text. The students stop the tape recording whenever a miscue occurs and mark the text. After the students finish marking the miscues, we meet with them to discuss the kinds of miscues and the effects (if any) they have on meaning. If the miscues do affect meaning, we might say things like, "Did the word make sense?" "Does that sound like language?" "I can see why you said that word because it looks like the author's word" and "Rereading a phrase isn't a bad thing to do when you are trying to figure out the author's meaning."

We review the types of miscues with an eye toward an explanation of why a reader would make that miscue. It is important to not say *error*. Although we agree that we learn from errors, miscues are not always negative. For example, if the reader says *rock fence* for *stone fence*, *huge yacht* instead of *enormous yacht*, or *grain* for *wheat*, there is little or no change in meaning. By looking back at miscues, a reader can gain confidence in his or her ability and know that synonyms are often rich miscues that don't interfere with meaning.

The following are miscues we want to discuss with our students:

1. **Substitutions** One word is substituted for another word, usually because the reader was focused on meaning. Often the word has the same meaning as the replaced word.

   <u>Reaction to miscue:</u> If the meaning of the substituted word does not alter the meaning of the sentence, we point it out to the reader. If the meaning is changed, the reader should skip the word or reread and try to figure out the word and its meaning through context. Looking closely at the graphophonic clues and known chunks may help a reader in the pronunciation of the word.

2. **Omissions** Readers sometimes leave out or skip over words they don't know. In some cases, the omitted word isn't necessary to understanding the meaning of the sentence. Other times, leaving a word out can result in a sentence that doesn't sound like language.

   <u>Reaction to miscue:</u> Ask if the omission affected meaning. If the reader always skips words that are unknown or are multisyllabic, bring this to the child's attention. Encourage him or her to attempt to figure out the word through context, syntax, and graphophonics.

3. **Self-corrections** When a reader utters a word that isn't the author's word and then immediately changes the word to the author's word, there is obviously no change in meaning. It can be interesting to speculate about why the reader made the miscue in the first place.

   <u>Reaction to miscue:</u> No action is necessary since there was no meaning lost.

4. **Repetitions** The reader rereads the same word, phrase, or sentence more than once. Repeating words in a text does not change the meaning.

   <u>Reaction to miscue:</u> A repetition of the author's words is acceptable. One can argue that repetitions interfere with meaning if they are numerous. Our experience indicates that students minimize repetitions as they mature as readers.

As we mentioned previously, engaging in retrospective miscue is not only helpful to the reader but to the peer who is helping with the analysis. Students come to understand that reading isn't a word-by-word process in which the reader always says each word in order, and also that good readers can make miscues. The difference between proficient and less-than-proficient readers is the quality of the miscues.

When many children in the classroom understand retrospective miscue, we can have rich focus lessons about the reasons for miscues. We can laugh about funny miscues and recognize miscues that have similar meanings, such as *house* and *home*. We can also notice miscues involving words such as *moose* and *mouse*, which are graphophonically similar and sound almost the same but differ in meaning. As more members of the class understand the reading process through retrospective miscue analysis, more progress will be made in reading development. We have never heard a teacher say that retrospective miscue wasn't helpful, especially with students who weren't focused on meaning.

There are several books and articles explaining retrospective miscue, and we recommend that you read one of them. Goodman and Marek (1996) have an excellent book that we reference.

Independent Engagement

This is the time when students are reading appropriate quality children's literature to further their reading development. If you have a mandated program, we hope it has an anthology of good fiction and nonfiction in different genres that you can use in a flexible manner. By second grade, almost every child can read connected text and is monitoring comprehension.

Challenges of Self-Selection

Throughout the reading block, you are encouraging students to assume responsibility as they become readers and writers. We wish all students could read self-selected literature, but that isn't always possible for a variety of reasons.

1. Children choose books that are not appropriate. We like to borrow Jobe and Dayton-Sakari's (2002) analogy of baby bear choosing the porridge that was "just right" when the subject is choosing a book for reading. Baby bear tasted all the porridge and sometimes it was too cold (too easy and offering no challenge). Other times the porridge was too hot (too difficult, so students can't understand what they are reading). Then there was the porridge that was just right (at the right level of difficulty, so students can understand what is being read but are still challenged). Jobe and Dayton-Sakari offer an activity for students to sort books with a "three bears" leveling system.

2. Leveling of text is not an exact science. There are several accurate and helpful text gradient type systems, such as *The Fountas and Pinnell Leveled Book List K–8* (2006), which Scholastic uses for organizing its leveled classroom books. The

Reading Recovery Council's *Reading Recovery Book List* (2008) is also an excellent resource, if you are a member. Although there are many variables for classifying a book at a particular level, vocabulary, sentence length, concept load, and the way the text is laid out on the pages are the essential ones. Because each reader must possess the necessary content knowledge to construct meaning, it is impossible to level a book so it is perfect for every child.

3. Availability of books is limited by money and space. Not every book in your classroom or school library will be interesting to all students. If you had all the money in the world to buy books, you wouldn't have the space to store them. Nonfiction books don't exist on all topics, especially obscure ones, although more and more come out each year.

It's important that the majority of the students' time during this period is spent reading real books and increasing their volume of reading; however, there are several other activities children can engage in during this time. These activities are all related to the books they are reading, but we caution you to make sure that your children are spending more time reading rather than always responding to literature.

Preparing for Literature Discussion Groups

Many of your students can participate in literature discussion groups by reading the chapter(s) they are asked to read before the next session. They maintain their reading response journals during a literature discussion group just as they do during independent reading, which means they follow the reading journal guidelines for fiction and non-fiction texts (Resources 4-4 and 4-5) or the bookmark (Resource 4-6). They record a list of words they don't know and can't pronounce along with page numbers.

See Resource 4-4, Fiction and Nonfiction Literature Response Journal Guidelines for Second Grade, p. 157.

See Resource 4-5, Reading Journal Guidelines, p. 158.

Writing in Literature Response Journals

A short summary of a chunk of text or a response (e.g., text-to-self, text-to-text, and text-to-world connections) can aid reading comprehension and increase the amount of writing students accomplish. We especially like literature response journals because they give students a chance to summarize in writing what they have read and/or respond personally to the text. Other suggestions for responding to texts are included on the student bookmarks (Resource 4-6).

See Resource 4-6, Getting to Know Your Book bookmarks, p. 159

See Resource 4-7, Tracks of Thinking While Reading Text, p. 160.

Gayle has developed the book-marks as an aid to students as they write in their reading response journals. Gayle's Tracks of Thinking form (Resource 4-7) is an excellent tool for students to use to monitor comprehension of text they are reading. The journals can be as simple as half sheets of paper stapled together with a construction-paper cover or composition notebooks.

The "Growing as a Reader" pages (see Figure 3.2, page 100) are in the back of the journal. As concepts are introduced in focus lessons, they are added to these pages. For example, if the focus lesson is on contractions, then a page is labeled "Contractions," and students identify two in each of their books and post on these pages.

**Fiction and Nonfiction Literature Response
Journal Guidelines for Second Grade**

1. Fiction

Date: _____

Title: _____

Author: _____

1. Make **prediction** before reading.
2. Write down **unknown words** with page numbers.
3. **Chapter books**—write a **short summary** after you have read half of the book.
   Predict what will happen next.
4. Was **prediction** in #1 right or wrong? **Why?**
5. Make a **connection**—text to text, text to self, text to world.
6. After reading, **write a letter** to the teacher.
7. Complete **"Growing as a Reader" pages** in back of notebook.

2. Nonfiction

Date: _____

Title: _____

Author: _____

1. Make **prediction** before reading.
2. Write down **unknown words** with page numbers.
3. Write down **five facts** learned.
4. Was **prediction** in #1 right or wrong? **Why?**
5. Make a **connection**—text to text, text to self, text to world.
6. After reading, **write a letter** to the teacher.
7. Complete **"Growing as a Reader" pages** in back of notebook.

■ Resource 4-4: *Fiction and Nonfiction Literature Response Journal Guidelines for Second Grade*

Creating Word Logs

During independent reading time, children also use their literature response journals to make lists of words they can't pronounce or don't understand, as well as words that are used in interesting ways. Asking children to always record the page number is important because during discussion you will want them to go back and read the word in context.

We have a preference for journals rather than sticky notes or narrow strips of paper because they are more permanent. "Tracks" of a student's thinking tend to get lost when small pieces of paper or sticky notes are used. You can study the accumulation of words to determine the types of words that aren't known and the words the students find interesting. You can also notice if the same words are written over and over or if learning about the word once is enough.

Writing Book Critiques

Second graders like to share their opinions about books with others, and good questions can stimulate their thinking. The list below can be cut down or children may choose three or four questions to guide their response.

- Did you like the book?

- What are the reasons for your answer?

- What parts of the book did you find interesting?

- Are there places in the book that you would like to reread?

- Did the book have any lessons?

- Would you recommend that others read the book?

The responses can be shared at the community closing. Although this is a valuable reading–writing connection, the critique shouldn't follow every book that you read in class.

Resource 4-5

Second Grade ■ Resource 4-5
Reading Journal Guidelines

Reading Journal Guidelines

1. Make a prediction BEFORE you read the book.

2. Write down all unknown words and make sure you write down the page numbers. Make inferences for unknown words. (What do you think it means?)

3. CHAPTER BOOKS ONLY: Write down the MAIN IDEA of each chapter. Predict what you think is going to happen in the next chapter.

4. Tell how your prediction before you read the book was correct or incorrect.

5. Make a connection (text to text, text to self, text to world)

6. Complete one of the following:
Written retelling
Bookmark
Oral retelling
Teacher's choice
Student's choice

7. Check "Growing as a Reader" pages and make entries.

158   The Literacy Block

■ Resource 4-5: *Reading Journal Guidelines*

Independent Research

Second graders can and should do research on questions that interest them. The questions can come from any area of the curriculum or from a school or home experience. It can be a science or social studies question, a question from a book that was read aloud, a question from a television show, or one from many other sources.

We recommend that you first demonstrate the research process during a time outside of the reading block. Gayle demonstrates this process during her theme immersion.

1. Students choose the topic of butterflies for Gayle to demonstrate the research process.

2. Students go around the room gathering the various texts and media related to butterflies.

3. Students choose *Monarch Butterfly* by Gail Gibbons from the collection to read aloud.

4. Gayle conducts the read-aloud, and the class identifies the most important facts from the book.

5. Gayle posts the facts on the research chart, demonstrating how to take notes.

6. The next day, working together, the class chooses a Web site from the list of possible media sources in the text and media set, and the whole class watches a virtual tour on the topic.

7. The students discuss what they learned from the Web site and take notes on the most important facts, which are added to the notes on the chart.

Squirrels live in *dreys*. Dreys have two rooms. One of the two rooms is a nursery.

8.

■ Fig. 4.2: *Sample of second-grade research—squirrels*

8. During the next day's theme immersion, the class watches a video on butterflies, and Gayle adds the resulting discussion notes to the research chart.

9. The class rereads the chart to determine if there is any repetition of facts, and Gayle deletes any duplicated information.

10. Once the content of the chart is set, Gayle types each fact on a separate page, and groups of students illustrate their book.

Small groups and individuals engage in this process, making references to the whole-class research project during the independent and peer interaction components of the block. An example of part of a second-grade research project is shown in Figure 4.2.

The Literacy Block

Peer Interaction

Most of the block should be devoted to independent reading, but social interaction among peers is valuable for several reasons. Exchanging points of view is what helps our students reach higher levels of thinking. Experiences such as reading discussion groups, constructing graphic organizers with peers, and researching together provide time for sharing different viewpoints, spur thinking, and increase content knowledge.

Although many peer interactions spur thinking, group experiences such as Readers Theater, rereading texts, and reading poems together directly increase reading fluency. New knowledge is expressed through visual arts representations and technology projects.

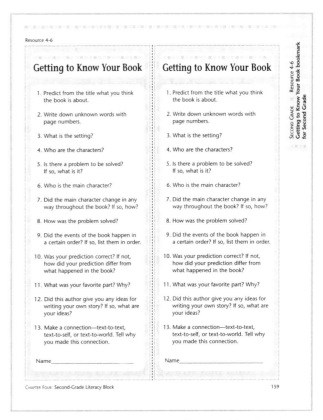

Resource 4-6: *Getting to Know Your Book bookmarks*

You will find many different options for peer interaction during the reading block in the Community Sharing section of this chapter. You can also add your own favorites, which can be equally productive.

Dramatizations

Drama gives our students an opportunity to express their knowledge about a story. So much can be learned in the process of acting out a story. There is no one right way to have students perform a text, so they aren't constrained by any rules. Some of the best memories many children have of the primary grades involve acting out stories. Little is needed for dramatization except simple props; a label pinned to a shirt or blouse can suffice as a costume. Acting out a story, a chapter, or

Programs such as Kidpix and Kidspiration also allow students to develop graphic organizers on the books they have just read. Story maps are just one example of what can be done. Students can print a hard copy of the organizer or it can be stored in a file folder for you to preview later.

Other uses of technology include the following:

- Children can make podcasts of themselves reading their favorite stories for parents to access and enjoy.

- Online book clubs can be conducted with classes around the world.

- iPods enable students to record their oral reading for retrospective miscue analysis with the teacher.

- Reading response journal entries can be made in Word documents and accumulated over time in each student's individual folder.

- Kids can publish and post student-authored digital books online at RealeBooks and RealeLibraries.

Literature Discussion Groups

The peer interaction component is the time to discuss reactions, interpretations, conclusions, predictions, comparisons, and so many other strategies. In pairs or triads, students discuss what they have read, having prepared during the independent component. For example, students who have read a chapter in a mystery book may not have yet determined the problem. Discussing what they perceive to be the problem will be the focus of the next discussion meeting. These discussions come from entries made in their literature response journals during independent reading.

Book series are very popular because they provide additional layers of support for the students, who enjoy revisiting the same characters and familiar "book world" across titles. Junie B. Jones, Nate the Great, and Bailey Street Kids are among the most popular series for second graders.

Community Sharing

The last few minutes of each reading block are usually devoted to community building and sharing. We say *usually* because some of us are having intentional teaching, and students are reading and writing up to the last minute, so on some days you will decide not to have a community gathering. When possible, we recommend having one because it contributes so much to the building of community.

We know this from personal experience. The book club that we three authors belong to is a community. The 12 members come together once a month to discuss books we have all read. You wouldn't believe the differences in our individual opinions about the books we read! The discussions form bonds among all of us, and we leave each meeting refreshed and ready to read the next book.

Purposes for the gathering include our desire to celebrate what students have read, share the thinking about texts, and share expressions of knowledge. The only requirement for the gathering is that it must include the whole group. Some teachers we know have a sign-up sheet posted so students who want to present at the gathering can plan on doing so. Readers Theater, a reenactment of a scene from a book, or the unveiling of a piece of visual art representing ideas from a text are good ideas for such representations. There is no order to the happenings, and often you're not sure what the students are going to share until they get up and present.

Here are a few questions that tend to evoke a lot of discussion:

- "Who would like to read aloud a paragraph that had special meaning?"

- "Who has finished reading a book that you think others should consider reading? Share your reasons with all of us."

- "Has any pair finished a Venn diagram comparing two books by the same author?"

- "Does anyone have some incredible illustrations they would like to share with everyone?"

The following ideas have proven successful for sharing during the community gathering.

SECOND GRADE ■ Resource 4-1
Reading Progression Chart

Reading Progression Chart

Gayle's Suggestions for Emphasizing Meaning Throughout Second Grade

Grading Period for Introduction (May Vary)	Focus of Reading Instruction	Date of Intentional Instruction (whole group, small group)	Date of Practice (literacy centers, peer interactions)	Date of Independent Application (e.g., literature journals, conferences)
1	–Review Making Predictions/Validating			
	–Review Making Connections			
	–Review Elements of Story			
2	–Review Visualizing			
	–Review Main Idea			
	–Review Details			
	–Review Wondering/Questioning			
3	–Plot/Story Beginning, Middle, End			
	–Cause–Effect			
	–Synonyms			
	–Antonyms			
	–Multiple-Meaning Words			
	–Determining Important Ideas			
4	–Comparing/Contrasting			
	–Inference			
	–Drawing Conclusions			
	–Homonyms			
	–Understanding Text Structure			

Creating the Best Literacy Block Ever © 2009 by Maryann Manning, Gayle Morrison, and Deborah Camp: Scholastic Professional

Creating the Best Literacy Block Ever © 2009 by Maryann Manning, Gayle Morrison, and Deborah Camp: Scholastic Professional

Gayle's Reading Conference Form for Second Grade

Name _____

Date _____

	*	**	***			*	**	***
Text 1 _____ Level__ F UF			F N	Text 4 _____ Level__ F UF				F N
Text 2 _____ Level__ F UF			F N	Text 5 _____ Level__ F UF				F N
Text 3 _____ Level__ F UF			F N	Text 6 _____ Level__ F UF				F N

Comments

**Insert bk. # next to concept demonstrated.

Fiction Oral Retelling
Demonstrates:
Sequential Retelling ___
Beginning: Setting__ Characters__
Middle: Problem_____
Ending: Solution_____
Character Change_____
Main Idea_____

Nonfiction Oral Retelling
Recalled 5 facts____ More____

Comments

Instruction Based on Conference

Bk. #	Miscue	Semantics — Meaning Change?		Syntax — Structure Change?		Graphophonic Similarity — Visual		Graphophonic Similarity — Sound	
		Yes	No	Yes	No	Y	N	Y	N
Totals									

* If leveled books are used, record level.
** F is for books that are familiar and UF is for books that are unfamiliar.
*** Genre that includes fiction or nonfiction.

Gayle's Reading Strategies Conference Form for Second Grade

Name _____

Date _____

		*	**	***

Text 1 _____ Level___F UF   F N   Text 4 _____ Level___F UF   F N

Text 2 _____ Level___F UF   F N   Text 5 _____ Level___F UF   F N

Text 3 _____ Level___F UF   F N   Text 6 _____ Level___F UF   F N

Comments

**Insert bk. # next to concept demonstrated.

Fiction Oral Retelling

Demonstrates:

1. Sequential Retelling ___
Beginning: Setting__ Characters___
Middle: Problem_____
Ending: Solution_____
Character Change_____
Main Idea_____
2. Making Connections/Using Prior Knowledge_____
3. Visualizing_____
4. Questioning_____
5. Making Inferences_____
6. Determining Important Ideas____
7. Understanding Text Structure_____
8. Summarizing____

Nonfiction Oral Retelling

Recalled 5 facts____ More____

Demonstrates:

1. Identified Main Idea_____
2. Determined Important Ideas____
3. Understanding of Text Structure_____
4. Summarizing_____

Instruction Based on Conference

Bk. #	Miscue	Semantics — Meaning Change?		Syntax — Structure Change?		Graphophonic Similarity Visual		Sound	
		Yes	No	Yes	No	Y	N	Y	N
Totals									

  * If leveled books are used, record level.
 ** F is for books that are familiar and UF is for books that are unfamiliar.
*** Genre that includes fiction or nonfiction.

Creating the Best Literacy Block Ever © 2009 by Maryann Manning, Gayle Morrison, and Deborah Camp: Scholastic Professional

Creating the Best Literacy Block Ever © 2009 by Maryann Manning, Gayle Morrison, and Deborah Camp: Scholastic Professional

Fiction and Nonfiction Literature Response Journal Guidelines for Second Grade

1. Fiction

Date: _____

Title: _____

Author: _____

1. Make **prediction** before reading.

2. Write down **unknown words** with page numbers.

3. **Chapter books**—write a **short summary** after you have read half of the book.

   Predict what will happen next.

4. Was **prediction** in #1 right or wrong? **Why?**

5. Make a **connection**—text to text, text to self, text to world.

6. After reading, **write a letter** to the teacher.

7. Complete **"Growing as a Reader" pages** in back of notebook.

2. Nonfiction

Date: _____

Title: _____

Author: _____

1. Make **prediction** before reading.

2. Write down **unknown words** with page numbers.

3. Write down **five facts** learned.

4. Was **prediction** in #1 right or wrong? **Why?**

5. Make a **connection**—text to text, text to self, text to world.

6. After reading, **write a letter** to the teacher.

7. Complete **"Growing as a Reader" pages** in back of notebook.

Reading Journal Guidelines

1. Make a prediction BEFORE you read the book.

2. Write down all unknown words and make sure you write down the page numbers. Make inferences for unknown words. (What do you think it means?)

3. CHAPTER BOOKS ONLY: Write down the MAIN IDEA of each chapter. Predict what you think is going to happen in the next chapter.

4. Tell how your prediction before you read the book was correct or incorrect.

5. Make a connection (text to text, text to self, text to world)

6. Complete one of the following:
   Written retelling
   Bookmark
   Oral retelling
   Teacher's choice
   Student's choice

7. Check "Growing as a Reader" pages and make entries.

Creating the Best Literacy Block Ever © 2009 by Maryann Manning, Gayle Morrison, and Deborah Camp: Scholastic Professional

Resource 4-6

Getting to Know Your Book

1. Predict from the title what you think the book is about.

2. Write down unknown words with page numbers.

3. What is the setting?

4. Who are the characters?

5. Is there a problem to be solved? If so, what is it?

6. Who is the main character?

7. Did the main character change in any way throughout the book? If so, how?

8. How was the problem solved?

9. Did the events of the book happen in a certain order? If so, list them in order.

10. Was your prediction correct? If not, how did your prediction differ from what happened in the book?

11. What was your favorite part? Why?

12. Did this author give you any ideas for writing your own story? If so, what are your ideas?

13. Make a connection—text-to-text, text-to-self, or text-to-world. Tell why you made this connection.

Name_____

Getting to Know Your Book

1. Predict from the title what you think the book is about.

2. Write down unknown words with page numbers.

3. What is the setting?

4. Who are the characters?

5. Is there a problem to be solved? If so, what is it?

6. Who is the main character?

7. Did the main character change in any way throughout the book? If so, how?

8. How was the problem solved?

9. Did the events of the book happen in a certain order? If so, list them in order.

10. Was your prediction correct? If not, how did your prediction differ from what happened in the book?

11. What was your favorite part? Why?

12. Did this author give you any ideas for writing your own story? If so, what are your ideas?

13. Make a connection—text-to-text, text-to-self, or text-to-world. Tell why you made this connection.

Name_____

Creating the Best Literacy Block Ever © 2009 by Maryann Manning, Gayle Morrison, and Deborah Camp: Scholastic Professional

Tracks of Thinking While Reading Text

Title of Book _____

Name _____ Date _____

Before-Reading Questions

Questions Answered?

During-Reading Questions

After-Reading Questions

Unfamiliar Word	What I Think It Means	Context Clues	Meaning

Creating the Best Literacy Block Ever © 2009 by Maryann Manning, Gayle Morrison, and Deborah Camp: Scholastic Professional

Third-Grade Literacy Block

Community Gathering Suggested time: up to 15 minutes

- Read-aloud of short texts
- Shared reading of enlarged texts
- Focus lessons
- Interactive writing
- Author studies
- Vocabulary

Intentional Teaching Suggested time: 30–45 minutes.
Activities in all columns are occurring simultaneously during workshop.

Teacher/student interaction	Independent engagement	Peer interaction
- Discussion of texts - Think-alouds - Reading assessments - Reading conferences - Shared reading - Guided reading - Focus lessons - Literature circles - Rove the room	- Independent reading of appropriate self-selected text (usually beyond emergent level) - Preparation for literature circles - Book logs - Reading response journals - Interesting words logs - Book critiques - Independent research - Technology projects - Listening stations - Word work - Sketch books/sketch to stretch - Fine-arts representations	- Literature circles - Readers Theater - Dramatizations - Graphic organizers - Technology projects - Word work - Shared reading of big books - Partner reading - Fine-arts representations

(Optional) Community Sharing Suggested time: up to 10 minutes

- Rereading a big book
- Student reading of selected passages
- Role-playing/dramatizations
- Discussion of texts and/or reading processes

CHAPTER 5

Third-Grade Literacy Block

It's 9:00 and Randy asks his third graders to move back to the carpet for the reading block community gathering, which lasts about 15 minutes. Once they are seated, he asks each literature circle group, partners, and individual readers to report where they are in their reading and posts it on the status-of-the-class chart. Once the updates are complete, the class notices that one of the literature circle groups is not making as much progress in their reading as the others.

When asked if they encountered a problem, group member Josh replies, "There were a lot of vocabulary words we didn't know, and it took a lot of time to figure them out." This made sense to Randy because they were reading a nonfiction book, *Big Cats* by Seymour Simon. When others were asked if they were having vocabulary issues, a large majority said yes. Randy asked everyone to make notes of vocabulary concerns in their reading response journals during their reading that day and to bring them back to the community sharing. Randy immediately knew that word strategies would be the topic for mini-lessons for the rest of the week.

Once all updates were posted and discussed, students moved to their choice of spots in the room and began reading and talking about books for the next 45 to 60 minutes. Randy spends this time conferencing and roaming the room making observations. During each student's weekly conference, the student reads and discusses texts, and Randy conducts a miscue analysis on oral reading. During deep discussions, he notes if the student is making meaning or if there are reading obstacles that need to be removed. These conferences direct the teacher's instruction on an individual basis. All conferences are documented on conference forms, and texts read are recorded on an instructional text progression form. At the end of reading time, the students come back together for community sharing and discuss any vocabulary issues they encountered that day. Randy writes all vocabulary concerns on a chart, making mental notes to address them in his focus lessons that week.

The Block in Third Grade ~

Most third graders are independent or nearly independent in their reading and writing, and they usually have a preferred genre as well as distinctive interests in either fiction or nonfiction. You may have some students who are reading below their grade level. Refer to the previous chapters for guidance in developing intentional teaching for these students. Some of the students are definitely bookworms who want to be left alone to read. We know their comprehension will be enhanced in small-group discussions, and though some may want to forgo interaction with peers, we must ensure that they participate.

Some students are likely to be "word callers" (they read the words without thinking about the meaning) who desperately need revaluing (Goodman & Marek 1996) as readers. In other words, we need these students to understand reading as a meaning-making process and to revalue the reading skills they already possess and use them to become strong, confident meaning-makers. During the block we can provide support to students at all levels.

The strategies that follow throughout this chapter are ones we have used in our classrooms, but by no means are we providing an all-inclusive list.

Community Gathering

During this time we establish rituals, routines, and procedures that are especially critical for those students who haven't experienced similar reading settings in lower primary grades. All children have opinions, but third graders have many well-defined notions about the texts they read. Conducting discussions about the relationships that students have made with book characters often interests other classmates. Even though students have been identifying story elements for several years, we still need to help them think about the sequence of events in a story, conflict and resolution, and other important literary elements that enhance students' comprehension abilities.

For years, Gayle has hung a world map behind her community gathering space. Her students put a sticky note with the book title on the place where they think the story occurred. Some fiction isn't explicit about setting, and it is left up to the reader to make an inference based on text clues. If the book is nonfiction, the students place the sticky note on a region where the events *could* have taken place. Following are some literacy experiences that can occur during this time.

Read-Alouds

The reading block isn't the time for major read-alouds. A chapter book can be read aloud at another designated time during the day, a nonfiction book can be read aloud during social studies and/or science, and other texts can be interspersed during daily events such as the writing workshop. Even though most third graders are independent readers, they still need to hear texts read aloud because it demonstrates fluent reading. The texts chosen for the reading block are short pieces of literature with some special attribute that adds to the students' reading development. Poetry is an excellent genre to share because its concise, evocative language conjures up vivid visual images. Picture books are also a good choice. We are always on the lookout for short text passages that promote reading development to use during the community gathering of the reading block.

Short passages from the text provide the opportunity to think aloud and demonstrate reading strategies. After reading the text, we discuss it with the students and isolate certain comprehension strategies used to better understand the text. We then ask students to demonstrate awareness of the strategy by writing entries in their reading journals or as they interact with peers.

For a list of some of Gayle's favorite third-grade read-alouds, please go to page 185.

Shared Reading

The amount of shared reading decreases as students need less and less supportive reading, but shared reading is appropriate sometimes at all grade levels.

Shared reading with nonfiction big books allows us the opportunity to demonstrate how this genre works. We introduce text structures that students will encounter in content reading. These more sophisticated texts introduce new vocabulary, offer opportunities to practice comprehension skills, and share powerful literature that would otherwise be inaccessible to many of the students. With third graders, big books do not have to be the preferred format of texts. You can use an overhead projector or a document camera to enlarge the print for whole-class viewing. For a list of books Gayle recommends for shared reading, please go to page 185.

Focus Lessons

A focus lesson is another name for a mini-lesson, although the terms mean different things to each teacher and authority on the topic. Focus lessons are short, from five to ten minutes long, and they address only one teaching point. We begin by telling students the purpose of the focus lesson, giving examples and demonstrations as needed. The focus lesson topic can then be practiced in the peer interaction or independent engagement components of the literacy block. The following is an example of a third-grade focus lesson on inference.

> We read the beginning of Joy Cowley's new book *Chicken Feathers*: "Tucker and Elizabeth Miller were serious about life. Maybe it was something to do with living on a farm with three thousand chickens or maybe it was because their hearts were as soft as the new-laid eggs they took to the market."
>
> We then ask students to tell why living on the farm and having hearts as soft as new-laid eggs would make them serious about life. Students use their prior knowledge to make inferences. Once we finish reading this chapter (which is likely to take place over several days), the students will revisit their inferences to find out if their thinking is compatible with the author's or if it is still just between them and the text.

This focus lesson was an example of one used with a large group. During the intentional teaching component of the literacy block, focus lessons are conducted with individuals, pairs, or small groups. A focus lesson during the community gathering typically consists of strategies students really need to know. During this time, we also want to use more general focus lessons that most students need and are ready to learn. Your district and state standards are the basis for these lessons. Gayle has developed a reading progression for third grade, based on district and state standards, which guides teachers in developing these focus lessons (Resource 5-1). Reading and writing strategies become more complex as texts become more difficult. We teach more advanced focus lessons that develop critical thinking and deep structure strategies such as synthesizing, determining importance, and making inferences so students can mature as readers.

See Resource 5-1, Reading Progression Chart for Third Grade, p. 186.

Reading strategy books that have been helpful to us include *Reading with Meaning* by Debbie Miller (2002), *Strategies That Work* (2000) and *The Comprehension Toolkit: Grades 3–6* (2005) by Stephanie Harvey and Anne Goudvis, and Developmental Studies Center's (2006) *Making Meaning*. Refer to Gayle's conference forms (Resources 5-2 and 5-3) for a list of strategies that can guide your focus lessons.

See Resource 5-2, Gayle's Reading Conference Form for Third Grade, p. 187.

See Resource 5-3, Gayle's Strategies Conference Form for Third Grade, p. 188.

Author Studies

Because of time limitations of the community gathering, we suggest mini-author studies. For example, after reading a few works by the same author, briefly draw attention to the author's style and biographical information. Third graders enjoy David Harrison's works, such as *Glaciers: Nature's Icy Caps* and *Sounds of Rain: Poems of the Amazon*. After reading aloud these books, show students copies of other books he has written, such as *Wild Country: Outdoor Poems for Young Children* and *Mountains: The Tops of the World*.

During independent reading and peer interaction components, the students can explore the author's online autobiography, read about his interesting life, and learn more about this prolific author's books of fiction, nonfiction, and poetry at mowrites4kids.drury.edu/authors/harrison. If students want to write to the author, we encourage them to tell him *why* they enjoyed his books and to encourage him to continue writing wonderful works, a subtle way of letting him know that no reply is expected.

Resource 5-1: *Reading Progression Chart for Third Grade*

Vocabulary Study

Studying vocabulary together as a community can be enjoyable for students if it is done in short spurts. While learning unfamiliar words intrigues many of our students, some may not engage voluntarily in vocabulary study. We recommend having word study during the gathering segment for a few minutes at least once during the week. New vocabulary words are learned through read-alouds, focus lessons, and wide reading. We believe we should teach vocabulary all day long, through intentional teaching and incidental opportunities. We embed vocabulary instruction within the context of texts shared naturally with students.

Isabel Beck, Margaret McKeown, and Linda Kucan's book *Bringing Words to Life: Robust Vocabulary Instruction* (2002) and Peter Johnston's *Choice Words* (2004) suggest that not all unknown words are worth knowing. We want to choose words that will help students understand what they read and express themselves in writing. Beck and her colleagues organize vocabulary words into three categories, or tiers. Tier One words are those that are in native-speaking children's receptive and expressive language; examples include words such as *school*, *baby*, *jump*, and *pretty*. Tier Two words are more sophisticated words that are less likely to be familiar to students. Examples of Tier Two words are *organize*, *vehicle*, *outrageous*, and *trudge*. Tier Three words are those associated with the science, social studies, and math content areas. We agree with these authors that teachers should concentrate on the intentional teaching of Tier Two words (they will learn Tier Three in content-area studies).

Although most new words are learned through context, either as we read or as we listen to others speak, we recognize the need to discuss unfamiliar words as they occur in read-alouds and conversations. We provide user-friendly definitions, make an ongoing class chart of these words accessible to the students, and provide opportunities for children to apply their understanding of these words through speaking and writing. We also teach children to use context clues to help determine the meaning of new words; however, many children do not develop this ability easily and need us to demonstrate how to use the other words in the sentence or paragraph, as well as syntax, to predict meanings. In their literature response journals, the students are asked to infer the meaning of unknown words based on context. Gayle's literature response guidelines (Resources 5-4 and 4-5)

Resource 5-2: *Gayle's Reading Conference Form for Third Grade*

See Resource 5-4, Fiction and Nonfiction Literature Response Journal Guidelines for Third Grade, p. 189.

See Resource 4-5, Reading Journal Guidelines, p. 158.

help students with these responses. If the text being read is context-lean and the surrounding text does not provide context clues, then using the dictionary is a final option for many students.

Think-Alouds

Third graders profit from think-alouds following the reading of a text. Discussing what you do when you come to a word you don't know provides students with important information. First of all, some students believe that a teacher never comes to a word she doesn't know and that she doesn't substitute synonyms for unknown words. Also, when we think out loud about our reading process, we share how we use content knowledge and context clues to help us understand texts.

THIRD GRADE ■ Resource 5-3
Gayle's Strategies Conference Form for Third Grade

Resource 5-3

Gayle's Strategies Conference Form for Third Grade

Name _____				Comments
Date _____		* ** ***		
Text 1 _____Level__F UF		F N		
Text 2 _____Level__F UF		F N		
Text 3 _____Level__F UF		F N		

**Insert bk. # next to concept demonstrated.

Fiction Oral Retelling Demonstrates:		Miscue	Semantics Meaning Change?		Syntax Structure Change?		Graphophonic Similarity			
							Visual		Sound	
1. Sequential Retelling ___ Beginning: Setting__Characters_ Middle: Problem__ Ending: Solution__ Plot____ Char. Change___	Bk. #		Yes	No	Yes	No	Y	N	Y	N
2. Main Idea__										
3. Making Connections/Using Prior Knowledge_____										
4. Visualizing_____										
5. Questioning_____										
6. Making Inferences___										
7. Determining Important Ideas___										
8. Understanding Text Structure___										
9. Summarizing_____										
Nonfiction Oral Retelling Recalled 5 Facts____ More___ Demonstrates:										
1. Main Idea___										
2. Determining Important Ideas___										
3. Understanding Text Structure___										
4. Summarizing___										
Instruction Based on Conference										
Totals										

* If leveled books are used, record level.
** F is for books that are familiar, and UF is for books that are unfamiliar.
*** Genre that includes fiction or nonfiction.

188   The Literacy Block

■ Resource 5-3: *Gayle's Strategies Conference Form for Third Grade*

In *Saturdays and Teacakes* Lester Laminack (2004) describes mowing the grass at his Mammaw's (grandmother's) house. He writes, "From time to time the mower choked on mouthfuls of wet grass that clung to the blades and to my bare legs. But by early afternoon the dew-pearls were gone, the grass was mowed and dry, and I was soaked with sweat." As we read the book, we pause after this paragraph and say, "Did you notice I paused after one of the words in the last paragraph? I have never read the word *dew-pearls* before. I caught myself trying to visualize the dew and what would make it look like a pearl, and then I thought of dew drops, which helped me to understand the author's use of this word."

Intentional Instruction

This critical component of the reading block requires more time than the other elements. Intentional teaching is based on observations of student learning as well as informal assessments. At the third-grade level, children's span of reading development will be wide. Some students can read several years above their grade level, while those who are several levels below are in serious need of what Yetta Goodman and Ann Marek (1996) refer to as "revaluing" their reading by examining their own miscues. This is different from remedial reading because the process concentrates on the thoughts of the reader. For those students several levels below where they should be, you may want to administer Gayle's Phonics Inventory (addressed in Chapter 8, page 232), which identifies the gaps in a student's reading development. These identified gaps are posted onto a Phonics Inventory Chart to guide the teacher in the intentional teaching lessons (Resource 5-5).

During the intentional teaching segment of the reading block, both individual and small-group instruction occurs. Small-group work does not equate with the traditional three reading groups based on proficiency (i.e., high, medium, and low readers). Although some group instruction might be based on similar reading ability and needs among the group members, other small groups are based on student interests. Three students who have an intense interest in volcanoes, for example, can read appropriate text on the topic to satisfy their curiosity.

We study all of our assessments to determine how we will spend our time during intentional teaching. Through the use of excellent children's literature and other texts such as magazines and newspapers, our knowledge of strategies, our understanding of the reading process, and our assessments, we have an impact on the reading of our students.

Fiction and Nonfiction Literature Response Journal Guidelines for Third Grade

1. Fiction

Date: _____

Title: _____

Author: _____

1. Make **prediction** before reading.
2. Write down **unknown words** with page numbers.
3. **Chapter books**—write **a short summary** after you have read half of the book.
   Predict what will happen next.
4. Was **prediction** in #1 right or wrong? **Why?**
5. Make a **connection**—text to text, text to self, text to world.
6. After reading, **write a letter** to the teacher.
7. Complete **"Growing as a Reader" pages** in back of notebook.

2. Nonfiction

Date: _____

Title: _____

Author: _____

1. Make **prediction** before reading.
2. Write down **unknown words** with page numbers.
3. Write down **seven facts** learned.
4. Was **prediction** in #1 right or wrong? **Why?**
5. Make a **connection**—text to text, text to self, text to world.
6. After reading, **write a letter** to the teacher.
7. Complete **"Growing as a Reader" pages** in back of notebook.

CHAPTER FIVE: Third-Grade Literacy Block   189

■ Resource 5-4: *Fiction and Nonfiction Literature Response Journal Guidelines for Third Grade*

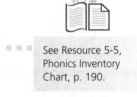

See Resource 5-5, Phonics Inventory Chart, p. 190.

Discussion of Texts

It's fun to discuss text with third graders because they are passionate about defending their opinions. Some students can read almost anything, while a few are "word callers" who don't understand what they read. Sometimes the students who aren't comprehending the text are the ones who benefit the most from discussions because they hear other students share their thought processes and the ways they use content knowledge to build meaning.

The goal of all text discussions is the same—to help our students achieve maximum understanding of what they read. Questions about characters, setting, and conflict and resolution are almost always good for fiction. The questions to ask during nonfiction are not quite as predictable. Discussions can be enhanced and extended by asking questions that result from listening to the last response the child gave. Gayle's questioning bookmark (Resource 2-10) is helpful for student and teacher discussions. Open-ended questioning helps students develop critical thinking skills.

See Resource 2-10, Questions for Developing Deeper Thinking, p. 80.

Resource 5-5

Phonics Inventory Chart
Third Grade

Teacher _____ Date _____

S–Secure in Application　　　　　D–Developing　　　　　N–Needs Intervention

Phonics Inventory Items	Student Names							
Alphabet Names								
Consonant Sounds								
Consonant Digraphs								
Consonant Blends								
Vowel Names								
Short Vowels (aural)								
Double Vowels								
Final "e"								
Diphthongs								
Read Short-Vowel Words								
Reversals								
Prefixes								
Suffixes								
Compound Words								
Silent Letters								
Vowel + "r"								
Syllabication								

* This Inventory is given ONLY to those students who have gaps in their reading development. This assessment can guide intentional instruction.

190　　　　　　　　　　　　　　　　　　　　　　The Literacy Block

■ Resource 5-5: *Phonics Inventory Chart*

Reading Conferences

At the heart of your literacy block are reading conferences. The five to ten minutes that we try to find a couple of times each week for conferences will be instrumental in increasing the amount of reading a child does independently and supporting his or her reading development in general. It is a time for us to observe the reading process, and it is our most influential instructional time. We ask questions that will help a student move to higher levels of comprehension. In addition, we draw attention to the strengths the child possesses as a reader as well as those that need to be developed.

When we sit down with a
student, we look at the last
conference notes to make sure that
we address any skill that was to be
worked on before this conference.
We then check the literature
response journal to make sure the
student practiced applying the skill.
For example, Latasha was having
difficulty reading contractions, and
her miscues in this area altered
meaning, so she was asked to
work on this skill before her next
conference by locating contractions
in her reading and then writing
them in her "Growing as a Reader"
pages in the back of her journal.
Through this review of Latasha's
journal, Gayle is able to ascertain
that she has a good understanding of
contractions. Then Latasha reads
from her favorite book for the week,

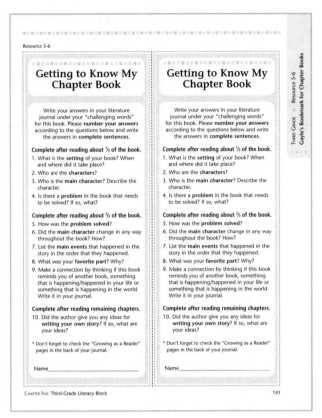

■ Resource 5-6: *Getting to Know My Chapter Book bookmark*

and Gayle notes the miscues to inform her instruction and how they interfere with
Latasha's comprehension of the text. She also posts the books she and Latasha
discuss to the Text Progression Form (see Resource 2-16 on page 86) and
completes today's conference form (Resource 5-2 on page 187). Both student
records are housed in the teacher's reading binder. Gayle also checks Latasha's
journal to see if there were any words she didn't understand during her independent reading that need to be addressed.

Shared Reading

Shared reading is a strategy to use with third-grade students who are what we call
Type V readers (see Chapter 8, page 227, for more information) because they focus
only on decoding. Shared reading is a way for a small group to look at enlarged
text such as a big book and learn many things. Using big books and other enlarged
text can help students think about observing punctuation and being expressive

when reading aloud. By masking (covering all or part of a word), we can help students learn the power of context. Greg, for example, attends to the initial consonant only when reading unfamiliar words, which often results in a loss of meaning; preparing text by masking initial consonants on some words forces him to read for meaning. Shared reading is also an opportune time to develop word strategies.

Guided Reading

Most third graders have become independent in reading a variety of texts, but many still need support with comprehension. Some students need help self-monitoring their reading and need to be encouraged to continually ask themselves if what they have read makes sense and sounds like language. The most extensive work in this area is that of Irene Fountas and Gay Su Pinnell (1996), the most prolific authors on guided reading.

Guided reading takes place with a small group of students (usually six or fewer). The texts are individual copies of children's literature on an appropriate level for the students. In accordance with the Fountas and Pinnell text gradient (2006), books are leveled for vocabulary, sentence length, and complexity of ideas. The books are arranged from simple to more complex so students can be progressively presented with texts that become more challenging. In special cases, guided reading can also take place with just one reader.

Many publishers provide well-written and attractive leveled reading books in both fiction and nonfiction. Some excellent publishers are Scholastic, Red Brick, Mondo, Benchmark, Okapi, and Heinemann Rain Tree. Many different sources exist to help teachers determine reading levels. Scholastic's Web site Teacher Book Wizard (bookwizard.scholastic.com), indexes thousands of children's books and supports customized searches based on interest, genre, and reading level. A print resource for determining reading levels is *The Fountas and Pinnell Leveled Book List, K–8*. No list of leveled books, however, is totally accurate because students bring varying degrees of background knowledge to the texts they read, and a child with extensive background knowledge on the content of text will more easily comprehend the text than another child with limited background knowledge.

Making meaning is the focus of our questions to the students as they practice monitoring their comprehension. Repeated guided learning will continue to increase students' comprehension as they become more mature independent readers.

Focus Lessons

Focus lessons take place during individual reading conferences or small-group supportive reading lessons. We use both formal and informal assessments to determine the focus lessons for particular children. Refer to the Focus Lessons discussion under the community gathering component on page 165.

Strategy Lessons

Strategy lessons were mentioned in the community gathering, but they are also very effective during the intentional teaching section. The brilliant *Reading Strategies: Focus on Comprehension* (1996) by Goodman, Watson, and Burke is one of the best sources of strategy lessons you will ever find. The lessons are organized according to the cueing system—graphophonic, syntactic, semantic, or pragmatic—they focus on. (Gayle's conference forms on pages 187 and 188 aid the teacher in determining cueing systems that need intentional instruction.) All the lessons include companion text, some of which will be too difficult or too easy for particular third graders. For those students, you can often find appropriate text at the primary level in magazines and anthologies of short, complete text.

Another publication that is brimming over with strategy lessons is *The Comprehension Toolkit: Grades 3–6* by Harvey and Goudvis (2005). This rich resource has numerous pieces of nonfiction that help to build comprehension. *Making Meaning* by the Developmental Studies Center (2006) is another commercial resource that possesses many of the same qualities as the *Toolkit* but can be used for both fiction and nonfiction.

Retrospective Miscue Analysis

Retrospective miscue analysis is an instructional strategy in which both the student and the teacher identify and analyze miscues from an oral reading passage.

Students tape-record themselves reading a passage of text, either self-selected or assigned by the teacher. (If an iPod with a recording device is available, the student can use that instead of a tape recorder.) In the beginning, the teacher and the student listen to the recording together while looking at the text, and the teacher instructing the student to stop the recording anytime a miscue occurs. With each stop, the teacher and student talk about the different types of miscues, focusing on why deviations from the text aren't errors but miscues, which aren't negative if the meaning is not affected. We ask, "Did the miscue change the meaning?" and then follow it with a discussion about the cause of the miscue. After working with the teacher, groups of children who are comfortable with one another and not embarrassed by sharing miscues can engage in retrospective miscue without teacher guidance. Group discussions of the principles of miscue analysis can also be beneficial. Please refer to Chapter 4, pages 140–142 for a complete discussion on the types of miscues you might encounter.

Retrospective miscue analysis helps all readers better understand their reading processes, but it is especially helpful for students who have difficulty focusing on meaning. Also, having a large number of students who have a good understanding of the reading process creates very interesting discussions about miscues. See Yetta Goodman and Ann Marek's (1996) *Retrospective Miscue Analysis: Revaluing Readers and Reading* for more on this powerful tool.

Literature Circles

Literature circles are an enjoyable way for students to read chapter books and discuss with one another the meanings they have constructed. Although these groups are largely student-driven, there are important reasons for us to meet with them.

- **Launching literature circles** Literature circles don't just happen all by themselves; teachers demonstrate in the beginning and act as a member of the group for at least one book. We recommend starting one group and getting it going before starting the second group. After everyone is lit circling, we can reorganize the students and even have student-selected circles based on common interests.

- **Assessing literature circle process** We want to keep an eye on whether all students are participating in the circle, and the best way to know is to meet with them occasionally. We can easily determine who is reading and prepared for the circle, who comes to the circle with questions, and who is exerting leadership. We do not favor students following rigid roles, but from time to time we will want to sit in on literature circles to determine if the purpose of the literature circle is being met.

- **Celebrating closure** The completion of a literature circle provides a perfect opportunity to spend a few minutes discussing whether readers liked or didn't like the book, if they think other students should read it, and if there are other books by the same author that they want to read.

Independent Engagement

Third graders are readers with a wide range of abilities. You have students who can decode almost any text, but we still want to make sure comprehension is taking place during the reading. We are especially concerned that they are reading quality children's literature throughout the block so that all texts further reading development. If you use a mandated program, we hope it is flexible and contains outstanding children's literature because most of this time should be spent engaging as readers.

Keeping a record of the books that each child reads is important, and students should maintain an up-to-date list in their reading journals. You can also use the list in parent–teacher conferences to show the range and depth of the child's reading as well as to identify his or her interests. As students grow as readers and writers, you encourage them to assume more responsibility, and one area of responsibility is text selection.

Challenges of Self-Selection

We wish all children could self-select texts, but that isn't always possible. Here are some of the issues to consider.

1. Children choose books that are not appropriate. We especially like Jobe and Sakari's analogy of choosing books as being like baby bear tasting his porridge (1999). Baby bear doesn't want his porridge to be too hot (too difficult to build meaning when reading the text) or too cold (too easy, with no challenging text). Baby bear wants his porridge just right (at the level of difficulty so students can build meaning but still be offered a challenge). In *Reluctant Readers: Connecting Students and Books for Successful Reading Experiences*, Jobe and Sakari (1999) provide an activity that encourages students to sort books with a "three bears" leveling system.

2. Leveling of text is not an exact science. There are several helpful and accurate text gradient–type systems. *The Fountas and Pinnell Leveled Book List K–8* and Scholastic's online Teacher Book Wizard (bookwizard.scholastic.com/tbw) are two that we have used, but there are others that are helpful. We agree that you can classify a book on a particular level according to many variables such as vocabulary, sentence length, concept load, and text features, but we are psycholinguists and therefore believe that content knowledge is absolutely necessary for understanding of a text. For that reason, we think you should consult the systems only for guidance because we believe it isn't possible to level a book so accurately that it is perfect for all children at a certain level. Maryann's article for *Teaching K–8*, "On the Level" addresses abuses of leveling (Manning, 2006).

3. Availability of books is limited by money and space. Most of us believe that we never have enough books in our classroom libraries and that the school library could use more books as well. Each year more and more nonfiction books are published, which improves the selection and enables us to meet more individual interests. Below we discuss some things that students can do as they are reading real books.

Preparing for Literature Discussion Groups

Preparing for literature circles takes place during independent reading. (See the Intentional Instruction section of this chapter for more discussion of literature circles.) We rarely encounter a third grader who isn't ready to participate in a literature circle. Students prepare by reading silently the chapters agreed upon by the circle before the next session. We find it advantageous to ask students to keep lists of words they either don't know the meaning of or can't pronounce (along with page numbers on which the words appear) in their literature response journals. We also ask them to follow the literature response guidelines (Resources 5-4 and 4-5) in their literature response journals or their bookmark (Resources 2-10 and 5-6) as they are reading the book independently. *Literature Circles Resource Guide* by Hill, Schlick Noe, and Johnson (2001), is a good reference on the subject.

Writing in Literature Response Journals

Journals can be a commercially bound notebook or a stack of stapled half-sheets of paper with a construction paper cover. We like literature response journals for a number of reasons, but primarily because students can write a summary of what they have just read. You will find the bookmarks that Gayle has developed helpful to children as they write responses. Personal responses about connections (text to self, text to text, and text to world) are also important reading–writing experiences that are included on the bookmarks. "Growing as a Reader" pages (see Figure 3.2 on page 100), kept in the back of reading journals, are good places for students to demonstrate their understanding of a skill or strategy by finding an example in their reading and posting it in this section. If a student is having difficulty decoding and determining the meaning of words with prefixes, for example, the teacher may set up a prefix page in the "Growing as a Reader" section and have the student post two words with prefixes and their meaning from each book they read. With chapter books, we ask students to post five words. By making these entries and discussing them during conferences, the teacher can determine if the student understands the concepts.

Creating Word Logs

When children read independently, it is helpful for them to record lists of words they can't pronounce, words they don't know the meaning of, and words they find especially interesting. The page number needs to be written by each word so it can easily be found and read in context for strategy and vocabulary development.

For maintaining these logs, we prefer notebooks or journals rather than separate lists and sticky notes, because they last longer and aren't easily lost. Compiled over time, they provide valuable vocabulary study. By individualizing the lists, you can base instruction on need. The lists may signal a need for intentional teaching of prefixes or suffixes.

Writing Book Critiques

Third-grade children have very definite opinions about books and want to express them. The following general list of prompts can be minimized, or children can choose three or four questions about a book. You can also add more questions to this list.

- Did you like the book? Explain why or why not.
- What parts of the book did you find interesting?
- Are there places in the book that you would like to reread?
- Did the book have any lessons?
- Would you recommend that others read the book?

The responses can be shared at the community closing. Although this is a valuable reading–writing connection, a critique shouldn't follow every book that is read.

Independent Research

Third graders can conduct research on topics that interest them. Their natural curiosity can lead them into asking questions about any area of the curriculum.

It might be a science or social studies question, a question that arose from a read-aloud, a question from a television show, or one from many other sources. A page from a third-grade research project is shown at right.

We recommend that you demonstrate how you conduct research so your students can understand the process. Post the process in the room for reference. Isolate a question, read, and view your information while taking notes on the overhead or document camera. Write your report in front of the children so you demystify the process. *Theme Immersion: Inquiry-Based Curriculum in Elementary and Middle Schools* (Manning, Manning, & Long, 1994) is a book that many teachers find helpful with student research. Refer to the grade 2 Independent Research section in Chapter 4 (pages 145–146) for more details.

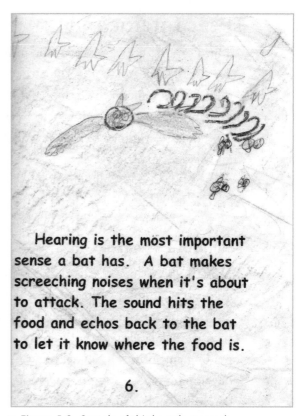

Hearing is the most important sense a bat has. A bat makes screeching noises when it's about to attack. The sound hits the food and echos back to the bat to let it know where the food is.

6.

Figure 5.2: *Sample of third-grade research*

Graphic Organizers

Many students at this level don't need adult help to develop graphic organizers as they make representations of their thinking, but some need for us to reteach the process. It is during intentional teaching that we take the time to explain to students how to display their knowledge about a subject or story. Outlines of major points or Venn diagrams help our students think deeply. We think it is better to use only a few organizers rather than a different one each day because we want students to focus on meaning and not on learning how to use a new organizer. Other examples include K-W-L charts, the 5 W's, T-charts, and story maps. Sources for information about using graphic organizers in content areas can be found in Linda Hoyt's (2002) *Make It Real: Strategies for Success With Informational Texts*.

Peer Interaction

Third graders are very social, and although much of the reading block should be devoted to independent reading, they enjoy and profit from social interaction with their peers. Some of these opportunities contribute to deeper thinking because exchanging divergent points of view is essential in building new knowledge.

Some peer interaction experiences are for the purpose of expressing new knowledge. Artistic visual representations, writing, and technology projects help our students express the new knowledge they have constructed. Using a variety of experiences helps our students stay engaged in their reading.

Readers Theater

Most children enjoy participating in Readers Theater. Children like the social aspect of reading together, sharing a story or poem with other students, and maybe performing for the class. There is nothing new about Readers Theater, other than the availability of more commercial products than in years past. Numerous reading authorities have identified Readers Theater as a good strategy for developing oral reading fluency, and publishers have provided numerous fiction and nonfiction scripts.

One of our favorite Readers Theater books is *It's Show Time: Poetry from the Page to the Stage* by Allan Wolf (1993). Poems from the book that work well with third graders are "Sometimes I Feel This Way" and "Mummy Slept Late and Daddy Fixed Breakfast" by John Ciardi and "Wynken, Blynken, and Nod" by Eugene Field. The last poem can be scripted so that the entire class can participate.

Caroline Feller Bauer's (1987) book *Presenting Reader's Theater: Plays and Poems to Read Aloud* contains several excellent scripts for third graders, including "The Skipping Pot," a Danish folktale, and "Ali Baba and Princess Farrah" from a Johanna Hurwitz book. The book also contains numerous scripted poems, such as "Using Subtraction" by Allan Jacobs and Leland Jacobs, "The Greedy Man's Week" by Beatrice Schenk de Regniers, and "A Bug" by Karla Kuskin.

Another good resource for Readers Theater scripts are the books of Suzanne Barcher, including *More Readers Theatre for Beginning Readers* (2006), *Readers Theatre for Beginning Readers* (1993), and *Multicultural Folktales: Readers Theatre for Elementary Students* (2000). The first two books contain folk- and fairy tales such as "Cinderella" and "Henny Penny." The multicultural book provides many unfamiliar yet interesting folktales from around the world.

Another great resource for Readers Theater scripts is Aaron Shepard's Web site at www.aaronshep.com. A fun story for third graders is "Three Sideways Stories from Wayside School," which is adapted from Louis Sachar's book *Sideways Stories From Wayside School*. This Web site contains many folktales from around the world.

Dramatizations

Third graders are not too old to act out stories. While it is true that not all children want to perform stories, drama should be offered as a choice. Reading a script deepens comprehension and increases fluency, and acting out a story expands oral language. Students may act out their favorite read-aloud or concepts that are being learned in the classroom. *Miss Alaineus: A Vocabulary Disaster* by Debra Frasier is a good book to use to demonstrate acting out vocabulary.

Wordless picture books are another source for dramatizations. Students use the pictures to determine both narration and dialogue. Some wordless picture books that work well for this experience are David Wiesner's *Tuesday*, *Flotsam*, and *Sector 7*. Visit Wiesner's Web site at www.houghtonmifflinbooks.com/authors/wiesner for more wordless books to use for Readers Theater.

Demonstrating Our Engagements With Literacy

To portray a character and act out a story, the student must understand the story, so drama supports comprehension. There is no need for costumes, and very simple props can be made with a word on a piece of paper. Most children enjoy acting, although as they get older, they often become self-conscious. The source of the text to be dramatized can come from a literature circle selection, a read-aloud, or a book several children have read. Fiction is usually a good choice, but some nonfiction also lends itself to dramatization.

Technology Projects

Our students can use technology in a number of ways during the reading block. Virtual libraries have greatly increased the amount of text available to our students for little or no cost. BookFlix (teacher.scholastic.com/products/book flixfreetrial) is one such collection of books available on the Internet for a nominal fee. Authors can visit our classroom via their Web sites; examples are authors Jon Scieszka (www.jsworldwide.com) and Andrew Clements (www.andrewclements.com). Our students can express their knowledge about the text they have read through technology projects using programs such as Kidpix and Kidspiration.

Other uses of technology during the reading block include:

- Creating graphic organizes to express thoughts
- Making podcasts
- Developing a Web site for books the class has read
- Making electronic journal entries

Literature Discussion Groups

The peer interaction component of the reading block is the time the literature groups come together and discuss what they read during the independent component since their last meeting. Each member refers to his or her literature response journal and shares vocabulary, questions, predictions, and other strategies used to make meaning of the text. Before the discussion ends, the group decides on the focus for discussion at the next meeting. It might be characters' strengths and weaknesses or predictions about the conclusion of the story. Sometimes the discussions bring disequilibrium to some of the participants, but that causes the readers to think beyond surface knowledge and consider other opinions.

Some popular books for third-grade literature circles are the Judy Moody series by Megan McDonald, the Maximum Boy series by Dan Greenburg, the Animal Ark series by Ben Baglio, and the Magic Tree House chapter books by Mary Pope Osborne.

Community Sharing

The last few minutes of the reading workshop are devoted to community sharing, attended by everyone for the purpose of celebrating reading. Some teachers we know have a gathering every day, others choose to have three per week, and still others schedule one whenever students have something to present. There is great value in having gatherings because of the community building that takes place. Laughing, thinking, and crying together provide a common bond that permeates the community.

Having an opportunity to talk about books and express opinions is enjoyable and increases comprehension. The three of us belong to a book club that meets once a month. There are a dozen adults who have all read a book and have formed their individual meanings about it. Few books win the approval of all members of the club, and the differing reactions are amazing. We would not expect any less diversity within a class of third graders.

There are no set procedures for the gathering because each day will be different. Some days will feature presentations by groups or individuals, and on some days there will be discussions of texts. You will need to observe who hasn't contributed for several days so you can encourage those students to participate. There will be other students who enjoy verbalizing so much they will need to be reminded to share the stage with others.

On the days that you are discussing books, some of these questions will evoke a lot of discussion:

- Can you think of two books by the same author to which you had different responses?

- What is the most compelling opening line to a book that you can remember?

- Is there one perfect book to recommend to other third graders that you can guarantee they will enjoy? If not, why doesn't such a book exist?

- If a friend was going on a long trip and wanted a good book to read, what would you recommend?

The following are ideas we have found to be successful for sharing during the community gathering.

Artistic

Illustrations
Costumes of characters
Character mobiles
Book posters

Drama

Readers Theater
Improvisations
Monologues
Plays
Puppet plays
Skits

Literary-Style Sharing

Author biographies
Character analyses
Fictional diaries
Dust jackets
Lists of facts
Eyewitness accounts
Raps

Speech Forms

Demonstrations
Oral reports

Symbolic Presentations

Cartoons

Charts

Diagrams

Graphs

Maps

Timelines

Three-Dimensional Art

Constructions

Diorama

Sculptures

Shadow boxes

Technology

PowerPoint presentations

Virtual tours of settings

In Conclusion ⁓

In this chapter, we have shared our ideas about a third-grade literacy block. Because most third graders can read independently, they can read for longer periods of time, so peer interaction and intentional teaching can take place throughout the reading block. We continually focus on comprehension as our students move to higher levels in their thinking and increase their content knowledge.

Some of Gayle's favorite third-grade read-alouds include:

Brimner, L. (2002). *The littlest wolf*

Bryan, A. (1980). *Beat the story-drum, pum-pum*

Bryan, A. (1987). *The dancing granny*

Bryan, A. (1989). *Turtle knows your name*

Bunting, E. (2000). *The memory string*

Carle, E. (1999). *The very clumsy click beetle*

Cronin, D. (2003). *Diary of a worm*

Cronin, D. (2005). *Diary of a spider*

Pinkney, A. D. (1998). *Duke Ellington*

Fleming, C. (2004). *Gator gumbo*

Fox, M. (2002). *The magic hat*

Frasier, D. (2000). *Miss Alaineus: A vocabulary disaster*

Haseley, D. (2002). *A story for bear*

Hoose, P., & Hoose, H. (1998). *Hey, little ant*

Johnston, T. (2000). *The barn owls*

Laminack, L. (2004). *Saturdays and teacakes*

Levenson, G. (1999). *Pumpkin circle: The story of a garden*

Lewis, K. (2002). *My truck is stuck!*

Moulton, M. (2005). *Scarecrow Pete*

Munson, D. (2000). *Enemy pie*

Nickle, J. (1999). *The ant bully*

Palatini, M. (2002). *Earthquack!*

Polacco, P. (1993). *The bee tree*

Polacco, P. (2005). *Emma Kate*

Posada, J. (2006). *Play ball!*

Raven, M. T. (2005). *America's white table*

Scieszka, J. (2001). *Baloney Henry P*

Van Allsburg, C. (2006). *Probuditi!*

Waldman, N. (1999). *The Starry Night*

Watt, M. (2006). *Scaredy Squirrel*

Watt, M. (2007). *Chester*

Watt, M. (2007). *Scaredy Squirrel makes a friend*

Watt, M. (2008). *Scaredy Squirrel at the beach*

Wheeler, L. (2002). *Turk and Runt*

Wiesner, D. (2006). *Flotsam*

Wood, A. (1996). *The Bunyans*

Woodson, J. (2005). *Show way*

Wyeth, S. D. (1998). *Something beautiful*

Some of Gayle's favorite short texts for shared reading include:

Cowcher, H. (1993). *Whistling thorn*

Fox, M. (1989). *Night noises*

Greeley, V. (1990). *White is the moon*

Heller, R. (1999). *The reason for a flower*

Hoberman, M. A. (2007). *A house is a house for me*

Jakab, C., & Keystone, D. (1995). *What on earth*

THIRD GRADE ■ Resource 5-1
Reading Progression Chart for Third Grade

Reading Progression Chart for Third Grade

Gayle's Suggestions for Emphasizing Meaning Throughout the Year

Grading Period for Introduction (May vary)	Focus of Reading Instruction	Date of Intentional Instruction (whole group, small group)	Date of Practice (literacy encounters, peer interactions)	Date of Independent Application (e.g., literature journals, conferences)
1	Use: -Previewing and predicting			
	-Knowledge of word meaning			
	-Text features			
	-Visualizing			
	-Wondering /questioning			
	Demonstrate literal understanding: -Details			
	-Sequence events			
	-Text structure			
2	Interpret Passages: -Main idea			
	-Draw conclusions			
	-Cause and effect			
	-Fact and opinion			
	-Summarizing			
	-Author's purpose			
	-Make inferences			
	-Determine important ideas			
3	Analyze and Identify: -Character			
	-Setting			
	-Plot			
	-Problem and solution			
	-Point of view			
4	Self-Monitor: -Accessing prior knowledge and experience			
	-Rereading			
	-Using context clues			
	-Self-questioning			

Creating the Best Literacy Block Ever © 2009 by Maryann Manning, Gayle Morrison, and Deborah Camp: Scholastic Professional

Gayle's Reading Conference Form for Third Grade

Name _____

Date _____

	*	**	***	
Text 1 _____ Level___	F	UF	F	N
Text 2 _____ Level___	F	UF	F	N
Text 3 _____ Level___	F	UF	F	N

Conference Comments

**Insert bk. # next to concept demonstrated.

Fiction Oral Retelling

Sequentially Retold ___

Beginning: Setting__ Characters__

Middle: Problem_____

Ending: Solution_____

Plot_____   Char. Change?_____

Main Idea_____

Nonfiction Oral Retelling

Recalled 5 facts____ More____

Identified Main Idea___

Determined Important Ideas_____

Comments

Instruction Based on Conference

	Miscue	Semantics Meaning Change?		Syntax Structure Change?		Graphophonic Similarity			
						Visual		Sound	
Bk. #		Yes	No	Yes	No	Y	N	Y	N
Totals									

* If leveled books are used, record level.
** F is for books that are familiar and UF is for books that are unfamiliar.
*** Genre that includes fiction or nonfiction.

Creating the Best Literacy Block Ever © 2009 by Maryann Manning, Gayle Morrison, and Deborah Camp: Scholastic Professional

Resource 5-3

Gayle's Strategies Conference Form for Third Grade

Name _____

Date _____

	*	**	***
Text 1 _____	Level___	F UF	F N
Text 2 _____	Level___	F UF	F N
Text 3 _____	Level___	F UF	F N

Comments

**Insert bk. # next to concept demonstrated.

Fiction Oral Retelling
Demonstrates:
1. Sequential Retelling ___
Beginning: Setting__Characters__
Middle: Problem___
Ending: Solution___
Plot_____   Char. Change_____
2. Main Idea_____
3. Making Connections/Using Prior
        Knowledge_____
4. Visualizing_____
5. Questioning_____
6. Making Inferences_____
7. Determining Important Ideas____
8. Understanding Text
        Structure_____
9. Summarizing_____

Nonfiction Oral Retelling
Recalled 5 Facts____ More___
        Demonstrates:
1. Main Idea___
2. Determining Important Ideas___
3. Understanding Text
        Structure___
4. Summarizing___

Instruction Based on Conference

		Miscue	Semantics Meaning Change?		Syntax Structure Change?		Graphophonic Similarity			
							Visual		Sound	
Bk. #			Yes	No	Yes	No	Y	N	Y	N
	Totals									

* If leveled books are used, record level.
** F is for books that are familiar and UF is for books that are unfamiliar.
*** Genre that includes fiction or nonfiction.

Creating the Best Literacy Block Ever © 2009 by Maryann Manning, Gayle Morrison, and Deborah Camp: Scholastic Professional

THIRD GRADE ▪ Resource 5-4
Fiction and Nonfiction Literature Response Journal
Guidelines for Third Grade

Fiction and Nonfiction Literature Response Journal Guidelines for Third Grade

1. Fiction

Date: _____

Title: _____

Author: _____

1. Make **prediction** before reading.

2. Write down **unknown words** with page numbers.

3. **Chapter books**—write a **short summary** after you have read half of the book.

   Predict what will happen next.

4. Was **prediction** in #1 right or wrong? **Why?**

5. Make a **connection**—text to text, text to self, text to world.

6. After reading, **write a letter** to the teacher.

7. Complete **"Growing as a Reader" pages** in back of notebook.

2. Nonfiction

Date: _____

Title: _____

Author: _____

1. Make **prediction** before reading.

2. Write down **unknown words** with page numbers.

3. Write down **seven facts** learned.

4. Was **prediction** in #1 right or wrong? **Why?**

5. Make a **connection**—text to text, text to self, text to world.

6. After reading, **write a letter** to the teacher.

7. Complete **"Growing as a Reader" pages** in back of notebook.

Creating the Best Literacy Block Ever © 2009 by Maryann Manning, Gayle Morrison, and Deborah Camp: Scholastic Professional

THIRD GRADE ▪ Resource 5-5
Phonics Inventory Chart

Phonics Inventory Chart
Third Grade

Teacher _____ Date _____

S–Secure in Application   D–Developing   N–Needs Intervention

	Student Names							
Phonics Inventory Items								
Alphabet Names								
Consonant Sounds								
Consonant Digraphs								
Consonant Blends								
Vowel Names								
Short Vowels (aural)								
Double Vowels								
Final "e"								
Diphthongs								
Read Short-Vowel Words								
Reversals								
Prefixes								
Suffixes								
Compound Words								
Silent Letters								
Vowel + "r"								
Syllabication								

* This Inventory is given ONLY to those students who have gaps in their reading development. This assessment can guide intentional instruction.

Creating the Best Literacy Block Ever © 2009 by Maryann Manning, Gayle Morrison, and Deborah Camp: Scholastic Professional

Getting to Know My Chapter Book

Write your answers in your literature journal under your "challenging words" for this book. Please **number your answers** according to the questions below and write the answers in **complete sentences**.

Complete after reading about ⅓ of the book.

1. What is the **setting** of your book? When and where did it take place?

2. Who are the **characters**?

3. Who is the **main character**? Describe the character.

4. Is there a **problem** in the book that needs to be solved? If so, what?

Complete after reading about ⅔ of the book.

5. How was the **problem solved**?

6. Did the **main character** change in any way throughout the book? How?

7. List the **main events** that happened in the story in the order that they happened.

8. What was your **favorite part**? Why?

9. Make a connection by thinking if this book reminds you of another book, something that is happening/happened in your life or something that is happening in the world. Write it in your journal.

Complete after reading remaining chapters.

10. Did the author give you any ideas for **writing your own story**? If so, what are your ideas?

* Don't forget to check the "Growing as a Reader" pages in the back of your journal.

Name_____

Getting to Know My Chapter Book

Write your answers in your literature journal under your "challenging words" for this book. Please **number your answers** according to the questions below and write the answers in **complete sentences**.

Complete after reading about ⅓ of the book.

1. What is the **setting** of your book? When and where did it take place?

2. Who are the **characters**?

3. Who is the **main character**? Describe the character.

4. Is there a **problem** in the book that needs to be solved? If so, what?

Complete after reading about ⅔ of the book.

5. How was the **problem solved**?

6. Did the **main character** change in any way throughout the book? How?

7. List the **main events** that happened in the story in the order that they happened.

8. What was your **favorite part**? Why?

9. Make a connection by thinking if this book reminds you of another book, something that is happening/happened in your life or something that is happening in the world. Write it in your journal.

Complete after reading remaining chapters.

10. Did the author give you any ideas for **writing your own story**? If so, what are your ideas?

* Don't forget to check the "Growing as a Reader" pages in the back of your journal.

Name_____

Creating the Best Literacy Block Ever © 2009 by Maryann Manning, Gayle Morrison, and Deborah Camp: Scholastic Professional

■ CHAPTER 6 ■

Classroom Life

It is a little before 8:00 on Monday morning, and the school buses are unloading. Students are hurrying to their classrooms. From the opened door of Room 3A, a second-grade classroom, comes lively music. Inside children are writing their names on a chart tablet. Gayle is near the door greeting the children, accepting notes from parents and trading family and school news and information. She had sent home the class newspaper, *The Globetrotter News*, which included questions for family members, and this sparks additional conversation with parents. The children are now standing in front of several charts, checking their weekly committee assignments and signing up for literacy encounters.

Yolanda and Sylvia, who are on the Discovery Committee and serving as the Zoo Keepers for the week, check the hamsters' water bottle. Yolanda takes the water bottle out of the cage and goes over to the sink to wash it out. Gayle says, "That bottle wasn't very dirty. You probably don't need to wash it yet." Sylvia answers, "We like to drink from really clean glasses, so we don't want Jenny and Fred to drink out of a dirty bottle."

Melissa says to John, "Someone left a few books out of the shelves Friday, but we can put them back before anyone looks for them." John answers, "I don't believe the Book Committee last week would have left them out. I think someone must have taken them out after the committee checked their area. We all try to do a good job."

When Tiffany finally comes in, she still has sleep in her eyes. Hiko approaches her and says, "Is your little sister any better or is she still sick?" Tiffany answers, "Yes, but she is in a room where we can visit her. I took her the cards that everyone made for her last night and she was happy."

Jonathan seeks out Kyoko and says, "I really liked the sushi that your mother brought to our class yesterday. I thought all sushi had raw fish, but the avocado and cucumber your mother used really tasted good." Gayle is so pleased to overhear Jonathan's compliment. Kyoko's mother had brought in a piece of sushi for each child, and Gayle had been concerned that some of the children wouldn't taste the sushi or might make unkind remarks about the unusual food, but it turned out very well. The fruit cups Mrs. Kato brought were especially popular, and the children all seemed to enjoy the green tea. In the future, Gayle plans to share several read-alouds about Japan.

The children continue to do committee work, sign up for literacy encounters, and choose books from the class library for free reading time. When they finish these tasks, they move to their tables and write their weekly goals. Then they read the math problem of the day on the chart tablet and began to work in their math journals.

Gayle's Evolution ∼

These classroom routines haven't always been this smooth. Gayle's first few years teaching were marked by trial and error. She has moved from being teacher-centered to child-centered and from dictating rules to children to developing autonomy in children. She has changed because she reflected upon her teaching practices, read a lot of professional literature, and interacted with some really great teachers in districtwide meetings and at conferences. Now she works hard to help her students develop ownership of their actions, exercise freedom of choice, and demonstrate responsibility for themselves and others in their classroom community.

Peterson's Influence

Ralph Peterson's (1992) seminal book, *Life in a Crowded Place*, and his ideas about ceremony, ritual, rites, and celebration helped Gayle form a learning community in her classroom that closely resembles a family. Peterson's ideas helped her see how language can be used throughout the day to develop inquiry and extend literacy growth. She rereads his book every summer so she can reflect on her classroom community from the year before and think about refinements she wants to make to strengthen the learning community in the coming year.

Gayle believes that the psychological environment is dependent upon the collaborative efforts of the entire class in the construction of the physical environment. Gayle's students take pride in their classroom because they have responsibility for it and ownership of everything in it. The children understand the purposes behind what they are doing and can explain them to visitors. Because of the predictability of the day, the children feel safe and secure in taking risks to develop as human beings.

Gayle's Daily Schedule ～

A well-planned and neatly implemented daily schedule provides opportunities for children to follow consistent and predictable classroom rituals and routines. Students gain control of their own learning and depend less on the teacher to control and lead their learning. Students also develop a sense of ownership of their classroom. For example, at the beginning of the year Gayle would take their orders for school supplies and place them directly at the school office. By the end of the first semester, the students assumed responsibility for this process. The students, not Gayle, determined what supplies students needed, composed the list, collected the money, and made change for one another when they received the order.

A Walk Through the Schedule

This is a description of a typical day for Gayle at the beginning of the year. Keep in mind that the reading block is part of a sequence that affords many literacy opportunities throughout the day.

Visualize a busy beehive and you will have a picture of the students at the beginning of the day. Before the first whole-class gathering takes place,

A Sample Schedule

This schedule is one that Gayle developed and has used with her first and second graders.

7:45   Sign-In/Welcome

7:55   Committee Work
       Encounters Sign-Up
       Habitat Detectives' News II
       Get Five "Free Read" Books
       Check-in Materials/Homework
       Write/Check Goals

8:15   Math Journals: Problem of the Day

8:40   Habitat Detectives' Daily News
       Committee Reports

The Reading Literacy Block

9:00   Focus Lesson

9:15   Intentional Instruction, Peer Interaction, Independent Reading
       Reading Process: Choice, Literature Journals (Vocabulary, Retellings, Concept Pages, Connections, etc.), Guided Reading, Conferences (Running Records, Miscue Analysis)

10:20 Closing

10:30 Lunch

**11:00 Book Talk Read-Aloud; What Did You Notice/See?
       Wonderings/Questions, Reminds Me of Something in My Life or of Another Book
       Reflections in Book Talk Booklets

The Writing Block

11:30 Focus Lesson

11:45 Intentional Instruction, Peer Interaction, Independent Writing
       Writing Process: Choice

12:30 Research: Theme Immersion

1:30   Physical Education

2:00   Literacy Encounters

2:30   Closure of the Day: Author's Chair/Pass the Rock

2:45   Get Ready for Home

** Monday, 11:00: Art, Wednesday, 11:00: Music

Entering Gayle's classroom, the sign-in sheet can be seen on the right

students encounter eight routines that require their attention the minute they step into the classroom. The day unfolds in a sequential manner.

Sign-in As students enter the room, they sign in, acknowledging their presence at school that day.

Check community assignments Each child checks his or her community assignments for the week. These committees are Math, Opening, Discovery, Welcoming, Maintenance, and Book. The jobs rotate weekly, giving Gayle five days to observe each group and document how the students are applying their reading, writing, and math skills in authentic ways.

- The Math Committee takes attendance and counts the names on the sign-in sheet at the door to determine who is absent. These math activities provide real-world practice while developing concepts.

- The Opening Committee updates the calendar, weather, and number line, and shows how many days they have been in school. They also represent the number of days with coins. The math skills applied during the opening address both student needs and curriculum mandates.

The Classroom

- The Welcoming Committee writes a message on the message board outside the room informing visitors where the class is at all times of the day. During the writing block, this committee is responsible for writing the letter that visitors to the classroom receive. The Welcoming Committee members also serve as escorts for the visitors while they are in the room.

- The Discovery Committee is responsible for feeding the animals and updating the ongoing observation journals or experiments. The committee shares observations with the class during the whole-class gathering.

- The Book Committee is responsible for making sure that classroom books are kept in their proper place according to the class-initiated sorting guide.

- The Maintenance Committee is responsible for making sure the room is kept in order as the groups transition throughout the day. After each transition, the Maintenance Committee checks areas and recalls groups that may have left their area messy.

Literacy encounters The students sign up for a literacy encounter and document their choice on a literacy encounter form. The students rotate through all five encounters during the week:

- Computer

An orderly classroom, thanks to the Maintenance Committee

A student signs up for a literacy encounter

- Writing
- Reading
- Math
- Discovery

Daily news Each morning during the writing block, a different group is responsible for writing the daily news to share during the focus lesson.

Choose five texts Each child selects five texts from anywhere in the room to be used for free reading throughout the day.

Check-in Students check in materials, homework, and traveling friends. They also restock materials as necessary.

Weekly goals On Monday, each child writes his or her weekly goals. On other days, they date and check off their accomplished goals to determine the new day's goals. This routine allows them to be accountable for their work and set realistic goals that result in success. The weekly goal checklist is sent home on Friday so parents can share in their children's successes.

Problem of the day The students read the problem of the day on the chart, write it in their math journal, and start problem solving. The Whole group discusses Monday's problem on Wednesday, and Tuesday's problem on Thursday, leaving Friday for the discussion of both. Staggering the days gives everyone time to complete the problems and have something to contribute to the math talk. The math problem of the day requires students to use developmentally appropriate critical thinking skills.

These routines give children time to apply skills authentically while giving Gayle intentional teaching time with those who need it. During these morning routines, Gayle walks around the room and does the following:

- Talks with students
- Monitors student engagement
- Observes student interaction and activities
- Takes anecdotal notes
- Facilitates the different committees
- Clarifies any student misconceptions

Committee reports During this whole-class time, the Opening Committee reviews the date, weather, and number of days students have been in school. The Discovery Committee updates the class on ongoing experiments as well as observations made while feeding the animals. Gayle and her students write the Daily News; they also take dictation from a different group of students each day and post it in front of the room to be used throughout the day for reading and spelling. This modeled writing serves dual purposes for reading and writing because the students can read what they dictate and reuse the words they can read in their writing.

Transition to the literacy block Gayle uses music for transitions. Each year she chooses a different transition song, such as "It's a Small World." At the sound of the song, the students move to the community gathering, which usually begins with a focus lesson based on the needs of the children and curriculum guidelines. The needs of the children are determined by ongoing assessments such as those described in Chapter 8. The block lasts for 90 minutes, with much of the time spent on intentional teaching and the children reading texts.

A student hard at work during the literacy block

Lunch In Gayle's school, the children enjoy lunch/brunch at 10:30 am—early for many schools, but it works well for her students.

Read-alouds and book talk Use this time to help children make connections—to their lives, to other books, and to their questions or "wonderings." Demonstrate making connections in the teacher's book talk booklets for several weeks. After Gayle demonstrates how to use book talk booklets (blank papers stapled together), she gives her students their own booklets for recording and reflecting on the connections they make during the read-aloud.

Each day after returning from lunch, Gayle invites her students to listen to a read-aloud without conversation so the students can reflect on their own connections without being influenced by what Gayle has written or by what their classmates think. After connecting the read-aloud to their lives and to other books, Gayle shares her wonderings and then invites her students to record theirs in their book talk booklets. The children use their book talk booklets throughout the year to faster deeper thinking and reflections.

Writing Block At the sound of the transition song, the students gravitate back to the community gathering area for the focus lesson at the beginning of writing block. The bulk of time during these 60 minutes is spent with children writing on their topics of choice. During the writing block, the teacher is engaged in intentional teaching through conferencing, and the children are writing independently and having peer conferences. Sharing of published writing occurs during author's chair at the end of the day.

Theme immersion, inquiry, and research The next transition leads to the theme immersion/inquiry/research time. At the beginning of the year, the teacher leads the class in conducting a research project, modeling the stages of the process. An anchor bulletin board serves as a guide in the research process throughout the year.

Once students begin their own small-group research, they meet together first during this time so the teacher can conduct a status-of-the-class check. This check determines which group is at the following stages of the research:

- Gathering information
- Compiling
- Revising
- Editing
- Publishing

At the end of the theme immersion time, the students chart goals for the next day's research. This chart informs the teacher as to who needs conferences or additional texts and also which small group is ready for a content conference. The amount of reading, writing, and engagement during a theme immersion can be tremendous.

Literacy encounters After physical education, the students begin the literacy encounters they signed up for in the morning. During this time, Gayle also works with specific children who need targeted help, or gathers a small group for math and reading focus lessons based on the observations she made during opening activities and the reading block.

Author's chair and pass the rock After literacy encounters, the children transition to a class gathering area for author's chair and "pass the rock" (Peterson, 1992). Pass the rock is a ritual Gayle and her students perform at the end of the day when they all gather in the whole-group area, form a circle, and share something from their lives. It may be something that has happened that day in school, or at home, or it could be something that is going to happen in the future. The children pass the rock to the right and as each person receives the rock, he or she has the option of sharing with the group. Everyone respects the person with the rock by listening closely. One day when Harold, who is a very quiet, shy little 7-year-old, received the rock, he told how his classmate Andrew had squirted mustard on him at lunch and had not apologized. The incident had been bothering Harold all day. Andrew, who was sitting across from him in the circle, immediately apologized, and Harold felt much better. This is a bonding time when everyone feels safe sharing what is on their minds and in their hearts— it's a special community ritual.

Dismissal At this time, the students take out their math bags, traveling friends, parent bags, and science boxes and pick up their belongings as they prepare to go home, making sure the room is neat and tidy. In summary, students take pride in their classroom because they own—and are responsible for—all aspects of classroom life. The children understand the purposes behind what they are doing and can explain them to visitors. Because of the predictability of the day, the children feel safe and secure in taking risks to develop as creative, competent learners. A substitute teacher once remarked to Gayle that she (the substitute) almost wasn't needed because the children were so familiar with the expectations of the classroom community and how to conduct all classroom rituals and routines!

Gayle's Physical Classroom Environment ～

Let's take a tour of Gayle's classroom. From miles around, undergraduate students and experienced teachers alike arrive at Gayle's school to visit her classroom for ideas. When teachers hear that Gayle lets her students help design the classroom, they find it hard to believe. They are eager to discover how primary students can be involved in designing the layout of their room. Visitors soon discover that Gayle's students refer to "our room" and take great interest and pride in every detail of the classroom organization and layout. Everywhere classroom visitors turn, they see children engaged in literacy experiences—working on the floor, at

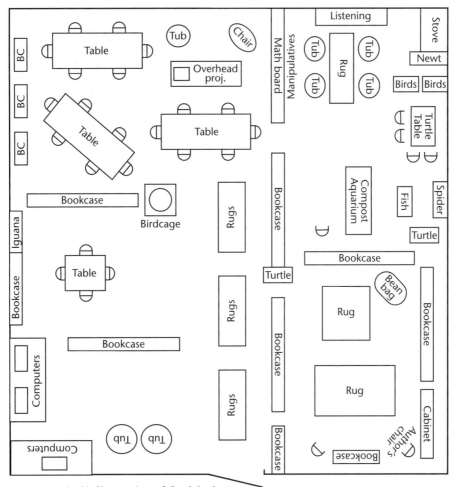

■ Figure 6.1: *Bird's-eye view of Gayle's classroom*

tables, under tables, or near the CD player, where they can hear the soft music that plays throughout the day. In order to maximize learning, the one rule about choosing a sitting place is that only two students can be in any area at one time.

Charts for Children

Everywhere you look you see charts on walls, ceilings, the backs of bookcases, tucked into every available open space. Here are some charts you'll see in Gayle's classroom:

- Poem and song charts on the walls
- An environmental print alphabet chart under the chalkboard
- Weekly student goal charts over tables

- Anchor charts produced by both Gayle and her students
- Class-made vocabulary charts from favorite books
- A "Riddle of the Day" chart near the door
- Charts that correspond with the class's current theme immersion, such as habitat detectives
- A large chart tablet for posing daily questions discussed at the end of the day, such as "Why do we have to have cold sandwiches instead of pizza?" and "Where does the green come from that is on the top of the dirt in the compost pile?"

Environmental Print Display

In addition to the environmental print alphabet, Gayle has a word wall of logos, labels, and other familiar print. The environmental print alphabet from the previous year is used as the beginning of the word wall for the next year.

Not Your Average Bulletin Board

The classroom bulletin boards appeal to Gayle's students because they generate the content and participate in the design of each board. These displays serve as references that help students develop independence in literacy activities. An example is the research bulletin board Gayle and her students created depicting each stage of a research project. Students refer to the visual as they are engaged in their own data gathering and report writing.

Gayle's a bulletin board devoted to the children and their families promotes home–school connections by keeping everyone informed about family happenings. This bulletin board often contains pictures of family reunions, christenings, birthday parties, and vacations.

Bookcases, Books, and Baskets

Bookcases with baskets and tubs of books are everywhere. What's in the book tubs? Here's a sampling:

- I Can Read books
- Magic Tree House series
- The Berenstain Bears books
- Clifford the Big Red Dog books
- The Bailey School Kids series
- Henry and Mudge series

Bookshelves are well stocked in Gayle's classroom.

Works by:

- Dr. Seuss
- Marc Brown
- Peggy Parish
- David Shannon
- Jack Prelutsky
- Eloise Greenfield
- Denise Fleming
- Lois Ehlert
- Ashley Bryan
- Rosemary Wells
- James Marshall

Other bookshelves contain:

- Multiple paperback copies of books by Patricia Polacco, Eve Bunting, Kevin Henkes, and Robert Munsch for buddy reading and literature circles
- Caldecott Medal and Honor books used in author and illustrator studies

One of many gathering areas in Gayle's classroom

- Fiction and nonfiction big books

- Books that have been read aloud during the year

- Children's magazines

- Student and class books published during the writing block and theme immersions

- Baskets with leveled texts and trade books coded according to the Fountas and Pinnell text gradient (2005)

- A book check-out basket containing a list of books that children have left at home. The children take home five books each night to share with parents or siblings. They can choose any book in the room except the leveled texts. The next day, the books that were taken home are free reading books for the day, and the process begins again as they choose five more books. Gayle also keeps a red wagon full of books the children want her to reread over and over, with a sign that reads, "Read these again, Mrs. M."

One year, Gayle's children organized the nonfiction books according to different categories, such as land animals, sea animals, and plants. Water books had blue stickers; land books, green; plant books, orange; insect/bug books, red; weather, purple; and miscellaneous books were tagged with white stickers.

The Home–School Connection

Every Monday morning the children proudly enter the classroom waving their newsbooks, showing them off to their friends.

Sarah announces, "My dad wrote about his fishing trip where he caught a big fish."

"Wait until you see the picture my mom drew of her and the dog she had when she was little!" Jerome says.

Jamise proudly proclaims, "My mother wrote about being the first African-American Girl Scout in Mobile County."

Tyree has his hands full with his newsbook and a science box he's returning. He smiles broadly as he talks about his work. "Wait until you see the outcome of our experiments on salt."

They all eagerly await author's chair time when they will share their newsbooks and other home–school projects. Lawrence says his mother is coming to read her own letter today during author's chair. "She wrote about my grandmother when she was a little girl living in Greenville," he tells us. The room is humming with excitement as the children check in all of their materials and go about their daily routines.

As Gayle observes the students signing their names on the chart to indicate that they have brought back their newsbooks, she can't help but reflect how far this project has come over the years in building a partnership with the parents and how it has shaped and enhanced student learning. This is evident not only in the number of parents who respond each week but also in the students' conversations while they are signing in their newsbooks.

Research and common sense tell us that a parent's involvement and visibility in their child's school foster success for the child. During the 18 years that Gayle taught in an inner-city school, parental involvement was a perpetual area of concern for her. Ninety-eight percent of her students were on free lunches, and parents often worked more than one job. She knew that developing a home–school connection was a challenging task, but she also knew it was essential to helping her students succeed in school. Not only did the students need Gayle's support, so did their parents. To this end, she began a three-year journey, working hard to develop a home–school connection that would inform parents as well as provide the support the students needed to become successful learners.

All administrators and teachers proclaim that they want more parent involvement, but often we get too busy in our instructional roles and forget home–school connections. Taking the time to involve families is an important investment, with a host of benefits for everyone involved.

The Benefits of Parent Involvement ~

Teachers benefit from interaction with parents in numerous ways because parents provide insights into the child's thinking, fears, joys, and interests (as well as key medical information). Parents also provide teachers with an understanding of the child's home life, thus enabling teachers to provide a culturally relevant pedagogy in the classroom.

Parents benefit because when we involve them intimately in the life of the classroom, they have a purpose for becoming involved in their child's education. They see the classroom as belonging to them as well as to their children.

Children benefit when they realize parents are participants and not mere observers of classroom happenings. Families often have talents and skills that teachers can tap to share with students during theme immersions or other units of study. Broadening the human circle to include parents in the classroom community adds to the children's perception that the classroom is truly a safe and special place where the child works, shares, and learns with other children and their families. Reading to, with, and by children in the home is an influential activity that brings families together around a joyful literacy experience.

Children also benefit when teachers provide the knowledge and skills necessary for families to support the teacher's efforts at home (see Figure 7.1 and the accompanying Resource 7-1 on page 219). Here are some topics we've addressed in parent education meetings and communications:

See Resource 7-1, Home Reading Partners form, p. 219.

- Reading aloud to children
- Supporting children's burgeoning literacy development
- Providing writing opportunities at home
- Joining the local public library

This information helps children discover that learning does not just occur in the classroom for seven hours each day, but is a lifelong endeavor.

Dear Parents and Guardians,

Your child will choose 5 books to bring home and share with you each night. You may read the books TO your child, or WITH your child, or the books may be read BY your child.

I hope you will enjoy this experience with your child. Please talk with your child about the books. Make predictions before the books are read and discuss the books after they are read. Were your predictions right?

Before your child brings the books back to school please take a moment and reflect on this experience by writing down any comments/concerns you have about your child's reading on the Home Reading Partners sheet. Please return this sheet and the books to school each day.

Remember that your child will learn to read by READING. By reading with your child every day you are insuring that he/she will become an independent reader.

I look forward to hearing from you.

Sincerely,

Gayle Morrison

Figure 7.1: *Letter to parents*

Home Reading Partners

Gayle's Home–School Reading Form

Date	Title of Book	Read to Child	Read with Child	Read by Child	Comments/Concerns	Initials

Resource 7-1

The Home–School Connections ▪ Resource 7-1
Home Reading Partners form

Chapter Seven: The Home–School Connections   219

Resource 7-1: *Home Reading Partners*

Involving Parents ～

Parents depend on us as expert professionals to show them how to help their children at home, but parents have as much to teach us as we have to teach them. We don't want them to view us as the almighty dispensers of knowledge; to make that clear, Gayle always asks parents to tell her about their children, and she relies on several tools to help her accomplish this goal.

Newsbooks

After Maryann returned from Australia with the newsbook idea she saw used in the upper grades there, she shared it with Gayle, who then developed the newsbook project for her primary students. The newsbook includes a weekly letter written by each student to their parents/

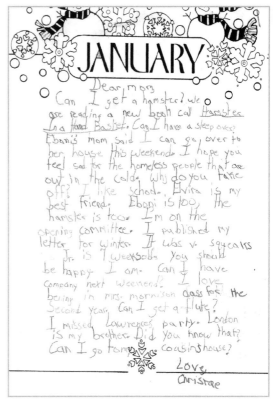

■ Figure 7.2: *Example of a child's letter*

guardians (see Figure 7.2), Gayle's weekly newsletter (Figure 7.3), and a blank piece of paper inserted for parents to write back to their child.

Parents' letters expressing their pride in their children's school accomplishments help foster their children's growth and self-confidence as learners.

In Gayle's newsletter (Figure 7.3) she explains what is happening in the classroom and lists ways parents can help their child by continuing the learning at home. Parents have an open invitation to come in and read their letters during author's chair or at a time of convenience for them. The newsbooks are also very helpful at parent conferences in showing the child's development as a reader and writer (Figure 7.4).

Wanted Posters and Guest Expert Days

Gayle also develops home–school relationships through something she calls wanted posters. These posters, drawn by the students, are a clever way to attract experts among the parents who are willing to visit the class, share their expertise with the students, and, in this way, enrich the curriculum and contribute to the classroom community. Gayle is always amazed and delighted with how many experts there are in any school community. Gayle has had nurses, firemen, policemen, ministers, teachers, homemakers, chefs, and zoo workers visit her classroom to demonstrate their expertise.

Gayle organized three Guest Expert Days throughout the year. After a parent/community expert visited the classroom, a committee would publish a book about the visit for the classroom library. The authors all signed a copy of the original book and presented it to the expert.

Traveling Friends

Students can check out one of the traveling friends for a week. The traveling friends might include Clifford, Arthur, D.W., Strega Nona, Corduroy, Berenstain Bears, Lily, Sylvester, Madeline, Frog and Toad, or Olivia. Each friend has a book, a journal, and an activity that parents can do with their child. The students record daily what happens while the traveling friend is visiting. Parents and other family members write in the journals, too.

Activities involving traveling friends that students and parents share include:

The Habitat Detectives' News

Dear Parents and Guardians,

These first few weeks of school have been very busy for us. We have learned a lot about each other and are beginning to become a community of learners who really care about each other.

We have many of our rituals, routines, and committees in tact, but we have a lot more work to do before our day is completely organized into the learning community we want. Ask your child to tell you about the committees and the responsibilities of each. As the weeks go along, the responsibilities will grow. Do you know the name of our community newspaper? Ask your child to tell you. Also, ask your child to tell you about the committees he/she has served on so far.

I'm sure your child has told you our class name this year is "The Habitat Detectives". We will be searching all year for homes and habitats of different animals and people. This theme immersion will involve all areas of the curriculum.

Everyone is making progress with the Mother Goose homework book. Some have moved out of it and into their first little homework book and there are four people who have moved into their Literature Journals. This is GREAT progress! PLEASE read with your child EVERY night. Reading EVERY night with your child is instrumental in your child's success in reading. Please take at least 15 minutes each night and find a place for you and your child to have some quality reading time together.

The little homework books will help your child develop a basic sight vocabulary that will enable him/her to read harder texts. If your child comes to a word he/she doesn't know, ask him/her to first look at the picture for clues. If he/she looks at the picture and makes a prediction, but it's not the word on the page, ask him/her to look at the beginning of the word and see if that is the sound that is heard at the beginning of the prediction made. These are two VERY important reading strategies that need to be learned early in order to help your child become an independent reader and make sense out of what is read. It's also VERY important that your child learns early that the purpose of reading is to make sense out of the words read, and not just to call out words on a page. Reading comprehension is VERY important, not the number of words read.

If your child does not know all of the letters of the alphabet, ask him/her to read the letters off of cereal boxes, candy wrappers, etc. It's much better for children to make associations with real objects in their environment when learning letters and sound/symbol correspondence. It is much easier for a child to get the beginning letter of the word "want" if he/she can make the connection with the sound at the

beginning of the word, Wal-Mart. We are in the process of making our environmental alphabet. Ask your child to tell you all about it. Later on, come in and see the finished product.

The children are doing very well with their math homework bags. It's important that children not only have one-to-one correspondence with each word as they read, but have one-to-one when counting. That's why dominoes make such a good tool for the homework bags. Written instructions will ALWAYS be inside the bags to explain the activity to you just in case your child forgets how to do the homework bag. PLEASE make sure all materials (directions, too) are put back into the bag before it's brought back to school the next day.

Has a Traveling Friend visited your home yet? Each bag will have a friend, at least one book and a journal in it. The children are to use their "best guess" spelling and tell all of the fun things they did with the friend overnight. PLEASE don't spell the words for your child in the journal. When they get back to school they can't read something that did not come out of their own heads. Remember that they are trying to make sense in their OWN WAY. Please allow your child to go through these learning stages at his/her own pace. I promise, you will not be disappointed by the end of the year.

I'm sure your child has told you all about the animals in our classroom. These animals are a great learning tool for the children. They introduce the children to the different animal family groups (reptile, mammal, amphibian, and foul).

Beginning next Thursday we will cook every Thursday. Be sure to ask your child to share the recipe with you.

Please review the Community Rules with your child. Several children are very close to having you come in for a conference about their behavior. THEY MUST LEARN THAT SCHOOL IS FOR LEARNING AND NOT PLAYING! Please help me with this.

Please feel free to come in anytime you feel there is a problem or if you have questions about anything. We would love for you to come in one day and read a book to us. You are a VERY important component to your child's success in school. I hope we can work together to form a very strong home/school connection.

If you have not done so, please send in a note telling me some things about your child that will help me be a better teacher to him/her this year. I need you to help me get to know your child better.

Thank you for your support and cooperation.

Gayle Morrison

■ Figure 7.3: *Gayle's weekly newsletter*

- Writing a story about their favorite character in the book

- Drawing pictures showing the sequence of the story

- Making a puppet and retelling the story

At the end of the week, parents are asked to come to school and share the book and activity with the other students. This is always a highlight of the week.

Traveling Science/ Discovery Boxes

Inside tin lunchboxes, parents will find everything they need to perform an experiment with their child based on a science topic the children are studying in the classroom. Science boxes typically include a book about the topic and a journal for daily notations about the experiment. Gayle sends home a letter explaining what parents should do (Figure 7.5).

Once the science project is completed, the parents visit the classroom so the student and parent can share the outcome with the entire class. There are five lunchboxes with the same experiment, so different outcomes might be shared each Friday, giving the students and parents a chance to discuss and wonder and ask new

Dear Parents and Guardians,

This notebook is our Newsbook. The first page each week will be a newsletter from me telling you about our activities for the past week as well as upcoming activities. I will also share with you some classroom practices that will help you when you are working with your child at home. The second page will be a letter or picture from your child. These letters are not edited because I want you to follow your child's reading and writing development throughout the year. Please talk with your child about his/her letter or picture and ask him/her to tell you about it. The next page in the Newsbook will be for you to write a letter back to your child for us to read at school.

Please remember that your child will learn to read and write the same way he/she learned to talk and walk—one step at a time with a lot of support and positive reinforcement from you. Learning to read and write can't be hurried or force-fed to your child. PLEASE BE PATIENT with your child and remember that in order to become an independent reader and writer he/she must go through each stage of reading development at his/her own pace. We all learn differently and we must determine the path your child needs to take in order for learning to take place. Please accept your child's "best guess" spellings and remember these "best guess" spellings will become standard spellings the more he/she reads and writes.

Behind this letter is a copy of the different stages of writing your child will go through. Please refer to this each week when you get the Newsbook, and you will be able to follow your child's development into an independent reader and writer.

The Newsbook will go home every Friday. PLEASE send the Newsbook back to school every Monday.

Thank you for your continued support and cooperation.

Gayle Morrison

- Figure 7.4: *Gayle's letter explaining the newsbooks*

Dear Parents and Guardians,

Beginning next week your child will start bringing home Discovery Boxes. The boxes may be kept at home for one week (from Monday until Friday). PLEASE make sure the boxes are returned EVERY Friday so I can get them ready for the next week.

Each box will contain supplies, sometimes a book and directions for you and your child to make scientific discoveries TOGETHER. Please talk with your child about each step as you work your way through the activity. It is VERY important that he/she becomes secure in verbalizing responses, as well as writing them down. PLEASE accept your child's approximations in oral and written language. Your child must feel like he/she is working in a risk free environment if learning is to take place.

Please make sure your child writes/draws his/her predictions about what will happen BEFORE the activity is done and writes/draws his/her observations AFTER the activity is completed. It is VERY important to the process that your child writes down WHY he/she thinks the experiment turned out the way it did.

REMEMBER: Understanding the PROCESS is MUCH MORE important than just getting a right answer and not understanding WHY. We want to develop lifelong problem solvers by giving your child experience in predicting, observing, drawing conclusions and confirming predictions.

Thank you for working with your child. It is VERY IMPORTANT that we keep the home and school connected for the sake of your child's education.

Gayle Morrison

- Figure 7.5: *Gayle's letter to families explaining the science boxes*

Family Bulletin Boards

Two bulletin board areas in the classroom are devoted to families. The one used primarily for keeping the class informed about family happenings is updated daily with birth announcements, church bulletins, and pictures. On the other, a family constructs its family history, which is celebrated in the classroom for a week. The child and parents bring in items that will help the class get to know their family, such as photographs and copies of newspaper clippings. At the end of the week, family members are invited to talk about their family history. This process was very informative for Gayle because she could immediately understand the whole child; what she learned helped her interact in a more compassionate manner with many children and their families.

In Conclusion ∼

In this chapter, we have provided many suggestions for involving parents in the life of the classroom. When students and parents are provided numerous methods for learning at home together and for sharing their family traditions and stories with the other students and families in the classroom, children develop pride in their classroom, in their families, and in their literacy development.

Resource 7-1

THE HOME-SCHOOL CONNECTIONS

Home Reading Partners form

Home Reading Partners
Gayle's Home–School Reading Form

Date	Title of Book	Read to Child	Read with Child	Read by Child	Comments/Concerns	Initials

Creating the Best Literacy Block Ever © 2009 by Maryann Manning, Gayle Morrison, and Deborah Camp: Scholastic Professional

■ CHAPTER 8 ■

Assessment-Informed Instruction

As Gayle's second graders are reading their self-selected books, she circulates through the room, recording on a chart the titles of the books the children are reading and takes notes about what she observes. Here's a sampling of her interactions with the children:

■ Asks Jerome to read aloud a poem from his book and makes a note to look for more poetry books to share with him

■ Listens to Gabriella read a paragraph from Barbara Park's *Junie B., First Grader (At Last!)* and notes a bit of choppiness but knows from the child's skillful retelling that she is comprehending well and that her fluency will improve with experience

■ Observes Michael writing in his response journal, compliments him on his attention to spelling, and makes a note to introduce him to the rule about doubling consonants in their next writing conference

The Value of Kidwatching ～

We believe Gayle is engaging in one of the most effective ways of assessing her students: the art of observation. Yetta Goodman (1985) calls it "kidwatching." We must avoid the tendency to focus solely on our own teaching performance or our use of instructional materials and neglect the most important component of teaching—the children! We challenge you to try this brief experiment the next time you are with your students. We know you've done it before, but it's beneficial to remind yourself of the process of kidwatching. Take just five minutes while the students are engaged in some literacy experience, such as a read-aloud, a discussion, or partner reading. Push every thought out of your mind and look closely at the children. Pay attention to what they are saying to you or to one another, the expressions on their faces, their body language. Resist the temptation to think ahead to the next transition of your day, how much longer until your break, or what you are going to cook for dinner. Focus all your energies for those five minutes on what your children are doing and saying. Just look and listen. At the end of those five minutes, make a mental note of what you learned about your children that you didn't know before.

Kidwatching allows us to understand our students deeply, not just as learners but as children—the same children who need us to know their dreams and their fears and to anticipate their academic, behavioral, and social needs. Classroom-based reading assessments are critical for diagnosing each child's reading strengths and areas for improvement, but we must never forget the power of kidwatching. Teachers who couple assessments with close teacher observation maximize their opportunities to know their students in several dimensions and increase student achievement (Black & Wiliam, 1998). As we discussed in Chapter 6, building a classroom community doesn't just mean that students respect their classmates and teacher; they also realize their teacher respects and cares for them as well.

Quantitative and Qualitative Reading Assessments ∼

While some educators believe classroom-based reading assessments are inferior to quantifiable measures, those of us in the field of literacy learning, know that qualitative measures tell us so much more about student growth. Quantitative tests give us student performance in numerical form. For example, a student can read 60 words per minute or scores in the 70th percentile for reading comprehension. These instruments can inform us in a broad-brush manner what children know and can do, but shed little or no light on how children are processing text and what strategies they are using or not using when they read. Qualitative instruments such as miscue analysis, running records, qualitative reading inventories, interviews, questionnaires, artifacts, field notes, conference notes, tape recordings, notes on predictions, and portfolios are respected assessments we will address in this chapter.

The Cyclical Nature of Reading Assessment~

Our beliefs about teaching and learning are important because they guide our assessments. We espouse the following beliefs:

- Teachers should create a mutually respectful classroom community, honor diversity, and promote a culturally responsive pedagogy.

- Comprehension is the goal of reading.

- Communication is the goal of writing.

- Students should experience a rich, integrated curriculum that fosters inquiry throughout the day. (What occurs outside the reading block contributes to the learning of content knowledge and the practicing of literacy processes.)

- Students should experience quality children's literature during read-alouds, shared reading, guided reading, and independent reading.

- Students should choose a significant portion of the texts they read.

- Teachers should support families as they partner in the education of their children.

- Authentic assessments should guide the selection of rich literacy experiences.

- Reading and writing are reciprocal processes.

These beliefs have helped us to understand the importance and practice of rich, classroom-based reading assessments. We have also discovered that the more we understand the reading process, the better we become at recognizing the development and needs of our students. An in-depth discussion of these beliefs follows in Chapter 11.

Gathering and Recording Assessment Data

As we have said, teacher observation enables you to collect student data all the time, but teachers need a routine for some of the data collection. Every teacher we know has a favorite way to record observational data. Maryann likes sticky notes, 4" x 6" cards, and steno pads; Gayle favors binders with tabs for each student; and Deborah prefers page-size forms that she attaches to her clipboard and later files in individual student folders.

Regardless of our record-keeping preferences, as busy teachers we need to store observational data in a place other than our heads because we can easily forget important information we have gathered. Determining when you are going to assess, what you are going to assess, and how you will record these assessments should be planned so you don't neglect any aspects of your students' literacy development.

Some teachers prefer to store these documents in file folders, one folder per child, often housed in a portable plastic box with a lid and a handle. The box is easily transported between a conference table to another work space. Other teachers, at home in the technological age, have a computer folder for each student.

While discussion of binders versus folders and index cards versus spiral-bound notebooks or hard drives may seem trivial, these are some of the most important organizational decisions we make as teachers. If the purpose of assessment is to help us make the best instructional decisions possible, then we must be able to put our hands on the collected documentation. Without an organizational system that is comfortable for you, and only you, expect to find documents and forms scattered from one end of your classroom to the backseat of your car to the den couch.

Don't hesitate to abandon a system if it doesn't feel right or if you are unable to find documentation easily. Also, make a pledge to yourself to file your documentation on a regular basis. A good time for this is when you are writing your plans for the next week.

> ### Assessment Data We Gather
> - Reading interviews
> - Marie Clay's Reading Observation Survey (from *An Observation Survey of Early Literary Achievement*, 2006) recording forms
> - Reading passages with a miscue analysis
> - Reading passages from a reading inventory
> - Reading conference notes
> - Writing samples
> - Kidwatching anecdotal notes
> - Individual reading intervention plan, if appropriate

mirrors the words children are familiar with from spoken language. Thus, most emergent texts contain very few words that are unfamiliar to children. The visual arrangement of words on the page is also simple, with large print and one sentence per page. Emergent readers need support from the teacher through previewing the text and from the side-by-side guidance the teacher provides during the oral reading of the text.

- Beginning readers are able to read texts that are more complex. The sentences are longer and may contain more unfamiliar words. The visual arrangement is often more complex, with smaller print and sentences that wrap around from one line to the next, and there may be fewer pictures to support the text. Beginning readers continue to need support from us in selecting texts that are appropriate for them—neither too easy nor too hard—and will need some "front-loading" support and monitoring of comprehension from us.

- Independent readers are just that—they can independently select appropriate books and read with understanding with little or no support from the teacher.

In every early childhood classroom, we see children reading at all developmental levels.

An Additional Method of Classifying Readers

There are other ways of classifying students' reading development. Based on many years of assessing children, Maryann has identified five types of readers. We use this system to determine which one of the five reader types each student is, and we determine what we will do to make a difference during the reading block. As you read this, you will probably begin classifying your students into one of the five types of readers.

Type I

Emergent, or Type I, readers are children who are learning to read. They possess varying knowledge about how written language works and about the four cueing systems (graphophonics, syntactic, semantic, and pragmatic) depending on their exposure to reading in classrooms and at home. In a typical kindergarten class, most students are emergent at the beginning of the year.

No student is an empty vessel devoid of knowledge about written language. All students notice the environmental print in their lives. Ferreiro & Teberosky

(1982) studied low-income preschool-age children in Argentina who had no schooling or exposure to reading in the home, and discovered that the only literacy experiences these children had was with environmental print in their communities.

Type II

These children demonstrate an effective reading process, utilizing all four cueing systems efficiently and reading age-appropriate text. These students usually score in the average range on standardized reading tests, and few teachers or parents worry about them because they are reading so-called grade-level text. With appropriate instruction, many of these students will progress throughout the year to reading more difficult texts and exploring more complex ideas.

Type III

These children demonstrate an effective reading process but are not reading grade-appropriate text. They often have a limited oral language facility, vocabulary, and content knowledge. But these students do know that reading is supposed to make sense and they often demonstrate the behaviors of good readers.

Type IV

These children demonstrate an effective reading process and are reading text that is considered above grade level. These are the students in our classrooms who always have their hands up, letting us all know that they know the answers to our questions. These are also the students who consistently perform well on standardized tests. Many of them are avid, curious, and self-directed readers. Often our challenge with these students is to help them choose texts that stimulate their thinking and to keep up with them as they read and grow.

Type V

A Type V decoder does not know how written language works, and they generally rely solely on graphophonic cues. These readers can be any age, from 5 to 62. Maryann recently tested a 20-year-old college football player who was was only able to say words that began with a given letter. He was obviously relying solely on graphophonic cues, and often made up words that didn't sound like the English language. These decoders don't consider the text as an aid in making meaning these children as pre-emergent.

Marie Clay's *An Observation Survey of Early Literacy Achievement* (1993) contains tasks designed to measure the following:

- Concepts of print
- Reading of continuous text
- Letter identification
- Word reading
- Writing vocabulary
- Hearing and recording sounds in words

A second edition of the book, published in 2006, contains simple directions and recording forms. Each assessment task is administered individually, and the recording of the child's performance is based on the teacher's observation of these literacy tasks. The book also includes tables of scaled scores and stanines of normed groups, enabling teachers to compare the child's scores with those of his or her peers.

Clay's survey measures 24 items and can be lengthy in its administration. We consider each child's background and decide whether we need to administer this task in its entirety or informally assess without the Clay task by asking questions such as "Where do you begin reading?" and "Show me a word." Whether we decide to assess concepts of print formally or informally, we think it is important to determine what children know in this area.

Letter Identification

We don't consider letter recognition as a reading prerequisite, but sound–letter correspondence knowledge is a necessary cueing system. Children need to know letter names for both reading and writing purposes, although some children learn letter names simultaneously while learning to read. Children with a wealth of literacy experiences prior to kindergarten often come to us with a working knowledge of upper- and lowercase letters. Also, since the advent of the *Sesame Street*, children have had more opportunities to learn letter names, and parents seem to place more emphasis on their preschool children learning letters and sounds.

We recommend administering the Clay survey's Letter Identification Task at the beginning of the year, midyear, and at the end of year. In this task, children are asked to identify 54 symbols: 26 lowercase letters, 26 uppercase letters, and the two ways of representing *a* and *g*. Marie Clay emphasized that this task is not designed to predict future literacy progress but "to be used as a guide for subsequent teaching" (2006, p. 89). Teachers can also observe knowledge of the alphabet in writing samples. Saving monthly journal entries and comparing spelling will reveal growth in your students' alphabet knowledge.

Phonemic Awareness

Phonemic awareness—the ability to hear and segment phonemes, the smallest units of sound in language—is a cognitive process that develops slowly over time. There are several tests of phonemic awareness, but you can easily assess it without one. One way is to just ask the child to say a word in "itty-bitty" parts. If you ask a child to say two-syllable words like *pony*, *tepee*, *daddy*, and *sofa* in itty-bitty parts, the child will have one of four responses. First, children provide no segmentation (*pony*); then they divide the word at the syllable juncture (*po-ny*). Third, the child will segment a phoneme in either the first or second syllable (*po-n-y* or *p-o-ny*); and finally, the child will segment all phonemes (*p-o-n-y*).

By closely observing invented spelling, you can determine a child's progression (Kamii & Manning, 2002). We recommend asking children to write these words: *ham, hamster, butter, butterfly, berry, strawberry, melon, watermelon*. Within spelling levels 1 and 2, children have no sound–symbol correspondence. Children's knowledge falls within a continuum of three levels.

- At level 1, the words they write are composed only of letter strings.

- At level 2, they know that *hamster* is a longer word than *ham* and, therefore, their symbolic representation of *hamster* is longer than *ham*.

- At level 3, consonants and letter-name vowels begin to appear, and the longer word of each pair continues to be represented by more letters. For example, *ham* and *hamster* are something like *hm* and *hmstr*. Eventually, the longer pair will be written something like *be* and *srbe* and a few months later, *bere* and *strbere*.

This assessment is not for studying conventional spelling but phonemic segmentation. Studying the invented writing in students' journals can also reveal phonemic segmentation abilities, and you can document their growth by administering the above assessment every six weeks to kindergartners and some first-grade children. Most children can segment before age 7, and this easy method allows for individual assessment.

If a child has receptive language but has yet to express this knowledge through speaking, we also need to make a referral to the speech and language therapist. There are several reasons why a child may not be talking, and the therapist is the best professional in the school to make a diagnosis or refer a child to an outside specialist.

Vocabulary

A child's vocabulary consists of words he or she understands when spoken by others, through speaking, in writing or reading. A child may also say or read a word without attaching meaning.

Many commercial standardized tests assess vocabulary, and many basal programs include word meaning tests, but it is our opinion that you can listen to children in informal conversation and in class discussions and make assumptions about the size of their vocabulary. You can informally assess a child's vocabulary knowledge during the following activities:

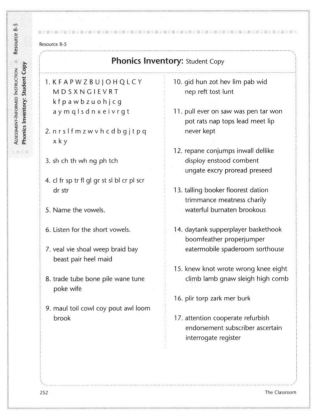

Phonics Inventory: Student Copy

1. K F A P W Z B U J O H Q L C Y
   M D S X N G I E V R T
   k f p a w b z u o h j c g
   a y m q l s d n x e i v r g t

2. n r s l f m z w v h c d b g j t p q
   x k y

3. sh ch th wh ng ph tch

4. cl fr sp tr fl gl gr st sl bl cr pl scr
   dr str

5. Name the vowels.

6. Listen for the short vowels.

7. veal vie shoal weep braid bay
   beast pair heel maid

8. trade tube bone pile wane tune
   poke wife

9. maul toil cowl coy pout awl loom
   brook

10. gid hun zot hev lim pab wid
    nep reft tost lunt

11. pull ever on saw was pen tar won
    pot rats nap tops lead meet lip
    never kept

12. repane conjumps inwall dellike
    disploy enstood combent
    ungate excry proread preseed

13. talling booker floorest dation
    trimmance meatness charily
    waterful burnaten brookous

14. daytank supperplayer baskethook
    boomfeather properjumper
    eatermobile spaderoom sorthouse

15. knew knot wrote wrong knee eight
    climb lamb gnaw sleigh high comb

16. plir torp zark mer burk

17. attention cooperate refurbish
    endorsement subscriber ascertain
    interrogate register

252   The Classroom

Resource 8-5: *Phonics Inventory: Student Copy*

- Read-alouds
- Shared reading
- Guided reading
- Individual reading conferences

Several different games also help determine a child's vocabulary size:

- Analogies (*Bird* is to *feather* as *bear* is to ___.)
- Synonyms (Another word for *run* is ___.)
- Charades

Assessing Story Schema

One definition of *schema* is "an organized chunk of knowledge or experience, often accompanied by feelings" (Weaver, 2002). Many children enter school with vast amounts of knowledge about how written language works. We've seen them sitting on the carpet saying things like "Once upon a time . . ." Because they have been read to from an early age, they use book language that will help them predict when reading. As children go through the early grades, they continue to add to their knowledge of story elements, the development of characters, and conflict resolution. Observing children's comments when you are reading stories aloud to them is the most efficient way to assess their understanding of story schema.

High-Frequency Words

These are words that students encounter most often in the primary texts. Many of them are "sight words," such as *school*, which are phonetically irregular and cannot be decoded. Children recall and recognize the meaning and the pronunciation of these words from their visual memory. Because few children come to kindergarten recognizing this type of written word, with the possible exception of their names, we do not recommend administering a word test to kindergartners until the end of the year, unless a child comes from an enriched literacy background and demonstrates the ability to read labels and signs in the room or examples of connected text on charts, big books, and trade books.

The word test we recommend at the end of kindergarten is Marie Clay's Word Reading Task. Two word lists are supplied: the New Zealand "Ready to Read" Word Reading and the Ohio Word Test. The first word list was developed for New Zealand children who were instructed using the Ready to Read series. The Ohio list is derived from the Dolch high-frequency word list, a list that has been used for half a century in the United States.

For most first-grade through third-grade children, we use the word lists found in the *Qualitative Reading Inventory–4* by Lauren Leslie and JoAnne Caldwell (2005). We are cautious about using sight-word testing because these measures only offer a quick measure of whether a child is beginning to build a repertoire of phonetically regular words as well as sight words. Word reading assessments only yield information on one of the four cueing systems.

Invented Spelling

So much can be learned from studying a child's invented spelling. Maryann has been researching spelling development with Constance Kamii (Kamii, Long, & Manning, 2001) for many years. Their research demonstrates how we can easily assess a child's invented spelling levels by using seven words and one sentence. The words which can be administered individually to a child at intervals of one or two months, are *cement, ocean, punishment, vacation, karate, motion,* and *tomato,* and the sentence is *The whale swims fast* (see figures 8.1 through 8.4).

This assessment yields five developmental levels:

Level One

A child will write in long letter strings with letters or symbols. There will be no letter–sound correspondence (see Figure 8.1).

■ Figure 8.1: *Invented spelling level 1*

Level Two

The length of the words is shorter, usually three to six letters (see Figure 8.2). Some letter–sound correspondence is demonstrated at the higher end of this level.

Level Three

At this level, you can read the child's invented spelling. All children don't use the same letters, but this level is called the consonantal level because students only use consonants and letter-name vowels. *Cement* will be similar to *cemt* or *semt*, and *ocean* will be similar to *oshn.* Level three readers demonstrate knowledge of sound–symbol correspondence, and usually they are beginning to read (see Figure 8.3).

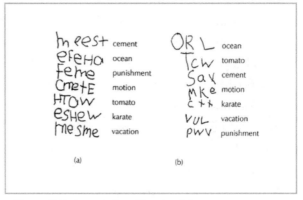

■ Figure 8.2: *Invented spelling level 2*

Level Four

This is called the alphabetic level because students use consonants and vowels. Words are still not conventional, but the majority of letters is correct, although some vowel confusion usually still exists (see Figure 8.4).

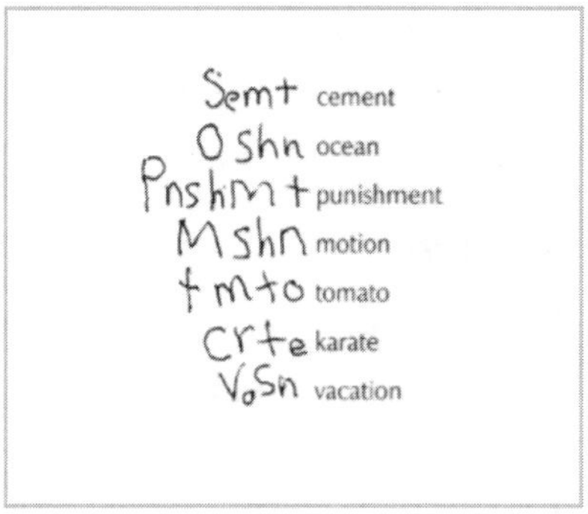

Level Five

At this level, students can spell words conventionally, and almost every word is spelled correctly.

In addition to using individual words, students show growth in the invented spelling in their journal writing. We classify any spelling sample using the above levels. There is no one age or grade level that a child should reach when spelling at these levels. Generally, the more experience a child has had with print, the earlier he or she demonstrates letter–sound correspondence.

When we administer these assessments depends on our analysis of the children's journal writing. If a child is demonstrating writing and spelling ability beyond the letter-string stage, then this assessment should be followed up with at least one additional assessment during the school year.

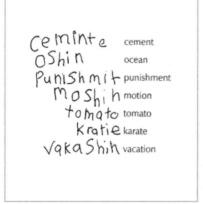

■ Figure 8.3: *Invented spelling level 3*

■ Figure 8.4: *Invented spelling level 4*

Conventional Spelling

To assess spelling, we recommend a developmental assessment developed by Kathy Ganske (2000) in her book *Word Journeys: Assessment-Guided Phonics, Spelling, and Vocabulary Instruction*. According to Ganske, the stages of spelling development are:

- Stage I: Emergent
- Stage II: Letter-Name
- Stage III: Within-Word Pattern
- Stage IV: Syllable Juncture
- Stage V: Derivational Constancy

Students in primary grades typically fall somewhere within the first three stages of the continuum. This assessment is easy to administer, and the book contains instructional suggestions for children at each developmental level.

Writing Vocabulary

To assess a kindergarten student's unaided ability to produce words on paper, we recommend the Clay Writing Vocabulary Observation task (2006). In this easy-to-administer, 10-minute task, you ask the student to write every word he or she knows, beginning with his or her own name. This deceptively easy task yields a multitude of information about a child:

- Directionality
- Knowledge of the alphabet
- Ability to physically form letters
- How letters are formed
- Which words a child has internalized through exposure to text

Most kindergarten children do not enter that grade with the ability to write words, so we recommend waiting to use this assessment until the latter part of the school year, unless you notice you have a number of precocious children in your classroom.

Comprehension of Oral Text

When the three of us first started teaching, the notion of "reading readiness" was prevalent. Many educators believed that a child must have certain prerequisite literacy skills in place before a teacher could even think about beginning reading instruction. As you might imagine, this knowledge consisted of low-level skills such as letter identification and letter–sound identification. We now know that phonemic awareness, phonics, and letter identification can develop simultaneously with the reading of connected text. We also know that a child begins constructing meaning from text the moment an adult begins reading aloud to that child. As adults, we communicate to children that the purpose for reading is to construct meaning, not just to decode and identify words.

In kindergarten, we begin to emphasize meaning making when we read aloud to children or involve them in a shared reading experience. Assessing children's understanding of texts we read aloud is where we use our kidwatching skills. We ask ourselves:

- Which children readily answer the questions we ask about the text?

- Which children seem tentative when asked to respond?

- Who can retell the story through drawing in a sketch journal?

- Who has difficulty recalling the plot of a book read the day before?

We make either "in the midst" notes immediately after an interactive read-aloud or shared reading or jot down observations at the end of the day, "after the fact."

As children mature through the early childhood grades and enter the emergent and beginning reading stages, you will continue to use your good judgment and observations to document progress, but there are other procedures and recording instruments for systematically recording your observations. These assessment procedures are appropriate for first, second, and third grades, but, if you have a child in kindergarten who is a precocious reader, then by all means begin gaining an understanding of his or her reading processes and abilities through the following instruments for measuring comprehension (see Chapters 3, 4, and 5 for tools):

- Running records

- Benchmark books

- Miscue analysis and retelling

- Reading inventories

Comprehension of Written Text

There are several methods for determining reading comprehension.

Retelling

One of the simplest tasks is to ask a child at the end of a passage to tell you everything he or she can remember (Tierney, 1979). A retelling is an important component of the miscue analysis process. (See also Retrospective Miscue Analysis section in Chapter 4, pages 140–142.)

Think-Aloud

Conducting a think-aloud session is another powerful method for assessing comprehension. To use this technique with a student, you first need to demonstrate how to think aloud. Choose a familiar text and begin reading aloud while the child follows along. When you come to a section of the text that might provide some difficulty with comprehension, describe your thinking. Discuss:

- What makes this section harder to understand

- What information the author has given you to help you understand

- What mental processes you used, such as visualizing and inferring

- What prior knowledge you bring to the text

- How you reread or slow your reading pace to help you understand

Then have the child read aloud the next section you designate and think aloud to you. Think-alouds not only serve as an assessment vehicle but provide an opportunity for rich instruction as well.

Informal Reading Inventory

A more systematic way of measuring comprehension is an informal reading inventory. We recommend the Qualitative Reading Inventory–4 (QRI-4; Leslie & Caldwell, 2005), which is an abbreviated version of miscue analysis. This inventory can yield similar types of information when you have limited time to assess. Like miscue analysis, the QRI-4 entails the examination of each error/miscue to determine if it changed the meaning. The QRI-4 contains the following:

- Word lists

- Prereading concept questions to determine prior knowledge

- Grade-level passages

- Unaided and aided retelling sections

- Post-reading questions

None of the passages is lengthy, and the inventory is organized at each grade in the following manner:

- The pre-primer level consists of four narrative passages and one expository passage. The expository passage and two of the narrative passages contain pictures.

- The primer level and the first-grade level consist of three narratives and two expository passages. Picture support is provided in most of the passages.

- The second-grade level contains three narrative and two expository passages, with pictures provided in three passages.

- The third-grade passages increase to three narrative and three expository, with no picture support.

- Fourth-grade through high school passages are provided for precocious readers.

The aided and unaided retelling on the QRI-4 can provide a lot of information about a child's use of the semantic cueing system and can help you determine appropriate leveled text for beginning readers. This assessment is not appropriate for children who are just beginning to read connected text.

Benchmark Assessments

We also recommend the Fountas and Pinnell Benchmark Assessment System (Fountas & Pinnell, 2008), 1, for grades K–2 and levels A–N. These assessments are similar to the QRI-4 in that you select a benchmark book, rather than a passage, for the child to read and then you code the text as the child reads aloud. In both assessments, you mark when a child makes substitutions, insertions, repetitions, and self-corrections. Whereas the QRI-4 most resembles a miscue analysis, the Benchmark Assessment System is more similar to Marie Clay's running record assessment. Running records and these assessments place more emphasis on the quantity of miscues, or as Clay calls them, "errors." The Benchmark Assessment System, however, does require that you qualitatively analyze the student's errors and determine what kinds of information the child is attending to or using to figure out words, such as meaning, structure, and visual/phonological cues. These categories of information are similar to the semantic, syntactic, and graphophonic cueing systems.

Following the oral reading of a benchmark book, you and the child engage in a conversation in which you determine how well the student is comprehending within the text, beyond the text, and about the text. Your analysis of the child's ability to read words and understand text using this system can help you guide students to choose appropriate books. We want to caution, however, against "over-leveling" students' reading materials. After all, we want them to learn to choose appropriate books on their own. We have found this assessment system easy for busy teachers to use.

Use of the Cueing Systems

For all readers who can read connected text that is at least 250 words long, we recommend doing a miscue analysis inventory using the QRI-4 to analyze children's miscues. *Reading Miscue Inventory* by Goodman, Watson, and Burke (2005) is helpful if you are unfamiliar with this assessment. Analyzing miscues allows you to determine how children are using the three cueing systems:

- Graphophonic
- Syntactic

- Pragmatic

After a student reads a passage, you then ask him or her to retell the passage to determine if the reader is understanding the text.

Completing a miscue analysis will help you determine how a child is processing text. What are the differences between processing abilities?

Proficient Readers

These children demonstrate the following:

- Make miscues that do not change the meaning of the phrase

- Self-correct miscues

- Provide a coherent unaided retelling

Readers Who Need Support

These students demonstrate the following:

- Make many miscues that change meaning

- Do not self-correct miscues

- Make many miscues in which the actual word and the miscue contain many of the same letters

- Demonstrate many misconceptions in the retelling

We provide a more in-depth explanation of the cueing systems in Chapter 4.

Use of Comprehension Strategies

Unfortunately, some educators feel that kindergarten teachers must place phonemic awareness, phonics, and alphabet instruction at the center of their reading program. They seem to be saying, how could you possibly expect 5- and 6-year-old children to think about the mental processes good readers use when grappling with text? But Debbie Miller (2002), in *Reading With Meaning*, shows us that even first graders who are at the emergent or beginning reading levels can use strategies such as predicting, visualizing, asking questions, and inferring to make sense of the texts they encounter. Several other authors in addition to Miller, such as Ellin Keene, Susan Zimmermann, Stephanie Harvey, Anne Goudvis, and Chris Tovani, have built upon the metacognition reading research conducted by P. David Pearson and others in the 1980s and 1990s (Pearson, Roehler, Doler, & Duffy, 1992).

In *Starting with Comprehension: Reading Strategies for the Youngest Learners*, Andie Cunningham and Ruth Shagoury (2005) extend Miller's work down to the kindergarten level, emphasizing that it is never too early to begin comprehension instruction. The authors even post sophisticated statements such as "Metacognition is thinking about our thinking," in their classrooms. The kindergartners practice metacognition of oral text not only through discussion but also through class charts, art, metaphors, and movement. We highly recommend that kindergarten teachers read this short but enlightening book.

For documentation of individual children's use of these strategies, again we rely on our observational skills and jot down anecdotal notes. We also note students' use of comprehension strategies on conference forms, including those in Chapters 2 through 5. The response activities Cunningham and Shagoury describe, such as the class charts, provide a useful method for recording each child's use of particular strategies.

Students' Interests

The most important information for us to discover is what interests each child. We have to be the very best kidwatchers we can be to figure out what those interests are. We watch for smiles when we are reading aloud, we listen for requests to read a book a second or third time, and we watch and listen for other signs throughout the entire day. When a child says, "That was a really funny book you read to us! Can I borrow it to take back to my desk?" or when we see a child's face light up while telling us about the baby hamster she received as a birthday present, we have clues that can help us help students choose books of interest to them. With younger children, we need to listen, watch, ask questions, and be attuned to interests they express daily. During social studies or science we often discover a bit of information that the student wants to know or a subject that seems interesting. If we can help a child find fascinating text, we ensure that the child has a pleasurable reason to read.

At the beginning of the year, Gayle sends home a question-naire to parents requesting information about their child's likes and dislikes and any other information that would help her be a better teacher of the child (Resource 8-6). This information helps Gayle add books to the classroom library and determine guest speakers.

We have included an interest inventory (Resource 8-7) with questions to ask children in an interview setting. Second- and third-grade children may be capable of completing the inventory

See Resource 8-6, Gayle's Questionnaire to parents, p. 253.

See Resource 8-7, Interest Inventory, p. 254.

comfortable with you and the other children in the room. The classroom must be a safe zone where you constantly communicate the message that mistakes are just another opportunity to learn.

Self-Confidence

A child's self-confidence when reading is something we value because self-confidence can lead to continued growth. You can assess self-confidence by observing if the child volunteers to read and willingly reads passages out loud to peer audiences. Observe if a child initiates discussion by bringing up books that have been read in class. Also observe what children say about their reading abilities. Obviously, a child who picks out a new book and immediately states, "I don't think I can read this by myself" is lacking in self-confidence.

Flow

We prefer to use the term *flow* rather than fluency. The term, coined by Alan Flurkey (1997), refers to more than just speed (which recently has become associated with fluency). Many students may be able to read fast, but their reading lacks fluidity. They don't slow down and speed up as they read, and they often read in a monotone. Although expression in oral reading is one characteristic of good readers, we are more concerned with the meaning that children make of the texts they read.

We are concerned with prosody, or flow, in oral reading because it relates to the reader's attention to punctuation and inflection. We believe readers should change their rate according to the purpose and type of the text. Good readers don't always read every word correctly; they often have some repetitions, no-meaning-loss substitutions, occasional omissions, and self-corrections. Flow is easy to measure by listening to a child read aloud during a reading conference or during a Readers Theater performance and recording notes on a conference sheet or in anecdotal notes.

Self-Assessment

The ability to self-reflect is difficult for many adults, much less primary children! Children grow in their ability to assess their progress independent of adult feedback as they progress through the grades, but it's never too early to ask children these questions regarding any reading task:

- How did you do?
- What can you do to get even better?

- Who can help you get better?

- How will you know when you have gotten better?

Self-assessment efforts in the primary grades can occur naturally when you are conferring with a child individually and can be noted on conference forms or anecdotal records.

In Conclusion ∼

Assessment is not just a matter of faithfully collecting documents to go in a binder. You are using this information to make decisions regarding instruction for your students. The more you practice administering these assessments and analyzing the results, the more you will value the assessment process. It won't be long before you will say, "How did I ever teach before I began assessing my students on a regular basis?"

Creating the Best Literacy Block Ever © 2009 by Maryann Manning, Gayle Morrison, and Deborah Camp: Scholastic Professional

Phonics Inventory: Teacher Instructions

1. **Alphabet Names**—Name the letters of the alphabet.

2. **Consonant Sounds**—What sounds do these letters make?

3. **Consonant Digraphs**—What sound do these letters make together?

4. **Consonant Blends**—What sound do these letters make together?

5. **Name Vowels**—DO NOT SHOW STUDENTS THESE LETTERS. Name the vowels.

6. **Vowel Sounds**—DO NOT SHOW STUDENTS THESE WORDS. Listen carefully to these words. What vowel do you hear in each word?

7. **Double Vowels**—What sound do you hear when two vowels come together in a word? Circle **knows rule** if child can tell you. Have student read the words, some are not real words, and circle **applies rule** if child is able to complete this activity with 90% accuracy.

8. **Final "e" Rule**—What usually happens when the vowel is in the middle of the word and the word ends with an "e"? Circle **knows rule** if the child can tell you the rule. Have student read the words and circle **applies rule** if the child is able to complete the activity with 90% accuracy.

9. **Diphthongs**—Some vowels make their own special sounds. Read these words.

10. **Short Vowels**—These are not real words. Read each of these using a short vowel sound.

11. **Reversals**—Read these words as quickly as you can.

12. **Prefixes**—Sometimes we add a prefix to the beginning of a word. Read these make-believe words.

13. **Suffixes**—Sometimes we add a suffix to the end of a word. Read these make-believe words.

14. **Compound Words**—Do you know what we call two words that are put together to make a new word? Read these make-believe words.

15. **Silent Letters**—Read these words.

16. **Vowel + R**—Read these make-believe words.

17. **Syllabication**—HAND THE STUDENT A PENCIL and have him/her mark **on your recording sheet.** Divide these words into syllables (parts) with your pencil after I say the word.

Resource 8-4

Phonics Inventory: Teacher Copy

Name _____

Date _____

	Test Number	Number Correct	Percentage	S–Secure 90–100%	D–Developing 79–89%	NI–Needs Improvement Below 79%
1. Alphabet Names: K F A P W Z B U J O H Q L C Y M D S X N G I E V R T k f p a w b z u o h j c g a y m q l s d n x e i v r g t	1.	51				
2. Consonant Sounds n r s l f m z w v h c d b g j t p q x k y	2.	21				
3. Consonant Digraphs wh ng ph sh ch ng th	3.	7				
4. Consonant Blends cl fr sp tr fl gl gr st sl bl cr pl scr dr str	4.	15				
5. Name the Vowels a e i o u y	5.	5				
6. Short Vowels (aural) sink___ clock____ trust___ stack___ bread___	6.	5				
7. Double Vowels veal vie shoal weep braid bay beast pair heel maid Circle: knows rule Circle: applies rule	7.	10				
8. Final "e" trade tube bone pile wane tune poke wife Circle: knows rule Circle: applies rule	8.	8				
9. Diphthongs maul toil cowl coy pout awl loom brook	9.	8				
10. Short Vowels fas gid hun zot hev lim pab wid nep reft tost lunt	10.	12				
11. Reversals pull ever on saw was pen tar won pot rats nap tops lead meet lip never kept	11.	17				
12. Prefixes repane conjumps inwall dellike display enstood combent ungate excry proread preseed	12.	11				
13. Suffixes talling booker floorest dation trimmance meatness charily waterful burnaten brookous	13.	10				
14. Compound Words daytank supperplayer baskethook boomfeather properjumper eatermobile spaderoom sorthouse	14.	8				
15. Silent Letters knew knot wrote wrong knee eight climb lamb gnaw sleigh high comb	15.	12				
16. Vowel + R plir torp zark mer burk	16.	5				
17. Syllabication attention cooperate refurbish endorsement subscriber ascertain interrogate register	17.	8				

Creating the Best Literacy Block Ever © 2009 by Maryann Manning, Gayle Morrison, and Deborah Camp: Scholastic Professional

Phonics Inventory: Student Copy

1. K F A P W Z B U J O H Q L C Y
   M D S X N G I E V R T
   k f p a w b z u o h j c g
   a y m q l s d n x e i v r g t

2. n r s l f m z w v h c d b g j t p q
   x k y

3. sh ch th wh ng ph tch

4. cl fr sp tr fl gl gr st sl bl cr pl scr
   dr str

5. Name the vowels.

6. Listen for the short vowels.

7. veal vie shoal weep braid bay
   beast pair heel maid

8. trade tube bone pile wane tune
   poke wife

9. maul toil cowl coy pout awl loom
   brook

10. gid hun zot hev lim pab wid
    nep reft tost lunt

11. pull ever on saw was pen tar won
    pot rats nap tops lead meet lip
    never kept

12. repane conjumps inwall dellike
    display enstood combent
    ungate excry proread preseed

13. talling booker floorest dation
    trimmance meatness charily
    waterful burnaten brookous

14. daytank supperplayer baskethook
    boomfeather properjumper
    eatermobile spaderoom sorthouse

15. knew knot wrote wrong knee eight
    climb lamb gnaw sleigh high comb

16. plir torp zark mer burk

17. attention cooperate refurbish
    endorsement subscriber ascertain
    interrogate register

Creating the Best Literacy Block Ever © 2009 by Maryann Manning, Gayle Morrison, and Deborah Camp: Scholastic Professional

Creating the Best Literacy Block Ever © 2009 by Maryann Manning, Gayle Morrison, and Deborah Camp: Scholastic Professional

Dear Parents,

Your child has had a very successful first week of school, and I look forward to working with your child and getting to know him or her better. It is very important for me to find out early in the school year what your child's interests are. This helps me help your child select interesting books, writing topics, and research projects. I would appreciate it if you would take a few minutes to answer this brief questionnaire about your child's interests and return it to me as soon as possible.

Your child's name: _____

What books does your child like you to read aloud? _____

_____

Are these books read before bed? _____

What are some things your child likes to read about (examples could be dogs,

airplanes, soccer, horses, bugs, etc.)? _____

_____

Does your child like to read books/look at pictures alone? _____

What is your child's favorite food? _____ Drink? _____

Does your child like to play with others or alone? _____

What was your child's favorite summer vacation? _____

What is your child's favorite toy? _____

What else would you like to tell me about your child? _____

_____

_____

1. What do you like to do when you get home from school?

2. What do you like to do on Saturday and Sunday?

3. What pets do you have?

4. What is the best trip you have ever taken?

5. What games do you like to play?

6. What are your favorite TV shows?

7. What do you like to do on the computer?

8. What sports do you play?

9. What are your favorite toys?

10. Who reads aloud to you at home?

11. What are the best books anyone has ever read to you?

12. Who are your favorite book characters?

13. Who are your favorite authors?

14. What are some books you like to read by yourself?

15. What do you want to learn this year in our class?

Creating the Best Literacy Block Ever © 2009 by Maryann Manning, Gayle Morrison, and Deborah Camp: Scholastic Professional

Elementary Reading Attitude Survey
Directions for use

The Elementary Reading Attitude Survey provides a quick indication of students attitudes toward reading. It consists of 20 items and can be administered to an entire classroom in about 10 minutes. Each item presents a brief, simply-worded statement about reading, followed by 4 pictures of Garfield. Each pose is designed to depict a different emotional state, ranging from very positive to very negative.

Administration
Begin by telling students that you wish to find out how they feel about reading. Emphasize that this is not a test and there are no "right" answers. Encourage sincerity.

Distribute the survey forms and, if you wish to monitor the attitudes of specific students, ask them to write their names in the space at the top. Hold up a copy of the survey so that the students can see the first page. Point to the picture of Garfield at the far left of the first item. Ask the students to look at this same picture on their own survey form. Discuss with them the mood Garfield seems to be in (very happy). Then move to the next picture and again discuss Garfield's mood (this time a little happy). In the same way, move to the third and fourth pictures and talk about Garfield's moods—a little upset and very upset. It is helpful to point out the position of Garfield's mouth. especially in the middle two figures.

Explain that together you will read some statements about reading and that the students should think about how they feel about each statement. They should then circle the picture of Garfield that is closest to their own feelings. (Emphasize that the students should respond according to their own feelings, not as Garfield might respond!) Read each item aloud slowly and distinctly; then read it a second time while students are thinking. Be sure to read the item number and remind students of page numbers when new pages are reached.

Scoring
To score the survey, count four points for each leftmost (happiest) Garfield circled, three for each slightly smiling Garfield, two for each mildly upset Garfield, and one point for each very upset (rightmost) Garfield. Three scores for each student can be obtained: the total for the first 10 items, the total for the second 10, and a composite total. The first half of the survey relates to attitude toward recreational reading; the second half relates to attitude toward academic aspects of reading.

Interpretation
You can interpret score in two ways. One is to note informally where the score falls as regard to the four nodes of the scale. A total score of 50, for example, would fall about mid-way on the scale, between the slightly happy and the slightly upset figures, therefore indicating a relatively indifferent overall attitude toward reading. The other approach is more formal. It involves converting the raw scores into percentile ranks by means of Table 1. Be sure to use the norms for the right grade level and to note the column headings (Rec = recreational reading, Aca = academic reading, Tot = total score). If you wish to determine the average percentile rank for your class, average the raw scores first; then use the table to locate the percentile rank corresponding to the raw score mean. Percentile ranks cannot be averages directly.

Garfield Attitude Survey/ ©Paws, Inc. The Garfield character is incorporated in this test with permission of Paws, Inc., and may be reproduced only in connection with the reproduction of the test in its entirety for classroom use until further notice by Paws, Inc., and any other reproduction or use without the express prior written consent of Paws is prohibited.

Creating the Best Literacy Block Ever © 2009 by Maryann Manning, Gayle Morrison, and Deborah Camp: Scholastic Professional

ELEMENTARY READING ATTITUDE SURVEY

School _____ **Grade** _____ **Name** _____

1. How do you feel when you read a book on a rainy Saturday?

2. How do you feel when you read a book in school during free time?

3. How do you feel about reading for fun at home?

4. How do you feel about getting a book for a present?

Page 1

Creating the Best Literacy Block Ever © 2009 by Maryann Manning, Gayle Morrison, and Deborah Camp: Scholastic Professional

Creating the Best Literacy Block Ever © 2009 by Maryann Manning, Gayle Morrison, and Deborah Camp: Scholastic Professional

5. How do you feel about spending free time reading?

6. How do you feel about starting a new book?

7. How do you feel about reading during summer vacation?

8. How do you feel about reading instead of playing?

Page 2

9. How do you feel about going to a bookstore?

10. How do you feel about reading different kinds of books?

11. How do you feel when the teacher asks you questions about what you read?

12. How do you feel about doing reading workbook pages and worksheets?

Page 3

Creating the Best Literacy Block Ever © 2009 by Maryann Manning, Gayle Morrison, and Deborah Camp: Scholastic Professional

Creating the Best Literacy Block Ever © 2009 by Maryann Manning, Gayle Morrison, and Deborah Camp: Scholastic Professional

13. How do you feel about reading in school?

14. How do you feel about reading your school books?

15. How do you feel about learning from a book?

16. How do you feel when it's time for reading class?

Page 4

Children Struggle for Many Reasons ∿

Most classroom teachers can expect to serve the following groups of struggling students:

- Children who have recently immigrated to this country and possess little or no listening, speaking, reading, or writing ability in English

- Children with neurological developmental delays in the areas of speech and language

- Children with specific learning disabilities

- Children with mental retardation

- Children with pervasive developmental disorders related to autism, Asperger's syndrome, and mental illness

- Children who were born prematurely and have some disabilities as a result

- Children whose family lives are in turmoil and require extra help

- Children who have been bounced around from one school to the next, often several times in the same year

- Children who have attended schools with poor teaching, or, as we term them, "curriculum-and-instruction-disabled" students

- Children we fondly call late bloomers

We teach and love these children, but we often feel overwhelmed by their cognitive, social, and behavioral needs—and guilty when these children seem to take so much of our time away from our other students.

Meeting Children's Special Needs ∿

We intend for this chapter to offer some practical advice on meeting the needs of struggling readers within the context of your regular classroom.

Integrate All Children Into Your Classroom Community

Federal, state, and district mandates increasingly call for the general classroom teacher to assume more and more responsibility for English language learners, special education children, and all children who experience learning difficulties. Gone are the days when teachers sent their struggling readers down the hall to the special education teachers to be taught a separate reading lesson. You may ask yourself, "How am I going to help these children? I don't feel prepared for this!" But when you think about it, who better to teach reading to a struggler than the teacher who is closest to that child, not just instructionally, but from the standpoint of community? When we pull a child out of our room, we are breaking that precious sense of community we have worked so hard to build with the child and that the child has built with others in the class.

Take Ownership of Them

With all that said, just how do we go about teaching children who present challenges to us? These children need time for careful planned instruction and appropriate instructional materials, but we contend that the first step we must take is to examine our mindsets. We must first view these children as "ours." Yes, we must seek outside assistance, but we are the ones ultimately responsible for assessing these children's strengths and weaknesses, planning their instruction, and their ultimate success.

Avoid Deficit Model Thinking

Do we view strugglers as a liability for us and the other children we teach? Do we only look at them as children with deficits to be remediated? The deficit model is the traditional approach to special education, which closely mimics a medical model based on diagnosis and prescription. What is wrong with the child? (diagnosis) and How can I fix him? (prescription): Although this model may work well when a child visits the doctor with a sore throat, it's a very clinical and sterile approach when dealing with children and their cognition. Children are so much more than what they demonstrate on a reading assessment. Instead of training a laser-like focus on all that a child can't do or doesn't know, first attend to what he or she *can* do and *does* know. Children do not come to us as blank slates or empty vessels. All children, except the most severely multihandicapped, bring literacy instruction, then we have a natural setting for differentiated instruction. If we have children reading interesting books at an appropriate level for them, then we are guaranteeing access to good curriculum and instruction. If we are teaching them based on the information our assessments yield, then we have an excellent chance of meeting the instructional needs of all our children, including the students who struggle.

Let Assessments Guide Your Decisions

Now that you know you have a structure in place for delivering instruction, let's focus on the children whose reading development worries us. In Chapter 8 is an explanation of a systematic assessment process. These assessments provide you with a clear method for identifying those children who are not yet at grade-level standards. But this assessment phase is easier than what needs to follow. Gathering the data is one thing, but deciding how to plan or change instruction for struggling children is quite another.

Knowing which instructional strategies to use and locating appropriate instructional materials and texts can be perplexing and time-consuming, but the more children you assess, the more intervention plans you develop, and the more instruction you deliver, the easier this task becomes. You will begin seeing common patterns in children, specifically children who might be Type III readers or Type V readers. As you recall, Type III readers are not reading on grade level because of limited vocabulary and oral language development, although they know that reading is supposed to make sense. Type V readers rely primarily on the graphophonic cueing system and do not realize that reading is supposed to sound like language and make sense. Resource 9-1 provides instructional suggestions for these and other types of readers.

See Resource 9-1, Appropriate Strategies for Reader Types, pp. 287–288.

Develop Individualized Plans

After we've finished assessing a struggling reader, we record the results of those tasks on an individual intervention plan for that child. We then begin the process of mapping out a course of instruction developing lessons that address the child's identified needs and gathering the necessary resources. We have included sample forms that Gayle and Deborah use in their school district. These forms were developed by the elementary reading coaches, but the format was primarily the brainchild of Kathy Snyder, an exemplary reading coach at Riverchase Elementary in Birmingham. The first form (Resource 9-2) can be used to develop an initial individual reading intervention plan for a child at the beginning of the year and

See Resource 9-2, Individual Intervention Plan (blank), p. 289.

See Resource 9-3, Sample Individual Intervention Plan, p. 290.

to update the plan as the child progresses. The form provides a structure for examining all assessment data and determining in what area or areas the child needs intervention.

Resource 9-3 is an example of a completed intervention plan that also includes directions for preparing it.

Once assessments are analyzed and student needs are determined, the intervention form serves as a basis for planning and guiding instruction during small-group or individual lessons. The form guides teachers in using gradual-release instruction to promote student independence in the application of the skill or strategy taught. We have listed six areas on the form:

- Phonological awareness
- Phonics/accuracy
- Flow
- Comprehension
- Reading dispositions
- Vocabulary

Some of these areas may overlap. For example, many children have difficulties with comprehension because they have a limited reading and speaking vocabulary,

---

Resource 9-1

Appropriate Strategies for Reader Types

STRATEGIES	READER TYPES				
	I	II	III	IV	V
Phonemic Awareness					
Writing	•				•
Turtle Talk	•				•
Itty-Bitty Bits Game	•				•
Graphophonic Knowledge					
Interactive Writing	•		•		•
Dictation	•		•		•
Writing	•	•	•	•	•
Masking During Supportive Reading	•	•			•
Environmental Print Activities	•				•
Alphabet	•				
Onset & Rimes	•				•
Word Walls	•		•		•
Games	•				•
Focus Lessons	•	•	•	•	•
Comprehension Strategies					
Reading Aloud	•	•	•	•	•
Think-Alouds	•	•	•	•	•
Shared Reading	•	•	•		
Supportive Reading	•	•	•		
Discussions: Teacher-led	•	•	•	•	•
Discussions: Student-led		•	•	•	
Focus Lessons	•	•	•	•	
Visualizing	•	•	•	•	•
Predicting	•	•	•	•	•
Questioning	•	•	•	•	•
Using Background Knowledge	•	•	•	•	•
Inferring	•	•	•	•	•
Conferences	•	•	•	•	•
Graphic Organizers		•	•	•	•
Literature Circles		•	•	•	•
Dramatization	•	•	•	•	•
Retrospective Miscue Analysis		•	•	•	
Independent Reading					
Personal Book Collections	•	•	•	•	•
Literature Circles		•	•	•	•
Sustained Silent Reading		•	•	•	•
Content Knowledge					
Reading Nonfiction Aloud	•	•	•	•	•
Theme Immersions	•	•	•	•	•

CHAPTER NINE: Students With Special Needs · · · · · · · 287

STUDENTS WITH SPECIAL NEEDS ■ Resource 9-1 Appropriate Strategies for Reader Types

■ Resource 9-1: *Appropriate Strategies for Reader Types*

or children may demonstrate a slow and choppy reading flow because of difficulties in quickly recognizing words. Some readers may need help with almost everything! We always make sure our instructional emphasis is on helping the child to understand that text is supposed to make sense. Too many remedial reading programs focus entirely on phonemic awareness and phonics to the exclusion of vocabulary and comprehension. We will discuss the importance of keeping intervention instruction rich and meaningful later in the chapter.

We sometimes have trouble deciding where to keep the long-term and short-term plans and the child's materials. Whether you use binders or folders matters not; what matters is that you can put our

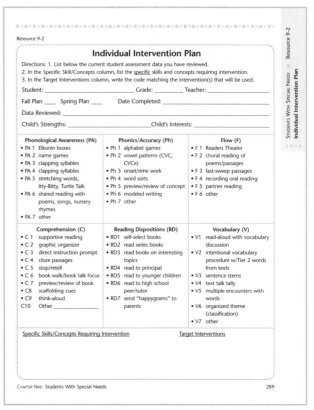

Resource 9-2: *Individual Intervention Plan*

hands on these documents and materials quickly when it is time for you to confer with a child or teach a small group of students. It is also important for you to maintain a record of the improvements your students are showing over time. Once a child is reading connected text, you need to administer a running record or have him or her read a benchmark book to determine if there is growth in their understanding of more complex text as well as recognition of new vocabulary. Although a running record is not as thorough as a miscue analysis, it is a much quicker method for busy lower-primary teachers to use in gauging progress among strugglers during intervention lessons. The children's miscue analysis or running record can also shed some light on how well they are using the cueing systems. Later in the chapter, we look at some common patterns among struggling readers and suggest some specific strategies and additional resources with regard to intervention.

> **Several resources for intervention strategies are:**
>
> Caldwell, J. S., & Leslie, L. (2004). *Intervention strategies to follow informal reading inventory assessment: So what do I do now?*
>
> Goodman, Y., Watson, D., & Burke, C. (1996). *Reading strategies: Focus on comprehension* (2nd ed.)
>
> Manning, M., Chumley, S., & Underbakke, C. (2006). *Scientific reading assessment: Targeted intervention and follow-up lessons*
>
> Strickland, K. (2005). *What's after assessment? Follow-up instruction for phonics, fluency, and comprehension*

Planning Intervention Lessons ~

We consider a child's interests to be paramount when designing intervention lessons. Every child we have ever taught was passionate about at least one thing. Younger children often express intense fascination with certain animals. As children begin playing sports and engaging in after-school activities, their interests may extend to soccer or tap dance. For children at the emergent level, we often have difficulty finding a large number of books on, say, snakes but sometimes we can provide the child with additional nonfiction books on this topic for browsing purposes or supply books-on-tape or iPod videos (e.g., from United Streaming) about snakes. Once children are at the beginning and independent stages of reading, finding books on areas of interest for them becomes less challenging. Also, children will begin developing preferences for authors or types of books, such as adventure or humorous stories. We recommend you help children discover a book series of interest to them. Series books are a valuable resource because once children have tackled the first book in the series, they then know the major characters, the setting, and the general nature of the author's plots. This familiarity can be comforting to children who are working harder than the average child and need the scaffolding a series book can provide. A study by Catherine Sheldrick Ross (1995) on early experience with series books among adults who read for pleasure concluded that, far from being harmful, series books can provide some readers an essential stage in their literacy development. Ross also studied the texts themselves and found evidence that series books teach beginning readers strategies for making sense out of extended text.

Find the Right Texts

We hear the voice of Richard Allington (2006) in our heads reminding us that we must carefully match struggling readers to appropriate books. Too often these children are reading books that are much too difficult for them. When students are grappling to understand a hard text, not only are they losing precious instructional or independent reading time, but they in danger of losing any confidence they may have in themselves as readers. To prevent this situation from occurring, we must have two things:

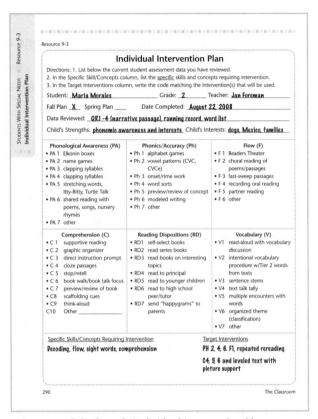

Resource 9-3: *Sample Individual Intervention Plan*

- Knowledge of an approximate level on the text gradient at which the child is comfortable

- A stack of appealing and appropriate books that the child can't wait to read!

We must know our kids and know books! We prefer to use the text gradient that Irene Fountas and Gay Su Pinnell (2005) developed to determine the difficulty of text and to correlate text levels to approximate grade levels. The "Fountas and Pinnell guided reading levels" differ from the readability levels that we used when we were beginning teachers. The old readability levels were based on the lengths of sentences and the number of multisyllabic words in a text. These guided reading levels represent more than just sentence length and word difficulty. They consider such characteristics as text layout, the complexity of the ideas and themes in the text, and use of literacy devices such as similes and metaphors. These reading levels range from A to Z, with A representing where a beginning kindergarten student would start, and level P representing the upper ranges of third grade.

Using Trade Books

You may ask yourself, "How can I be sure I am matching my students to the right books? Where am I going to find these leveled books?" Begin with the trade books in your classroom library, drawn from the plethora of great children's literature our students love to read, and determine the reading levels of the books. One resource for accomplishing this is *Leveled Books, K–8: Matching Texts to Readers for Effective Teaching* by Fountas and Pinnell (2005), in which the authors have cross-indexed thousands of books according to title, genre, and reading level.

The free Scholastic Book Wizard Web site (bookwizard. scholastic.com) allows you to search for texts to determine a given guided reading level, but you can also develop a customized reading list for a child that takes into account the interest level, book type (such as alphabet book or early chapter book), and genre.

Primary Series Books

A to Z Mysteries by Ron Roy

Amelia Bedelia by Peggy Parish and Herman Parish

Angelina Ballerina by Katharine Holabird

Arthur by Marc Brown

The Bailey School Kids by various authors

The Adventures of Benny and Watch by Gertrude Chandler Warner

Cam Jansen by David Adler

Captain Underpants by Dav Pilkey

Curious George by Margret and H. A. Rey

Dragon Slayers' Academy by Kate McMullan

Eloise by Kay Thompson

Frog and Toad by Arnold Lobel

Geronimo Stilton by Geronimo Stilton

Harriet Bean by Alexander McCall Smith

If You Take a Mouse by Laura Numeroff

Jackie Chan Adventures by Frank Squillace and Phil Weinstein

Judy Moody by Megan McDonald

Junie B. Jones by Barbara Park

Madeline by Ludwig Bemelmans

Magic Tree House by Mary Pope Osborne

Mercy Watson by Kate DiCamillo

Nate the Great by Marjorie Sharmat

The Kids of the Polk Street School by Patricia Reilly Giff

Using Leveled Text Series

Teachers sometimes ask us, "Which books should I use for struggling readers? Trade books or books from publishers who have developed leveled texts?" Our answer would be to use both. Scholastic publishes several A–Z guided reading

When the teacher is conducting guided reading lessons with struggling readers, however, it is critical that the children interact with texts they can understand. Also, when children read independently, we should ensure that they can make sense of the text. Nevertheless, prior knowledge plays a huge role in comprehension. A struggling reader may have knowledge of a subject such as iguanas because he has one for a pet and has direct experience with this subject. Consequently, he may be able to read a text at a higher level because of the information he brings to the book. Children can read above their assessed reading level if they are passionate about a subject, a book, or an author. Remember that matching books to readers is not an exact science.

Approximate Text Level Conversion Table

Grade Level/AR	Fountas & Pinell Guided Reading Levels	Lexile	Reading Recovery	DRA	Rigby Literacy Levels	Basal	Stage	Rigby PM/PM Plus Levels
K	A	-	A,B,1	A,1	1–2	Readiness	emergent	starters 1
K.5	B	-	2	2	3–4	Readiness	-	starters 2
1.0	C	-	3,4	3	5	Preprimer 1	-	3–4 red
1.1	D	100	5,6	4	6	Preprimer 2	-	5–6 red/yellow
1.2	E	-	7,8	6–8	7	Preprimer 3	-	7–8 yellow
1.4	F	200	9,10	10	8	Primer	early	9–10 blue
1.5	G	-	11,12	12	9	-	-	11–12 blue/green
1.7	H	300	13,14	14	10	grade 1	-	13–14 green
1.8	I	-	15,16	16	11	grade 1 (late)	-	15–16 orange
2.0	J	400	17,18	18	12	grade 2	-	17–18 turquoise
2.3	K	-	19,20	20	13	-	early fluent	19–20 purple
2.6	L	500	-	24	14–15	-	-	21 gold
2.9	M	-	-	28	16–17	-	-	22 gold
3.0	N	600	-	30	18	grade 3	-	23 silver
3.3	O	-	22	34	19	-	-	24 silver
3.6	P	-	-	38	20	-	-	25 emerald
4.0	Q	700	24	-	-	grade 4	-	26 emerald
4.3	R	-	-	40	-	-	fluent	27 ruby
4.6	S	-	26	-	-	-	-	28 ruby
4.8	T	800	-	44	-	-	-	29 sapphire
5.0	U	-	28	44	-	grade 5	-	30 sapphire
5.3	V	-	-	-	-	-	-	-
5.6	W	900	-	-	-	-	-	-
6.0	X	-	30	-	-	grade 6	-	-
6.5	Y	-	-	-	-	-	-	-
7+	Z	1000	32,34	-	-	-	-	-
-	-	1100	-	-	-	-	-	-
-	-	1200	-	-	-	-	-	-

Resource 9-4: *Approximate Text Level Conversion Table*

Make Instruction Rich and Engaging

Another criticism of intervention we have heard Allington (2006) and others make is that although struggling readers need carefully planned instruction, we should be mindful of keeping the instruction rich and meaningful. Too often, remedial instruction consists of the lowest level of skills instruction in which the teacher, rather than the student, does most of the talking, and student participation consists primarily of completing simple worksheets. Our struggling students need the benefit of rich literacy activities all day long. That is why we recommend the general classroom with a self-contained teacher as the best place for many of these students. They should not miss out on the wonderful read-alouds and shared reading sessions with the rest of the class. These common literacy experiences provide access to rich language and vocabulary, lively discussion, and demonstrations of complex thinking, which these children need in order to thrive. We incorporate art, drama, and music into our literacy curriculum because these fine-arts experiences can provide strugglers alternatives for expressing their understanding and representing the literature they read. Singing, drawing, sculpting, dancing, and acting are stimulating activities that allow children to experience literacy in many of the multiple intelligences that Howard Gardner (1983) promotes. We want our struggling readers to find our reading blocks to be so engaging and so much fun that they will run to our room every day excited about the many ways they can develop as readers.

In addition to these exciting large-group experiences, we want to keep our small-group and individual instruction lively as well. Nothing is more of a turnoff to a struggling reader than a steady diet of low-level drills on decontextualized skills. Most children this age are compliant because they want to please their teachers, but worksheets and flashcards do not make for memorable literacy events. Instead, we want to find the most engaging pictures and visuals, the most colorful and interesting texts, the funniest poems and plays, and combine these materials with our most enthusiastic selves to help these children discover the pleasures of reading. If we can create pleasurable experiences for these students, they are more likely to return for seconds and thirds.

Intervention Strategies ～

The scope of this book does not allow for us to expound on every intervention strategy we have used successfully with children, so we will select a few from the two Intervention Lessons charts for grades K–1 and grades 2–3 and explain them (Resources 9-5 and 9-6).

See Resource 9-5, Intervention Lessons: K–1, p. 292.

See Resource 9-6, Intervention Lessons: Grades 2–3, p. 293.

Phonemic Awareness

Phonemic awareness is the ability to hear and segment individual phonemes. Some children, for whom segmenting does not come naturally, profit from the activities discussed below.

Itty-Bitty Bits

These activities are helpful for children who have yet to distinguish the different phonemes in words and are especially helpful for English language learners who are struggling with unfamiliar sounds. For the first activity, we say to the child or small group, "We are going to play the Itty-Bitty Bits game. I'm going to say the word *pony*, but I'm going to stretch the sounds into itty-bitty bits. Listen to me: '/P/ /o/ /n/ /e/.' Now you say *pony* in little bitty bits." We continue to demonstrate with other simple words such as *like*, *dad*, *green*, etc. Once the children are familiar with the game, we ask them to suggest words and then have them speak in itty-bitty parts. We also like to select relevant words from read-aloud or shared reading texts the children have experienced.

Resource 9-5: *Intervention Lessons: K–1*

Turtle Talk

Turtle Talk is a game similar to Itty Bitty Bits; both games are designed to enhance phonemic awareness. With Turtle Talk, we tell the children we are pretending to talk like a turtle, very s-l-o-w-l-y. For example, *r-u-g*, *t-a-b-u-l*, *l-a-m-p*. We then ask the children to guess each word as we say it. These games are fun and engaging for the students, but we want to remind you that knowledge of sounds and sound–symbol correspondence is best attained through writing and repeated exposure to meaningful texts through shared and guided reading. These games should not comprise the bulk of a struggling learner's intervention lessons. They serve merely as a way to briefly isolate a skill, in this case segmenting sounds, from a richer literacy experience. The goal is to then embed it back into the richer experience. After playing the game with the children, we reread the page from the big book where the words appear.

Lots and Lots of Writing

One of the best ways for struggling primary readers to learn sound–symbol correspondence (graphophonic knowledge) is to do lots of writing, with support from us and also by themselves. Writing can be an extension of the Itty-Bitty Bits game and Turtle Talk. After practicing the segmentation of sounds, we like to practice writing these words with the children. First, we remind the children how we stretched the words out with our mouths. Next, we demonstrate through shared writing how to write the sounds we hear on paper. Finally, we encourage children to express their thoughts on paper through their own invented spelling of text.

Resource 9-6: *Intervention Lessons: Grades 2–3*

Phonics

Learning the alphabetic principle or letter correspondences is difficult for some students. We recommend embedded phonics rather than isolated instruction because we do not want to develop "word callers."

Word Sorts

Word sorts is a game that helps children who have demonstrated through miscue analysis that they have difficulty with graphophonic knowledge. Among the most common miscues we have seen are difficulties with discriminating consonant sounds, vowel patterns, and other tricky letters such as soft and hard *c* or *g*. We first learned of word sorts from *Words Their Way: Word Study for Phonics, Vocabulary, and Spelling Instruction* (Bear, Invernizzi, Templeton, & Johnston, 2000).

For primary children at the emergent level, picture sorts provide an engaging alternative to worksheets. All that is required for a picture sort of beginning consonant sounds are letter cards and picture cards. For example, if the children are having difficulty discriminating between *b* and *d*, we prepare picture cards with objects beginning with both these letters and sounds. We first demonstrate saying the name of a few of the picture cards aloud and sorting them into the two categories under the letter cards. We then ask the students to place the remainder of the picture cards underneath the correct letter. Although this task may seem a kindly form of "skill and drill," picture sorts differ from worksheets in that students are asked to determine similarities and differences between sounds, whereas most worksheets deal with the identification of one sound at a time.

Once students are beginning to develop a sight-word vocabulary, we move on to word sorts. Word sorts involve the same principle as picture sorts, only with word cards instead of picture cards. The process for sorting is the same because we identify word elements the child hasn't developed. For example, if we determine through observation that a child is having difficulty discriminating between short /o/ and long /o/, we prepare a set of one-syllable word cards with familiar words containing both short /o/ and long /o/ sounds. We also prepare two category cards to place at the top of each pile: short /o/ and long /o/. Again, we demonstrate the sorting process and then guide the children as they determine the similarities and differences between the words. When we provide children with the categories, it is called a closed sort. A more difficult variation is an open sort, in which we present the children with a set of word cards and ask them to determine the categories as well as sort the cards. Open sorts are most effective when children have had ample experiences with closed sorts. Children find picture sorts and word sorts a lively and engaging means of briefly analyzing word parts, and they rarely tire of repeating the same word sort assignment. As with Itty-Bitty Bits and Turtle Talk, we strongly recommend that you connect the words the students are practicing to words they are hearing, seeing, and reading in such settings such as shared and guided reading.

Creating sorts and cards can be very time-consuming. In lieu of making your own, we recommend Kathy Ganske's (2006) *Word Sorts and More: Sound, Pattern, and Meaning Explorations, K–3*.

Word Hunts

Students enjoy word hunts because they occur informally during individual or group settings. As the name implies, students look for words with the same letter or sound pattern during various reading experiences. Say that a student has conducted word sorts with the -*ai* vowel pattern. When he or she sees a word with this pattern, the student copies it onto a word hunt chart. Word hunts provide children with a fun opportunity to zero in on new knowledge and be on the lookout for certain words in their everyday reading.

Writing

Writing is an excellent strategy for acquiring graphophonic knowledge. When children write the letters of the sounds they hear and the spelling patterns they have learned to recognize through reading, they are applying their graphophonic knowledge.

Comprehension

Reading is comprehension, but word calling without meaning is just saying words. Most readers can enhance their comprehension of text by using the following strategies.

Repeated Rereadings

Once children begin to read connected text, an all-purpose, highly effective strategy is repeated rereadings. You know from your experiences with conducting read-alouds that children this age love to hear the same stories over and over again. Well, emergent and beginning readers also enjoy reading the same books over and over again. Not only do the children enjoy rereading a book you have introduced through shared reading, guided reading, or an individual lesson, they need the extra exposure to the words, the storyline, and the new information the author is presenting. Rereading helps children increase their knowledge bank of words, their familiarity with the characters and their interactions with one another; it gives them practice with flow and, above all, helps them learn that texts are supposed to have meaning. Repeated rereadings also increase children's confidence as they evolve from tentative cold readings to a proficient demonstration of word accuracy, smooth phrasing, and secure comprehension.

We concentrate on Tier 2 words selected from texts we are reading with kids. We introduce these words naturally by defining them in our own words. We then have the children practice using the words through shared writing, and we encourage them to use the words in their independent writing.

Flow

For most students, flow develops simultaneously with other reading abilities; however, some children really struggle with this. Through assessments in which we listen to children read aloud, we can determine whether a child's choppy reading is interfering with comprehension or if the child has the stamina to finish reading passages. If comprehension or stamina is affected, then this issue needs attention.

Call the child's attention to what flow is and how a well-flowing passage should sound. Ask the child to pay careful attention to how you sound when you read aloud and how the readers of stories on the computer or iPod sound. Engage the child in a conversation about what he or she notices. Then tell the child that you will be working together so that his or her reading sounds more like the reading that you discussed.

A child can use a tape recorder or an iPod to record him- or herself reading a familiar text. The child can then listen to the recording with an ear toward issues related to flow. Have the child read the passage again for practice without recording it, then have the child record the passage again, listen to it, and reevaluate. Has your oral reading improved? Is it smoother and less choppy? Are there long pauses within the text? Repeat the rereading and recording until the child recognizes that improvements have been made.

Readers Theater provides a fun and effective way for children to practice oral reading and listen to other students who read smoothly. Encourage children to read aloud to younger siblings at home as well.

Using Technology ∼

Teachers frequently ask us if we support the use of technology for struggling readers. Our answer is, "It depends." We recognize that when the early childhood students of today take their place in the work force, computer technology will be as ubiquitous as pencils and paper were when we began our careers. Technology will be the tool that they use to accomplish most of their work tasks. For that reason, we applaud the explosion of technology integration into early childhood classrooms. Young children are using the Internet to research topics of interest, creating podcasts of Readers Theater productions to share with parents, using digital cameras and software to create photo stories of field trip experiences, "Skyping" (using a webcam to communicate) with classrooms in remote villages in Alaska, and publishing their writing to larger audiences on the Web.

Young children must have frequent and sustained opportunities to use technology as they go about the important business of learning. Most children find the use of technology stimulating, and oftentimes struggling readers will more readily embrace a reading task that involves a computer or other technological device. We must ensure, however, that the nature of the technology experience is one that a child would not experience under ordinary circumstances. For example, is this a task a child could do in another format such as a paper-and-pencil assignments? If so, then the reading software program becomes nothing more than a set of high-tech worksheets. We recognize the temptation for a busy teacher (and we are all busy teachers!) to engage strugglers with remedial software programs in the bulk of their intervention lessons. We like to remember that software reading programs don't teach children. Teachers do. Computers and other hardware are effective supplements to that face-to-face instruction you deliver to the children.

We feel it is important that our struggling readers are not just consumers of text but also producers of information. Even first graders can use a digital camera to take pictures of a classroom experience and then type captions to accompany each picture in a word processing program. We certainly support the use of technology as part of intervention programs, but we try to be thoughtful about our children's experiences with technology.

Appropriate Software

Not all literacy software offers opportunities for students to practice and apply the strategies they need. After studying assessments, we can select the software that fulfills a purpose and doesn't just result in students hitting keys.

BookFlix

A software program we have found effective with all children, and especially with strugglers, is BookFlix by Scholastic (teacher.scholastic.com/products/bookflixfreetrial). BookFlix is a Web-based K–3 program that presents a wide variety of popular and high-quality children's literature in a video format accompanied by word-by-word highlighted text. Many of these videos are also in

Spanish. In addition, these titles are paired with related nonfiction eBooks produced by Scholastic. In essence, the children have easy access to a wide variety of the equivalent of books on tape, except these are books on the computer. When the children finish reading a book such as *Curious George Rides a Bike*, they can read a nonfiction text to learn more about monkeys and other mammals. The BookFlix site also contains biographies on popular authors and related Web sites for further exploration. Tumble Books is similar to BookFlix. You can sign up for a free trial at www.tumblebooks.com.

iPods

Students can use an iPod to record their oral reading, a Readers Theater performance, and to hear and see books. The Discovery Education Streaming Web site (streaming.discoveryeducation.com) contains a wonderful variety of short video clips of children's literature, both fiction and nonfiction. Some videos are close-captioned, enabling the children to view the words as well as hear the story and see the pictures. Using a converter software program, these video clips can also be downloaded onto iPods.

Collaborating Adults ∼

If the struggling readers in your room are special education students or English language learners, you will probably work with special education teachers, reading specialists, or ELL teachers. If you work in a Title I school, some of your children may receive the services of Title I teachers. It is critical that you ensure congruence in curriculum and instruction when these colleagues work with your struggling readers. For quite some time, general education teachers were led to believe that special educators could remove their strugglers from the classroom environment, transport them to a magical special education classroom, and in 45 minutes each day, could cure their ills. Of course, we all know that it's not that simple.

Struggling readers deserve a well-planned and aligned intervention program that doesn't waste a single minute of time. Students are more likely to make significant progress when the general classroom teacher takes the lead in planning, designing, and implementing intervention lessons and the additional teacher works to provide extra guidance and practice. Not only can students become confused when two adults are teaching totally different skills, strategies, and concepts with totally different types of texts, but precious and limited learning time is lost.

Response to Intervention ～

There is much discussion these days about Response to Intervention (RTI), a federal initiative that is contained in the latest reauthorization of the Individuals with Disabilities Education Act (IDEA). This initiative grew out of the concern that there might be overidentification of children with learning disabilities. Most states and districts have until recently used a discrepancy model to identify such children. Under this model, a child must progress far enough in school for school personnel to show a pattern of difficulties in the classroom and for assessments to indicate a discrepancy between the child's IQ and his or her performance on individually administered standardized tests (Fuchs, Fuchs, & Vaughn, 2008). Critics of the discrepancy model feel that too much time elapses between when teachers report that children are experiencing difficulties and their placement in a special education program. Often this occurs around third grade. Critics also feel that many children have received poor classroom literacy instruction, and that lack of instruction rather than biology is the cause of their "disability" (Allington & Walmsley, 2007).

The Response to intervention programs that are gaining popularity across the nation don't fit just one prototype. The model we have heard discussed the most is the three-tier model, in which children identified as experiencing difficulties in reading receive appropriate instruction during a first tier of instruction from their regular classroom teacher, followed by a second tier of instruction either delivered by the classroom teacher or another professional, and then a third tier of instruction if the first two tiers do not produce measurable results. Whereas intervention has traditionally been delivered after a child was identified as learning disabled, under RTI, intervention will start much earlier, such as in kindergarten. It is only after a child fails to respond to intervention that the child will be identified as learning disabled. Your state department of education or local school district may mandate RTI policies and procedures for you, and if the three-tier model is the chosen prototype, you will probably be sharing your struggling readers with a special education teacher or a reading specialist. As mentioned earlier, children benefit greatly if you and the other teacher make the time to talk and collaborate (Allington & Walmsley, 2007).

In Conclusion ⁓

Teaching struggling readers presents several challenges. The first challenge is time, because the clock is always ticking and we are always feeling that we have left things undone at the end of the day. This is normal and to be expected. Teaching children is not a finite task like stacking books on a shelf in the library. All children are complex, and those who struggle can be even more complex. We will never accomplish everything for every child in the classroom that needs to be done . . . ever. Even if we worked 24-7, there would always be tasks left undone and needs left unmet. We recommend you come to some type of peace about the time issue and affirm yourself for all the good things you do each day rather than focus on what is undone. Struggling readers also come to us with unique needs, and that requires us to be the very best kidwatcher, assessor, diagnostician, and reading teacher we can be. We encourage you to read the books we recommended in the chapter and heed the strategies (Resource 9-7) that deal strictly with developing implementation plans for children once you have assessed their reading performance. We know these books have helped us tremendously. By merely reading this chapter, you have shown a commitment to helping the neediest of the children you serve. We commend you for your dedication and encourage you to keep learning about children who struggle.

See Resource 9-7, Instructional Strategies and Materials, p. 294.

Resource 9-7

STUDENTS WITH SPECIAL NEEDS ▪ Resource 9-7
Instructional Strategies and Materials

Instructional Strategies and Materials

Grade Level	Phonemic Awareness	Phonics	Flow	Vocabulary	Comprehension	Student Interest
K–1	Itty-Bitty parts Turtle Talk Word stretching Appropriate software programs Rhyme books and Dr. Seuss books Clapping out syllables of names and words	Elkonin boxes Daily News and other writing demonstrations, activities Invented spelling Decoding by onsets and rimes/decoding by analogy Environmental print activities Word sorts Word hunts	Read books on independent level (silently and out loud) Repeated rereading of familiar text Readers Theater Partner-read (for short periods of time) Buddy-read (cross-aged groupings)	Conversations: Teacher-to-student and student-to-student Wide reading combined with instruction on Tier 2 words Kindergarten (building awareness): * Read-alouds * Writing (use of words) * Poetry * Interesting word records	Teachers demonstration of strategies: Read-alouds Think-alouds Retellings Predicting Questioning Making connections Visualizing Reading journals Increased time for independent reading, writing, and discussion Repeated rereading of familiar text	Student surveys Choice/self-selection Variety of materials: *Genre *Reading levels *Gender-specific literature
Grade Level	**Phonemic Awareness**	**Phonics**	**Flow**	**Vocabulary**	**Comprehension**	**Student Interest**
2–3	Unless needed for individual struggling readers	Daily News and other writing demonstrations, activities Invented spelling Environmental print activities Rhyme books Word sorts Word hunts	Read books on independent level (silently and out loud) Repeated rereading of familiar text Readers Theater Partner-read (for short periods of time) Buddy-read (cross-aged groupings)	Conversations: Teacher-to-student and student-to-student Tier 2 words Read-alouds	Teachers modeling/demonstration of deep structure strategies: • Making inferences • Determining • Importance • Synthesizing	Student surveys Choice/self-selection Variety of materials: * Genre * Reading levels * Gender specific literature

294   The Classroom

Resource 9-7: *Instructional Strategies and Materials*

Appropriate Strategies for Reader Types

STRATEGIES	I	II	III	IV	V
Phonemic Awareness					
Writing	•				•
Turtle Talk	•				•
Itty-Bitty Bits Game	•				•
Graphophonic Knowledge					
Interactive Writing	•		•		•
Dictation	•		•		•
Writing	•	•	•	•	•
Masking During Supportive Reading	•	•	•		•
Environmental Print Activities	•				•
Alphabet	•				•
Onset & Rimes	•				•
Word Walls	•		•		•
Games	•				•
Focus Lessons	•	•	•	•	•
Comprehension Strategies					
Reading Aloud	•	•	•	•	•
Think-Alouds	•	•	•	•	•
Shared Reading	•	•	•		•
Supportive Reading	•	•	•		•
Discussions: Teacher-led	•	•	•	•	•
Discussions: Student-led		•	•	•	
Focus Lessons	•	•	•	•	•
Visualizing	•	•	•	•	•
Predicting	•	•	•	•	•
Questioning	•	•	•	•	•
Using Background Knowledge	•	•	•	•	•
Inferring	•	•	•	•	•
Conferences	•	•	•	•	•
Graphic Organizers		•	•	•	•
Literature Circles		•	•	•	•
Dramatization	•	•	•	•	•
Retrospective Miscue Analysis		•	•	•	•
Independent Reading					
Personal Book Collections	•	•	•	•	•
Literature Circles		•	•	•	•
Sustained Silent Reading		•	•	•	•
Content Knowledge					
Reading Nonfiction Aloud	•	•	•	•	•
Theme Immersions	•	•	•	•	•

(READER TYPES)

Creating the Best Literacy Block Ever © 2009 by Maryann Manning, Gayle Morrison, and Deborah Camp: Scholastic Professional

STUDENTS WITH SPECIAL NEEDS ■ Individual Intervention Plan

Resource 9-3

Individual Intervention Plan

Directions: 1. List below the current student assessment data you have reviewed.

2. In the Specific Skill/Concepts column, list the <u>specific</u> skills and concepts requiring intervention.

3. In the Target Interventions column, write the code matching the intervention(s) that will be used.

Student: **Maria Morales**   Grade: **2**   Teacher: **Jan Foreman**

Fall Plan **X**   Spring Plan _____   Date Completed: **August 22, 2008**

Data Reviewed: **QRI-4 (narrative passage), running record, word list**

Child's Strengths: **phonemic awareness and interests** Child's Interests: **dogs, Mexico, families**

Phonological Awareness (PA)	Phonics/Accuracy (Ph)	Flow (F)
• PA 1 Elkonin boxes	• Ph 1 alphabet games	• F 1 Readers Theater
• PA 2 name games	• Ph 2 vowel patterns (CVC, CVCe)	• F 2 choral reading of poems/passages
• PA 3 clapping syllables	• Ph 3 onset/rime work	• F 3 fast-sweep passages
• PA 4 clapping syllables	• Ph 4 word sorts	• F 4 recording oral reading
• PA 5 stretching words, Itty-Bitty, Turtle Talk	• Ph 5 preview/review of concept	• F 5 partner reading
• PA 6 shared reading with poems, songs, nursery rhymes	• Ph 6 modeled writing	• F 6 other
• PA 7 other	• Ph 7 other	

Comprehension (C)	Reading Dispositions (RD)	Vocabulary (V)
• C 1 supportive reading	• RD1 self-select books	• V1 read-aloud with vocabulary discussion
• C 2 graphic organizer	• RD2 read series books	• V2 intentional vocabulary procedure w/Tier 2 words from texts
• C 3 direct instruction prompt	• RD3 read books on interesting topics	
• C 4 cloze passages	• RD4 read to principal	• V3 sentence stems
• C 5 stop/retell	• RD5 read to younger children	• V4 text talk tally
• C 6 book walk/book talk focus	• RD6 read to high school peer/tutor	• V5 multiple encounters with words
• C 7 preview/review of book	• RD7 send "happygrams" to parents	• V6 organized theme (classification)
• C8 scaffolding cues		• V7 other
• C9 think-aloud		
C10 Other _____		

Specific Skills/Concepts Requiring Intervention

Decoding, flow, sight words, comprehension

Target Interventions

PH 2, 4, 6. F1, repeated rereading

C4, 5, 6 and leveled text with picture support

Creating the Best Literacy Block Ever © 2009 by Maryann Manning, Gayle Morrison, and Deborah Camp: Scholastic Professional

Approximate Text Level Conversion Table

Grade Level/AR	Fountas & Pinell Guided Reading Levels	Lexile	Reading Recovery	DRA	Rigby Literacy Levels	Basal	Stage	Rigby PM/PM Plus Levels
K	A	-	A,B,1	A,1	1–2	Readiness	emergent	starters 1
K.5	B	-	2	2	3–4	Readiness	-	starters 2
1.0	C	-	3,4	3	5	Preprimer 1	-	3–4 red
1.1	D	100	5,6	4	6	Preprimer 2	-	5–6 red/yellow
1.2	E	-	7,8	6–8	7	Preprimer 3	-	7–8 yellow
1.4	F	200	9,10	10	8	Primer	early	9–10 blue
1.5	G	-	11,12	12	9	-	-	11–12 blue/green
1.7	H	300	13,14	14	10	grade 1	-	13–14 green
1.8	I	-	15,16	16	11	grade 1 (late)	-	15–16 orange
2.0	J	400	17,18	18	12	grade 2	-	17–18 turquoise
2.3	K	-	19,20	20	13	-	early fluent	19–20 purple
2.6	L	500	-	24	14–15	-	-	21 gold
2.9	M	-	-	28	16–17	-	-	22 gold
3.0	N	600	-	30	18	grade 3	-	23 silver
3.3	O	-	22	34	19	-	-	24 silver
3.6	P	-	-	38	20	-	-	25 emerald
4.0	Q	700	24	-	-	grade 4	-	26 emerald
4.3	R	-	-	40	-	-	fluent	27 ruby
4.6	S	-	26	-	-	-	-	28 ruby
4.8	T	800	-	44	-	-	-	29 sapphire
5.0	U	-	28	44	-	grade 5	-	30 sapphire
5.3	V	-	-	-	-	-	-	-
5.6	W	900	-	-	-	-	-	-
6.0	X	-	30	-	-	grade 6	-	-
6.5	Y	-	-	-	-	-	-	-
7+	Z	1000	32,34	-	-	-	-	-
-	-	1100	-	-	-	-	-	-
-	-	1200	-	-	-	-	-	-

Creating the Best Literacy Block Ever © 2009 by Maryann Manning, Gayle Morrison, and Deborah Camp: Scholastic Professional

STUDENTS WITH SPECIAL NEEDS ■ Intervention Lessons: K–1

Resource 9-5

Intervention Lessons: K–1

Student: _____ Month: _____ Year: _____

Intervention is Based on Fall _____ Winter _____ Assessments and Weekly Conferences

Lessons: Teacher (Intentional Instruction) **T**eacher/**S**tudent (Shared Application) **S**tudent (Independent Application)
Focus: V – Vocabulary   P – Phonics   C – Comprehension   F – Fluency   PA – Phonological Awareness

Week 1	Comments	Week 2	Comments
Monday Date _____ Focus: V P C F PA Materials/Activity: Outcome: Additional Reading:	T T/S S	Monday Date _____ Focus: V P C F PA Materials/Activity: Outcome: Additional Reading:	T T/S S
Tuesday Date _____ Focus: V P C F PA Materials/Activity: Outcome: Additional Reading	T T/S S	Tuesday Date _____ Focus: V P C F PA Materials/Activity: Outcome: Additional Reading	T T/S S
Wednesday Date _____ Focus: V P C F PA Materials/Activity: Outcome: Additional Reading	T T/S S	Wednesday Date _____ Focus: V P C F PA Materials/Activity: Outcome: Additional Reading	T T/S S
Thursday Date _____ Focus: V P C F PA Materials/Activity: Outcome: Additional Reading	T T/S S	Thursday Date _____ Focus: V P C F PA Materials/Activity: Outcome: Additional Reading	T T/S S
Friday Date _____ Focus: V P C F PA Materials/Activity: Outcome: Additional Reading:	T T/S S	Friday Date _____ Focus: V P C F PA Materials/Activity: Outcome: Additional Reading:	T T/S S

Creating the Best Literacy Block Ever © 2009 by Maryann Manning, Gayle Morrison, and Deborah Camp: Scholastic Professional

Intervention Lessons: Grades 2–3

Student: _____ Month: _____ Year: _____

Intervention is Based on Fall ____ Winter ____ Assessments and Weekly Conferences

Lessons: Teacher (Intentional Instruction) **T**eacher/**S**tudent (Shared Application) **S**tudent (Independent Application)

Focus: V – Vocabulary   P – Phonics   C – Comprehension   F – Fluency   PA – Phonological Awareness

Week 3	Comments	Week 4	Comments
Monday Date _____ Focus: V P C F PA Materials/Activity: Outcome: Additional Reading:	T T/S S	Monday Date _____ Focus: V P C F PA Materials/Activity: Outcome: Additional Reading:	T T/S S
Tuesday Date _____ Focus: V P C F PA Materials/Activity: Outcome: Additional Reading	T T/S S	Tuesday Date _____ Focus: V P C F PA Materials/Activity: Outcome: Additional Reading	T T/S S
Wednesday Date _____ Focus: V P C F PA Materials/Activity: Outcome: Additional Reading	T T/S S	Wednesday Date _____ Focus: V P C F PA Materials/Activity: Outcome: Additional Reading	T T/S S
Thursday Date _____ Focus: V P C F PA Materials/Activity: Outcome: Additional Reading	T T/S S	Thursday Date _____ Focus: V P C F PA Materials/Activity: Outcome: Additional Reading	T T/S S
Friday Date _____ Focus: V P C F PA Materials/Activity: Outcome: Additional Reading:	T T/S S	Friday Date _____ Focus: V P C F PA Materials/Activity: Outcome: Additional Reading:	T T/S S

Creating the Best Literacy Block Ever © 2009 by Maryann Manning, Gayle Morrison, and Deborah Camp: Scholastic Professional

Resource 9-7

Instructional Strategies and Materials

Grade Level	Phonemic Awareness	Phonics	Flow	Vocabulary	Comprehension	Student Interest
K–1	Itty-Bitty parts Turtle Talk Word stretching Appropriate software programs Rhyme books and Dr. Seuss books Clapping out syllables of names and words	Elkonin boxes Daily News and other writing demonstrations, activities Invented spelling Decoding by onsets and rimes/decoding by analogy Environmental print activities Word sorts Word hunts	Read books on independent level (silently and out loud) Repeated rereading of familiar text Readers Theater Partner-read (for short periods of time) Buddy-read (cross-aged groupings)	Conversations: Teacher-to-student and student-to-student Wide reading combined with instruction on Tier 2 words Kindergarten (building awareness): * Read-alouds * Writing (use of words) * Poetry * Interesting word records	Teachers demonstration of strategies: Read-alouds Think-alouds Retellings Predicting Questioning Making connections Visualizing Reading journals Increased time for independent reading, writing, and discussion Repeated rereading of familiar text	Student surveys Choice/self-selection Variety of materials: *Genre *Reading levels *Gender-specific literature
Grade Level	Phonemic Awareness	Phonics	Flow	Vocabulary	Comprehension	Student Interest
2–3	Unless needed for individual struggling readers	Daily News and other writing demonstrations, activities Invented spelling Environmental print activities Rhyme books Word sorts Word hunts	Read books on independent level (silently and out loud) Repeated rereading of familiar text Readers Theater Partner-read (for short periods of time) Buddy-read (cross-aged groupings)	Conversations: Teacher-to-student and student- to-student Tier 2 words Read-alouds	Teachers modeling/demonstration of deep structure strategies: • Making inferences • Determining • Importance • Synthesizing	Student surveys Choice/self-selection Variety of materials: * Genre * Reading levels * Gender specific literature

Creating the Best Literacy Block Ever © 2009 by Maryann Manning, Gayle Morrison, and Deborah Camp: Scholastic Professional

CHAPTER 10

Literacy Development

Becoming literate is simply the evolution of becoming more and more competent as a user of written language. Learning to read is the natural process that nonreaders goes through on the journey from first recognizing environmental print and one's name to becoming a reader who can construct meaning from age-appropriate text. Learning to write is the process of expressing knowledge and feelings; it begins as scribbles and moves to invented spelling and eventually conventional spelling.

The Evolution of the Reading Process ~

Throughout this chapter we discuss how children mature as readers during the reading block. We continue to grow in our understanding of the reading process as we interact with readers and reflect on the teachings of literacy educators.

Preschool Literacy Development

The seminal work on the evolution of literacy by Emilia Ferreiro and Anna Teberosky (1982) has taught us how preschool children first develop literacy by knowing that squiggles and marks on a page represent objects. Many researchers have studied how early readers produce invented spelling and how young children interpret text and have verified that literacy evolves quite similarly in different languages around the world. Maryann has spent many years researching early literacy with Constance Kamii, who was a student of Piaget. Together, Maryann and Connie replicated many of the studies of Ferreiro and Teberosky with English-speaking children (Kamii & Manning, 2002).

Four Levels of Readers

In a typical kindergarten class there are four levels of readers:

- Pre-emergent
- Emergent
- Beginning
- Independent

The development of these levels often begins before kindergarten. Most children move through predictable stages in their reading development, although children evolve in highly idiosyncratic ways. These stages, therefore, are not rigid, and some children may not follow such a neat and tidy progression in their literacy development.

Pre-Emergent Reader

A pre-emergent reader is beginning to develop concepts of print such as these:

- Text is read from left to right.
- Eyes make a return sweep at the end of a line.
- Words are read right-side up.
- The page is turned to read the next one.
- Readers attend to the punctuation on a page.

Pre-emergent readers may not understand that certain function words such as *the*, *of*, and *and* are even represented on paper, or may not see that individual words are part of a whole sentence. The child's writing consists of letter strings, and there is no evidence of letter–sound relations. The child, therefore, does not understand phonics instruction. Children at this level may have varying oral language capacities.

Emergent Reader

An emergent reader knows that all words in a sentence are represented on paper in a book or piece of text. Phonemic awareness is developing as the child moves from segmenting syllables to segmenting phonemes. The child is beginning to develop knowledge of letter–sound relationships. There writing demonstrates some letter–sound correspondences. During shared reading sessions, the child is beginning to notice concepts of print and the different shapes that letters have. When individually interacting with books, emergent readers will mimic page-handling behaviors, turning pages, looking at each page sequentially, and moving from front to back in the book.

Beginning Reader

A beginning reader has one-to-one correspondence, recognizing that each word read aloud from a book is represented by a written word on the page. The child can segment the phonemes in a two-syllable word, can remember some individual word, and read some predictable books. Picture clues help the child think about the meaning of the text (semantics), oral language helps with the prediction of words (syntax), and letter–sound knowledge assists in the decoding of new words (graphophonics). Spelling becomes more conventional.

This beginning reading level is not static because the child is continually developing and growing. Over time, the child depends less on pictures for meaning and more on graphophonic cues. The child takes risks in predicting words and self-corrects to monitor meaning.

Independent Reader

A child at the independent reading level can make meaning from unfamiliar text, although the child must possess background knowledge about the text for optimal comprehension. An independent reader only studies individual letters in words when experiencing difficulty figuring out a word through context and the use of the semantic and syntactic cueing system. A child at this level can understand age-appropriate and above-level text with ease.

Conditions for Literacy Development ~

Teaching reading involves preparing a literate environment that provides these essentials:

- Students choose materials and have time to engage with them.
- Growth is supported through large-group, small-group, and individual instruction in the use of the four cueing systems.

- Readers are challenged through teacher questioning and interactions and, when appropriate, more difficult texts.

We believe that learning to read and write isn't the big mystery that some policy makers and educators make it out to be. As teachers, we generally can predict which children will easily become readers when they enter school. If children have a rich literacy heritage, the greater the likelihood they will become readers within a reasonable period of time. Children with rich literacy heritages typically are "school-independent" children (Ladson-Billings, 2004). That is, their families read aloud to them, engage them in oral language opportunities, and provide enrichment experiences such as museum trips that build content knowledge. They come to school armed with more than their peers from non-reading environments.

For a majority of our students, the road to literacy is smooth. They move naturally from hearing texts and seeing illustrations on the laps of loving adults to experimenting with the writing of ideas to beginning to decipher texts to reading with the support of others to reading independently—and then to comprehending and evaluating more sophisticated texts as they mature as readers.

For some students, however, the journey isn't smooth due to several factors:

- Limited oral language development

- Lack of reading episodes prior to formal schooling

- A dearth of literate models

- Instruction with a phonics program before developing an understanding of part-to-whole relationships

These students need individual support from a knowledgeable teacher as they learn how language functions, rather than a daily regimen of isolated phonics drills and decodable books. Unfortunately, these students weren't 1,000-book kids. New Zealand primary teachers say that a child needs to hear 1,000 books read aloud before they come to school for reading to develop easily. If children have not had the 1,000-book experience, we need to make sure they do in our classrooms.

In some ways, teaching students reading is like hosting a dinner party. The host has to make sure to serve the guests healthy foods in a pleasant manner. We liken the food to quality children's literature and the pleasant manner to the classroom environment and the sequencing of the reading block. As the host, you ask your guests questions and create an amiable atmosphere with rich discussion. Just as you want your guests to enjoy the food, you want your students

Foundational Understandings

to devour the good books as well as relish the ambiance that you have worked hard to establish.

Beginning Reading Instruction ～

Two major views of the reading process exist: one is skills-based and the other is rooted in sociopsycholinguistics. In the skills-based approach, readers use one cueing system (graphophonics); in the sociopsycholinguistic approach, they simultaneously draw upon four cueing systems (graphophonics, semantics, syntax, and pragmatics). Skills-based versus the sociopsycholinguistics model can be further defined by:

- Top down versus bottom up
- Phonics first versus embedded phonics

The chart that follows (Figure 10.1) shows the major differences between a skills-based approach to reading and a sociopsycholinguistic view.

Sociopsycholinguistic View	Skills View
Uses quality literature as the basis of the reading program	Relies on commercial programs, including decodable text
Embeds phonics instruction in authentic daily reading and writing instruction	Teaches phonics in isolation
Focuses on students constructing meaning from text	Focuses on sounding out words and speed
Uses authentic reading and writing activities	Relies on worksheets and drills
Uses assessment to guide instruction	Assesses for reading grade level and report card grades
Demonstrates reading and writing frequently	Demonstrates reading and writing infrequently
Engages in read-alouds several times a day	Engages in read-alouds occasionally
Teaches vocabulary in context	Teaches vocabulary in isolation

- Figure 10.1: *Sociopsycholinguistic and skills view*

The Four Cueing Systems

We notice that proficient readers use all cueing systems simultaneously whenever we observe these readers processing text. Our views have been informed by the work of Kenneth Goodman (Goodman & Burke, 1973) and Frank Smith (1994). Supporting the four cueing systems as students mature as readers is our task during the reading block.

Graphophonic Cueing System

The phonological system relates to the sounds of oral language. The orthographic system relates to written language. The graphophonics cueing system refers to the systems of both oral and written language and the relationships between the two, or in other words, the relationship between letters and sounds.

Knowledge of sound–symbol relationships is necessary for reading, and many children come to kindergarten and first grade with this knowledge. Learning to match sounds with symbols and letter names isn't difficult for most 5- and 6-year-olds. We were amused when we heard about Alex, a grey parrot who makes sound–symbol connections. "Sssssss," he sounds when his teacher, biologist Irene Pepperberg, shows him a red plastic S-shaped refrigerator magnet. When she pushes an *H* next to it, Alex promptly says "Shhhhh." When she shows him the letters *O R*, Alex clearly enunciates "or" (Chandler, 1998). Unfortunately Alex died before he was able to master all sounds and symbols. Our point is that if a parrot can match letters and sounds, the task must not be difficult!

Children construct much of their knowledge about phonics from environmental print—McDonald's teaches the /m/ sound and Kellogg's teaches the /k/ sound that is often written as /c/. Children who have frequent writing opportunities begin to learn many sounds as they express their ideas on paper. Once, when Maryann and Gayle were speaking at an IRA conference to a large room full of teachers, an attendee asked Gayle how and when she taught phonics. Maryann stood there waiting nervously as Gayle thoughtfully responded. Gayle said simply, "I teach phonics whenever my students have a pencil in their hands, and that is almost all day." Certainly, students must learn the 44 letter–sound relationships in the English language, but this knowledge can be constructed during shared reading and interactive writing. Some of the most meaningful phonics instruction takes place during the writing workshop when students edit their writing.

Phonics instruction is generally limited to kindergarten and first grade. Most students have learned all the phonics they need by the end of first grade. Some publishers of commercial programs urge the explicit teaching of phonics rules but children intuit these rules and can apply them without the necessity of teaching them to name the rules. Time spent labeling spelling rules could better be spent reading books (Weaver, 2002).

Since we adhere to a sociopsycholinguistic view of reading, we believe that phonics instruction should be embedded within shared and guided readings, using whole texts and real words as opposed to nonsense words. Our experience has shown us that teaching children to decode words through analogy is more meaningful for them than teaching them to merely "sound and blend," a synthetic approach to phonics instruction. Decoding words through analogy with familiar words and word parts (Weaver, 2002) encourages children to look for chunks of smaller words or syllables within a word or to decode a word using onsets and rimes, which mimics what adult readers do.

We have heard skills-view educators argue that teaching children to chunk syllables in words is analogous to using nonsense words for phonics instruction. We argue that when we teach children to chunk words, we are teaching them a useful strategy to make sense of real words. Educators who believe in the validity of assessing children's phonics skills through the "reading" of nonsense words and who use drill work in nonsense words to prepare for the test are not teaching their children that words are supposed to make sense. We have also observed that many emergent readers who are administered a nonsense-word test attempt to make the pseudo-word into a real word, reading *milk* for *mik*, for example. When children are taught that reading is supposed to make sense, nonsense-word assessments and drills are unnecessary.

Discussions of phonics instruction often include references to "phonemic awareness." Phonemic awareness and phonological awareness are relatively new terms in the lexicon of reading instruction. Phonemic awareness, defined as the ability to segment words into phonemes, or units of sound, is a cognitive process that develops gradually. Initially, children cannot segment a word but can divide the word into syllables. Eventually, the child can divide or segment all phonemes in a word. The ability to segment moves from thinking the word *pony* is one unit to saying "po-ny," or two units, and eventually saying, "p-o-n-e," or four units. Initially, children will be able to segment one-syllable words but struggle with multisyllabic words. After a few months, children can segment longer and longer words.

Kamii and Manning (2002) view invented spelling as the way to assess phonemic awareness. Phonemic awareness is a natural cognitive process rather than a skill that needs to be taught. Although many researchers emphasize assessing phonemic awareness through reading, writing tells us a great deal about a child's awareness of units of sound within words. It is also important to encourage beginning readers to write because it requires them to analyze their own speech, a process that strengthens phonemic awareness.

Syntactic Cueing System

Proficient readers do not rely solely on their graphophonic knowledge to make meaning of text. Readers use their content knowledge, the context of the sentence, and their syntactical knowledge when they encounter unfamiliar words. Constance Weaver explains syntax as "syntactic cues—that is, grammatical cues like word order, function words, and word endings" (2002, p. 5). We have found that the term *grammar* is an easy way to remember what syntax is. Syntactical knowledge begins to develop when children start to talk. "I brush my teeth" and "The dog ran away" are simple sentences. Even though young children will not label *brush* as a verb or *dog* as a noun, they know where nouns and verbs belong in sentences. They acquire this knowledge through conversations with others and by listening to written language through read-alouds. They know intuitively when language sounds right. The interrelationship of words contributes to reading power because the reader can predict through word order and grammatical cues what part of speech is next. Readers use syntax and the context of the sentence to predict what word will come next in a sentence and then to confirm whether their prediction was correct or not. When we are reading with children and notice they are not using the syntactic cueing system, we need to ask them, "Does that sound like language?"

Semantic Cueing System

Without meaning, there is no reading process. Saying meaningless words isn't reading. Constructing meaning from text requires content knowledge; without this knowledge, there is no interaction between the author and the reader, and reading cannot take place. The transaction between the text, the reader, and the reader's prior knowledge enables effective readers to make predictions, to read the text, and then to confirm whether the prediction made sense.

Children begin making meaning of texts through read-alouds and shared reading. Through these early literacy experiences, children develop concepts of print.

Children also develop one-to-one correspondence, the knowledge that the written symbol composed of letters represents a word. On the first day of kindergarten, children must receive the message from teachers that reading is making meaning, not just correctly reading words.

As children begin reading connected text, we must encourage them to use the syntactic cueing system to make sense. Children at this stage tend to focus too much on their use of the graphophonic system, and unfortunately, many commercial programs emphasize decoding to the exclusion of comprehension. When we ask children to retell what they have read and continually encourage them to ask themselves, "Does this make sense?" when they read, we are helping them use the semantic cueing system.

Pragmatic Cueing System

Reading involves situational, social, and cultural factors. Students bring their cultural experiences and socioeconomic backgrounds to the reading task. For example, not all cultures view reading as a pleasurable activity, especially when economic conditions prevent the purchase of books and deny the leisure time to read them. Also, some cultures may demonstrate reading proficiency but do not consider reading a valuable leisure activity.

Children's reading processing can be influenced by the teacher's grouping of readers or other conditions such as the noise level in the classroom. Also, children may read differently based on the purposes they have for reading. For example, how a child reads for pleasure in a low-stakes situation may differ dramatically from how the child reads during informal or formal assessment settings.

Influencing Factors

Several other factors come into play with regard to reading development, including oral language development, content knowledge, flow, and desire.

Language Development and Vocabulary Size

We feel that language development is not emphasized enough in the teaching of reading. The same environment that fosters speaking also encourages children to become readers and writers. A baby's babbling begins to represent objects in his or her environment, and different sounds become units of meaning. We have all watched a young child progress from saying only a few words such as *ball, Mama,* and *Daddy* to demonstrating a large spoken vocabulary. How does this happen?

Brian Cambourne's research in Australia (1988) has helped us understand the conditions that must be present for language development. He identifies the following terms:

- Immersion
- Demonstrations
- Approximations
- Feedback (or response)
- Practice (or use)
- Expectations
- Responsibility

Children are surrounded by demonstrations of language in natural settings throughout their childhood. Approximations represent the acceptance of children's beginning attempts at learning to speak that parents and others provide; children are rewarded for coming close to the correct utterance rather than criticized for not getting it exactly right. Parents and others provide feedback immediately when it is needed, and children are encouraged to use and practice their language in various settings. Parents have expectations that their children will learn to talk, and children are responsible for progressing to an advanced state of language development.

Mem Fox (2001) documents the power of a large vocabulary. She tells us that the children of professionals generally possess larger vocabularies than children of nonprofessionals. The more words a child hears, attaches meaning to, and uses in speaking, the larger the child's vocabulary. When children are immersed in rich curriculum and language opportunities, their vocabulary can increase exponentially. If children possess an extensive oral vocabulary, they will likely be able to read the same words when they encounter them in texts. In general, there is a relationship between spoken and written language; the greater the language facility, the easier the transition into reading and writing.

Content Knowledge

Prior knowledge knowledge is necessary to being an effective reader. We organize our content knowledge into schemas, and the more we learn about a subject, the more detailed the schema. Each human being has had different experiences, so everyone's schema are different.

When we first read Kenneth Goodman's (1994) statement that you don't learn when you read, we disagreed because we thought we always learned when we read. What Goodman meant is that we must know something about a topic or we won't be able to understand what we are reading, and we agree that reading does not happen if a student can't connect the topic of a text to what he or she knows about the subject. For instance, none of us knows anything about nuclear fission, so even if we can say all the words when decoding text about that topic, we will not understand the words we are saying. Content knowledge is related to vocabulary development because when children learn about science, social studies, and other disciplines, they learn new words that enrich their vocabulary.

We are especially critical of the basic skills curriculum in some schools that serve children of poverty. Some policy makers believe that if children aren't reading well, the solution is for them to spend more time on reading skills. But there is no content learning when a child spends hours memorizing phonics rules or completing worksheets. Learning about about the specific content of all disciplines is necessary for students to mature as readers. Privileged children take vacations and go to cultural events as part of their family life. We believe that many of the children who supposedly have serious reading problems are actually struggling due to a paucity of content knowledge.

Flow

Flow is misunderstood and often confused with old-fashioned speed reading. In recent years, stopwatches have become a part of the landscape in early childhood classrooms, and we believe this misinterpretation of fluency is very harmful. We have observed students who begin a testing session by apologizing for reading at a slow rate and stating, "I only read at 90 words per minute, when my teacher says I should read 120 words." Parents call teachers and discuss the speed of their child's reading and ask how they can increase that speed. Our response to the reading speed issue is that without comprehension, the saying of words isn't reading.

Of course, we don't want students reading at a slow, laborious rate. We know that reading rate increases as students mature as readers. Research by Reutzel

CHAPTER 11

The Theory That Informs Our Practice

Time spent with students is limited and precious. In most districts, you have 180 days to support literacy development and to make a significant difference in the lives of students. In a classroom of 26 children, you have 26 different literacy histories to explore. Which students are read to at home and at preschool? What are their different levels of spelling development? What are their favorite books and characters? Which children already think of themselves as readers and writers? Although the individual differences among them are most dramatic in kindergarten, children in all grades enter our classroom with a range of literacy knowledge, varying degrees of intrinsic motivation, and a continuum of dispositions. You examine and accept these attributes and then spend the year making strides to support the children as they become self-monitoring and meaning-focused in their reading processes.

Setting Goals for Students ～

It is important to set broad, overarching goals for all our students. These goals encompass the knowledge, skills, and dispositions we want our children to walk away with at the end of their 180 days with us. These are the goals we have for our students:

- Develop oral language abilities
- Use all cueing systems efficiently (graphophonic, syntactic, semantic, and pragmatic)
- Read and write independently
- Develop and use a large vocabulary

- Think deeply and talk about the texts they read

- Develop a greater knowledge of genres and authors

- Expand content knowledge

- Read for personal meaning

- Read grade-appropriate text with confidence

- Develop the belief that one is a capable reader and do what capable readers do

- Read like a writer and write like a reader

- Develop prosody (the appropriate tone and rhythm for a particular text)

- Develop written communication

The Relationship of Goals and Beliefs

These goals stem from our own belief systems. Every teacher has beliefs about what children should experience during the instructional day, and those beliefs are reflected in how we spend our time. Since you are reading this book, you share our interest in learning as much as you can about teaching and learning. You may have read much of the same professional literature as we have and, like us, spent time reflecting on your beliefs. These beliefs form the foundation for all of our instructional decisions.

Because we subscribe to the view that minds develop progressively, we continually make revisions in our beliefs. For example, in recent years we have given more thought to the needs of English language learners because of the large number of Mexican-American children living in our area. Although we have always celebrated cultural diversity, we welcome the opportunity to learn more about the needs of and best practices for English language learners. Throughout our educational careers, we must continue to assess the newly arising needs of our students and address them accordingly. As society changes, so will the needs of the children we serve.

Beliefs Can Help With Classroom Challenges

Teachers implementing a classroom reading block face several challenges:

- Large class sizes

- A wide range of reading abilities, attitudes, and language development among students

- A shortage of classroom, school, and community resources
- Varying degrees of administrative support

One of the biggest challenges teachers voice to us is their difficulty in orchestrating the components of the reading workshop. We hear these questions frequently:

- How do I put all the pieces of my reading program together?
- How do I fit in shared reading, guided reading, independent reading, literature circles, word study, vocabulary instruction, and the reading–writing connection?
- How do I do all this and still make reading fun for my students?

We have asked ourselves those same questions. Before we came to manage and organize our reading block, we first had to examine our belief systems. Before we could articulate our beliefs, we were swaying and bending in the wind and trying out everything we saw at conferences and workshops. We were not standing on a firm foundational belief system. As we studied theorists, read other professional literature, observed our students, and became more experienced, over time we modified and established our beliefs. Now we know why we do what we are doing.

Theoretical Underpinnings ∼

Based on our evolution as teachers the following theoretical underpinnings represent our current beliefs.

- Comprehension is the goal of reading.
- Communication is the goal of writing.
- Students should experience a rich, integrated curriculum that fosters inquiry throughout the day. What occurs outside the reading/writing workshop contributes to the learning of content knowledge and the practice of literacy processes.
- Students should experience quality children's literature during read-alouds, shared reading, guided reading, and independent reading.

- Students should choose a significant portion of the texts they read.

- Teachers should support families as they partner in the education of their children.

- Authentic assessments should guide the selection of rich literacy experiences.

- Reading and writing are reciprocal processes.

Let us explain why each of these theoretical beliefs is so important to us.

Community, Diversity, and Culturally Responsive Pedagogy

We have referred frequently to Ralph Peterson's classic book *Life in a Crowded Place* (1992) throughout this book. Peterson's book has influenced us the most with regard to the importance of the classroom as a learning community. Prior to reading the book, we hadn't thought much about the purpose of classroom rituals, although we each could identify what our rituals were. Peterson helped us refine our use of rituals and routines and to reflect upon their importance and the impact they had on our students and their social environment.

If you haven't read *Life in a Crowded Place*, find it. We believe it will be forever relevant and is well worth your time. In the span of 139 pages and three chapters, Peterson explains the practices that create community and the importance of community in the development of readers and writers.

We agree with Peterson that rituals and routines provide the framework for developing a classroom community. Predictability and consistency afford students the security of a risk-free environment that allows them to participate in a democratic classroom where ownership is held by the students as well as the teacher. Gayle's class could almost operate without her presence, because her students are comfortable with the routines and feel they have ownership of their learning. They truly feel safe and secure because of their participation in developing the classroom community. This sense of responsibility empowers students to be decision makers in and out of school.

In *The Dreamkeepers: Successful Teachers of African American Children*, Gloria Ladson-Billings (1994) made us aware of the need for a culturally relevant curriculum. Knowing that schools are often enclaves of middle-class white values increased our sensitivity to children from other cultures. Also, classrooms usually contain both school-dependent and school-independent students. As mentioned in Chapter 10, school-independent children come to us with knowledge and

in making sense of text. In Chapter 10, we explored the reading process in detail and discussed why we feel that too often the acquisition of discrete skills and fluency is the goal of many current reading programs.

Writing Is for Communication

Although this book deals primarily with reading, we cannot separate reading from writing. Unfortunately, in too many classrooms, writing is relegated to a "when I can get around to it" status. In fact, the National Commission on Writing For America's Families, Schools and Colleges issued a report to Congress entitled *The Neglected "R": The Need for a Writing Revolution* (2003) to alert all policy makers about the need for a deliberate emphasis on appropriate writing instruction at all grade levels. We have observed that early childhood teachers often feel tentative about their ability to teach younger children writing strategies and skills. They often think that writing instruction might better be reserved for the intermediate and secondary grades. Much of the writing that occurs in some early childhood classrooms merely consists of copying handwriting lessons or filling in the blanks of a worksheet.

We believe the act of writing in early childhood classrooms is not merely the correct formation of letters or the copying of a poem from a chart. These actions do not further a child's self-expression. We consider writing to be the production of children's wonderful ideas. Teachers as well as children must reconsider writing as an act of communication rather than replication.

Along with the understanding that writing is communication, children need an audience wider than the classroom teacher for the sharing of their wonderful ideas. Children's writing must be shared with other children in the classroom, the school, the community, and even the world (easy to do if a teacher utilizes the power of the Internet). Children also need regular feedback from the teacher as well as their peers. Adults and peers can provide the scaffolding (Vygotsky, 1978) necessary to transform ordinary writing into good writing and good writing into exceptional pieces.

We also believe the goal of writing should not merely be for students to do well on a mandated writing assessment. Communicating one's ideas to others should be the goal, and if this communication is accompanied by skillful instruction and support, successful performance on mandated writing assessments will become a byproduct of classroom writing experiences.

Building Content Knowledge

Learning to read doesn't occur only during the reading workshop; literacy growth also happens throughout the day in other areas of the curriculum. Unfortunately, in many school districts we see a fragmentation and narrowing of the early childhood curriculum due to an overemphasis on what is measured on state assessments, which is reading and math. Science and social studies instruction are conspicuously absent unless tested. Beginning reading instruction has become a throwback to a skills-based approach, in many cases devoid of rich nonfiction texts. What teachers must do is integrate reading instruction during science and social studies units and infuse informational text into the reading block.

We hear teachers express that they don't have time to teach science and social studies, and we have observed students who don't see the relationships among the disciplines. We contend that the content knowledge learned in science and social studies instruction is necessary for a student to optimally understand texts. A content-rich curriculum benefits children's literacy development in several ways:

- When students acquire content knowledge, they develop the vocabulary necessary to read a wider variety of texts.

- The acquisition of content knowledge builds children's mental schemas, providing the background knowledge that allows them to better comprehend both narrative and informational texts.

- In a content-rich curriculum, students are filled with unanswered questions. The students' questions regarding a topic cause them to become inquirers.

When children turn to text—nonfiction books, magazines, Web sites—to find answers to questions, they are reading for meaning. To many children, nonfiction texts are more interesting than narratives. Every early childhood student is interested in some nonfiction topic, be it bats, firemen, the ocean, or trucks. Nonfiction can readily hook readers who are reluctant or lacking in confidence. We contend that some of the best reading practice occurs outside of the workshop—during content-area instruction and theme immersions.

Theme immersions are a vehicle for teachers to implement an interdisciplinary block of time each day. In theme immersions, students choose the topics they want to research, the questions they want to answer, and the texts they read to answer their questions about the topic. Not only do students enjoy having so much choice, they also experience many opportunities to practice reading and writing (Manning, et al., 1994).

Use Quality Children's Literature

The current volume of quality children's literature available for students to read is phenomenal. Each year, thousands of children's books are published and new authors emerge on the scene. Among this body of published texts, excellent books of every genre are just waiting to be placed in students' hands and minds. High-quality children's books provide pleasurable literacy experiences, rich and provocative ideas to ponder, lessons about life, new words to learn and practice, and models that students can use in their own writing pieces. Before children are able to read texts independently, they can enjoy and understand rich, interesting literature through read-alouds and shared reading experiences.

Once children begin reading independently, it is equally important that they continue their interaction with quality literature. Even books for emergent readers can be engaging, interesting, and written in natural-sounding language. Comprehension of authentic, as opposed to decodable, text is the goal of reading instruction. Decodable text like "Nan can fan the man" was prevalent in the 1970s primarily for special education students, but has staged a recent comeback as the text of choice of many educators for all emergent readers, not just those with identified learning problems. Many policy makers as well as educators believe that most, if not all, emergent reading materials should be decodable (Camp & Aldridge, 2007).

We cannot understand why decodable text has become so popular when the National Reading Panel's (2000) recently declared that "Surprisingly, very little research has attempted to determine the contribution of decodable books to the effectiveness of phonics programs" (p. 298). We believe that the best phonics instruction occurs within the context of shared reading, guided reading, independent reading, reading conferences, shared writing, and independent writing. No research exists demonstrating the superiority of decodable to predictable or other natural texts (National Reading Panel, 2000; Allington & Woodside-Jiron, 1998). And it has been our experience that children find decodable text not only uninteresting but confusing.

Children must not only authentic texts, but these books must also be comprehensible to them. Richard Allington (2006) has led the charge recently about the importance of providing children with books they can understand. Allington points out that often children choose books that are too difficult for them. We have observed this among our students as well, and feel we are doing our children a disservice if we don't gently nudge them into choosing more appropriate text, what many call "just-right" books. Otherwise, they are thwarted in fully developing as readers since their access to comprehensible text is limited.

We feel strongly that the texts children hear and those that they read independently must be interesting, well written, and written by real authors, at a level at which they can construct meaning. Children deserve a rich menu of high-quality books. As our good friend Roberta Long has always said, "We want children to fall in love with good books and authors." It is not phonics lessons, basal readers, or scripted programs that result in a child's love of reading. It is the quality of the literature menu we serve each day and the teacher's enthusiasm that creates a love of books and reading. With the plethora of quality books available today, there is no reason to avoid using good literature in every literacy encounter we provide for our children.

Let Students Choose

In addition to quality texts, self-selection is a critical ingredient in fostering a love of reading. If students are to become passionate about their own learning, they must have choice in the texts they read. Self-selection can promote students' emotional involvement. When our students become emotionally invested in their reading, they are more likely to grapple with the content, which in turn leads to an enhanced understanding of the text. It is unrealistic of us to expect children to become either cognitively or emotionally invested with a text when the teacher chooses all reading selections for them.

Think back on times in your life when you were assigned texts—in school or work assignments—and the reluctance you felt before and during the reading of the text. Contrast those experiences with the anticipation you feel walking into your public library or your favorite local bookstore to choose the books you, and maybe only you, want to read for pleasure and entertainment as well as to answer questions you might have about a topic of interest. Now imagine how you would feel if we limited your browsing to only one small shelf in the public library and the bookstore. You would be indignant and uninterested—and you would probably walk out. This is what we are doing to children when we deny them the opportunity to seize the texts that they care about. This does not mean that during the reading workshop you don't ask students to choose from a section of books or a tub that contains leveled books. You are still providing children a wide choice.

One way to promote self-selection is to provide students access to large classroom libraries and to a school library. This way, children have a wide choice of genres and authors to choose from for independent reading.

We consider reading a vehicle for personal growth, self-fulfillment, and enjoyment. Allowing children to self-select their independent reading texts is a critical element in helping them find this level of pleasure and growth.

Partner With Families

Families are often relegated to the fringes of our educational world, despite the best intentions of educators. In suburban districts, families can be limited to specific formal events, such as back-to-school night, open houses, PTA/PTO meetings, or parent conference days. In urban districts, where teachers sometimes comment on the scarcity of parent involvement at these formal events, we often don't do enough to actively pursue family participation. It's also possible that we haven't done enough to design our buildings as friendly environments. Because of security fears, our facilities can resemble fortresses, complete with locked front doors, metal detectors, and elaborate parent check-in and check-out systems. We must find a way in spite of these environmental barriers to convince parents that they are genuinely a part of the school and classroom family.

In Chapter 7, we describe the family bulletin board, which aims to involve all families and children in the classroom community. We also shared with you ways to involve parents from day one by establishing routines and practices that bring families into the big circle of the classroom community. When parents know that we not only care about their children but also about them, we build the trust needed to optimize teaching and learning.

Use Authentic Assessments

A current catchphrase we often hear is "data-driven instruction." We don't deny the importance of data, but what is most important is that teachers use data derived from rich, meaningful assessments. You cannot rely solely on summative assessments such as state tests to inform instruction. These scores should be considered "old data," collected months earlier and not reflective of children's current status. Besides, these assessments do not provide diagnostic information to help you plan appropriate reading instruction. Such "after the fact" data can only suggest general strengths and weaknesses. At best, standardized tests, whether norm referenced or criterion referenced, provide a broad-brush view of a child's performance. Unfortunately, policy makers judge children and base school reform efforts on these limited state assessments. We believe fill-in-the-bubble exercises and early childhood tests requiring the use of stop watches are not appropriate for reading assessment.

What teachers and children need instead are these conditions and supports:

- Well-designed, classroom-based assessments administered by you, the people who are closest to the children

- Professional development that prepares teachers to administer and analyze these assessments

- Help in translating this analysis into appropriate instructional decisions. Each child needs a teacher who can examine assessment data and answer the question "What does this child need from me based on the results of these assessments?"

Reading and Writing Are Reciprocal Processes

Reading and writing, though not identical, are reciprocal processes. Although reading is considered a receptive process in which we take in information, and writing an expressive process that conveys or gives out information, both actively involve using language to make meaning. Writing begins as the representation of knowledge, and reading begins as the deciphering of written language. If we emphasize writing within the reading program, reading and writing will develop simultaneously. Writing supports reading; when children write, they are using their knowledge of cueing systems. As they write, children apply knowledge of graphophonics through spelling, of syntax through grammar and word order, and of semantics through questioning whether the writing makes sense or not. When writers write, they read and reread their text, thus providing additional reading practice. When writers read, they see vocabulary words, crafting techniques, and standard grammar and spelling they can then use in their own writing. Oftentimes, we see that children who are good readers are also good writers.

Shared writing and interactive writing are classroom practices that are both receptive and expressive. Children are asked to help the teacher or to "share the pen" when composing their thoughts, and then to read what they've written. When children are writing, they are reading the words on the page. When children are reading, they are examining the writing of others. Shared writing, then, provides young children the opportunity to practice both writing and reading skills.

	Title	Page
2-21	Reading Journals: Nonfiction Level D–E	91
2-22	Getting to Know My Book bookmark	92
2-23	Kindergarten Reading Journal Guidelines	93
3-1	Gayle's Phonics Progression Chart for First Grade	121
3-2	Gayle's Conference Form for First Grade	122
3-3	Gayle's Strategies Conference Form for First Grade	123
3-4	Assessment Summary Forms—Phonological Awareness and Phonics	124
3-5	Sample Summary of Assessments—Phonological Awareness and Phonics	125
3-6	My Reading Responses bookmarks	126
3-7	Thinking About My Book	127
4-1	Reading Progression Chart for Second Grade	154
4-2	Gayle's Reading Conference Form for Second Grade	155
4-3	Gayle's Reading Strategies Conference Form for Second Grade	156
4-4	Fiction and Nonfiction Literature Response Journal Guidelines for Second Grade	157
4-5	Reading Journal Guidelines	158
4-6	Getting to Know Your Book bookmarks	159
4-7	Tracks of Thinking While Reading Text	160
5-1	Reading Progression Chart for Third Grade	186
5-2	Gayle's Reading Conference Form for Third Grade	187
5-3	Gayle's Strategies Conference Form for Third Grade	188
5-4	Fiction and Nonfiction Literature Response Journal Guidelines for Third Grade	189
5-5	Phonics Inventory Chart	190

	Title	Page
5-6	Gayle's Chapter Book bookmarks	191
7-1	Gayle's Home–School Reading Form	219
8-1	Anecdotal Record Form	248
8-2	Appropriate Assessments for Primary-Age Children	249
8-3	Phonics Inventory: Teacher Instructions	250
8-4	Phonics Inventory: Teacher Copy	251
8-5	Phonics Inventory: Student Copy	252
8-6	Parent Questionnaire	253
8-7	Interest Inventory	254
8-8	Garfield Attitude Survey	255–260
9-1	Appropriate Strategies for Reader Types	288
9-2	Individual Intervention Plan (blank)	289
9-3	Individual Reading Intervention Plan (sample)	290
9-4	Approximate Text Level Conversion Table	291
9-5	Intervention Lessons: K–1	292
9-5	Intervention Lessons: Grades 2–3	293
9-7	Instructional Strategies and Materials	294

Professional References

Adams, M. J. (1990). *Beginning to read: Thinking and learning about print.* Cambridge, MA: MIT Press.

Allington, R. L. (2005a). NCLB, Reading First, and whither the future? *Reading Today, 23*(2), 18.

Allington, R. L. (2005b). *What really matters for struggling readers: Designing research-based programs* (2nd ed.). Boston: Allyn & Bacon.

Allington, R. L. (2006). *What really matters for struggling readers: Designing research-based programs* (2nd ed.). Boston: Allyn & Bacon.

Allington, R. L. (2008). *What really matters in fluency: Research-based practices across the curriculum.* New York: Allyn & Bacon.

Allington, R., & Walmsley, S. (2007). *No quick fix, the RTI edition: Rethinking literacy programs in America's elementary schools.* New York: Teachers College Press.

Allington, R. L., & Woodside-Jiron, H. (1998). Decodable texts in beginning reading: Are mandates based on research? *ERS Spectrum, 16,* 3–11.

Barchers, S. I. (1993). *Readers theatre for beginning readers.* Englewood, CO: Teacher Ideas Press.

Barchers, S. I. (2000). *Multicultural folktales: Readers theatre for elementary students.* Englewood, CO: Teacher Ideas Press.

Barchers, S. I. (2006). *More readers theatre for beginning readers.* Westport, CT: Libraries Unlimited.

Bauer, C. F. (1987). *Presenting reader's theater: Plays and poems to read aloud.* New York: Wilson.

Bear, D. R., Invernizzi, M., Templeton, S., & Johnston, F. (2000). *Words their way: Word study for phonics, vocabulary, and spelling instruction* (2nd ed.). Upper Saddle River, NJ: Prentice Hall.

Beck, I. L., McKeown, M. G., & Kucan, L. (2002). *Bringing words to life: Robust vocabulary instruction*. New York: Guilford Press.

Black, P., & Wiliam, D. (1998). *Assessment and classroom learning: Assessment in Education, 5*(1) 7–74.

Britton, J. (1970). *Language and learning: The importance of speech in children's development*. New York: Penguin.

Caldwell, J. S., & Leslie, L. (2004). *Intervention strategies to follow informal reading inventory assessment: So what do I do now?* Boston: Allyn & Bacon.

Cambourne, B. (1988). *The whole story: Natural learning and the acquisition of literacy in the classroom*. New York: Scholastic.

Camp, D., & Aldridge, J. (2007). Rethinking dyslexia, scripted reading, and federal mandates: The more things change, the more they stay the same. *Journal of Instructional Psychology, 34*(1), 3–12.

Chandler, D. L. (1998, May 18). This bird talks, counts, and reads—a little. *The Boston Globe*. Retrieved May 1, 2008, from http://pubpages.unh.edu/~jel/video/alex.html.

Clay, M. (2006). *An observation survey of early literacy achievement* (rev. 2nd ed.). Portsmouth, NH: Heinemann.

Cunningham, A., & Shagoury, R. (2005). *Starting with comprehension: Reading strategies for the youngest learners*. Portland, ME: Stenhouse.

Developmental Studies Center. (2006). *Making Meaning*. Oakland, CA: Author.

Dewey, J. (1998). My pedagogic creed. In *The essential Dewey* (pp. 229–235). Bloomington: Indiana University Press.

Ferreiro, E., & Teberosky, A. (1982). *Literacy before schooling*. Portsmouth, NH: Heinemann.

Fisher, B., & Medvic, E. F. (2000). *Perspectives on shared reading: Planning and practice*. Portsmouth, NH: Heinemann.

Flurkey, A. D. (1997). *Reading as flow: A linguistic alternative to fluency*. Unpublished doctoral dissertation. University of Arizona–Tucson.

Fountas, I. C., & Pinnell, G. S. (1996). *Guided reading: Good first teaching for all children*. Portsmouth, NH: Heinemann.

Fountas, I. C., & Pinnell, G. S. (1999). *Matching books to readers: Using leveled books in guided reading, K–3*. Portsmouth, NH: Heinemann.

Fountas, I. C., & Pinnell, G. S. (2005). *Leveled books, K–8: Matching texts to readers for effective teaching*. Portsmouth, NH: Heinemann.

Fountas, I. C., & Pinnell, G. S. (2006). *The Fountas and Pinnell leveled book list K–8*. Portsmouth, NH: Heinemann.

Fountas, I. C., & Pinnell, G. S. (2008). *Fountas and Pinnell benchmark assessment system 1*. Portsmouth, NH: Heinemann.

Fox, M. (2001). *Reading magic: Why reading aloud to our children will change their lives forever*. San Diego, CA: Harcourt.

Fox, M. (2003). Presentation at MidSouth Reading and Writing Institute, Birmingham, AL.

Fuchs, D., Fuchs, L., & Vaughn, S. (2008). *Response to intervention*. Newark, DE: International Reading Association.

Ganske, K. (2000). *Word journeys: Assessment-guided phonics, spelling, and vocabulary instruction*. New York: Guilford Press.

Ganske, K. (2006). *Word sorts and more: Sound, pattern, and meaning explorations K–3*. New York: Guilford Press.

Gardner, H. (1983). *Frames of mind: The theory of multiple intelligences*. New York: Basic Books.

Goodman, K. S. (1994). Reading, writing, and written texts: A transactional sociopsycho-linguistic view. In R. B. Ruddell, M. R. Ruddell, & H. Singer (Eds.), *Theoretical models and processes of reading* (4th ed.). Newark, DE: International Reading Association.

Goodman, K. S., & Burke, C. L. (1973). *Theoretically based studies of patterns of miscues in oral reading performance.* Detroit: Wayne State University. Retrieved August 26, 2008, from the ERIC database.

Goodman, Y. (1985). Kidwatching: Observing children in the classroom. In A. Jaggar and M. T. Smith-Burke (Eds.), *Observing the language learner* (pp. 9–18). Newark, DE: International Reading Association.

Goodman, Y. (Ed.). (1986). *How children construct literacy: Piagetion perspectives.* Newark, DE: International Reading Association.

Goodman, Y., & Marek, A. (1996). *Retrospective miscue analysis: Revaluing readers and reading.* Katonah, NY: Owen.

Goodman, Y., Watson, D., & Burke, C. (1996). *Reading strategies: Focus on comprehension* (2nd ed.). Katonah, NY: Owen.

Goodman, Y., Watson, D., & Burke, C. (2005). *Reading miscue inventory.* Katonah, NY: Owen.

Harvey, S., & Goudvis, A. (2000). *Strategies that work: Teaching comprehension to enhance understanding.* Portland, ME: Stenhouse.

Harvey, S., & Goudvis, A. (2005). *The comprehension toolkit: Grades 3–6.* Portsmouth, NH: Heinemann.

Harvey, S., & Goudvis, A. (2008). *The primary comprehension toolkit: Grades K–2.* Portsmouth, NH: Heinemann.

Hill, B. C., Schlick Noe, K. L., & Johnson, N. J. (2001). *Literature circles resource guide: Teaching suggestions, forms, sample book lists, and database.* Norwood, MA: Christopher-Gordon.

Peterson, R., & Eeds, M. (1990). *Grand conversations: Literature groups in action.* New York: Scholastic.

Piaget, J. (1971). *Biology and knowledge* (B. Walsh, Trans.). Chicago: University of Chicago Press.

Power, B. M. (1996). *Taking note: Improving your observational notetaking.* Portland, ME: Stenhouse.

Reading Recovery Council of North America. (2008). *Reading Recovery Book List.* Can be retrieved by subscription at http://readingrecovery.org/rrena/membership/books.asp.

Reutzel, D. R., Hollingsworth, P. M., & Eldredge, J. L. (1994). Oral reading instruction: The impact on student reading development. *Reading Research Quarterly, 29*(1), 40–62.

Rosenblatt, L. (1994). *The reader, the text, the poem: The transactional theory of the literary work.* Carbondale: Southern Illinois University Press.

Ross, C. S. (1995). "If they read Nancy Drew, so what?": Series book readers talk back. *Library and Information Science Research, 17*(3), 201–236.

Routman, R. (1999). *Conversations: Strategies for teaching, learning, and evaluating.* Portsmouth, NH: Heinemann.

Routman, R. (2003). *Reading essentials: The specifics you need to teach reading well.* Portsmouth, NH: Heinemann.

Smith, F. (1994). *Understanding reading: A psycholinguistic analysis of reading and learning to read* (5th ed.). Hillsdale, NJ: Erlbaum.

Strickland, K. (2005). *What's after assessment? Follow-up instruction for phonics, fluency, and comprehension.* Portsmouth, NH: Heinemann.

Tate, J. (2005). *Teaching reading in New Zealand.* Presentation at MidSouth Reading and Writing Institute, Birmingham, AL.

Tierney, R. (1979). The discourse processing operations of children. *Reading Research Quarterly 14*(4), pp. 539–573.

Trelease, J. (2001). *The read-aloud handbook* (5th ed.). New York: Penguin Books.

Veatch, J. (1967). *Reading in the elementary school.* New York: Ronald Press Co.

Vygotsky, L. S. (1978). Mind in society. In *The development of higher psychological processes.* Cambridge, MA: Harvard University Press.

Weaver, C. (2002). *Reading process and practice* (3rd ed.). Portsmouth, NH: Heinemann.

Wilde, S. (2000). *Miscue analysis made easy: Building on student strengths.* Portsmouth, NH: Heinemann.

Wolf, A. (1993). *It's show time: Poetry from the page to the stage.* Asheville, NC: Poetry Alive!

Zimmermann, S., & Hutchins, C. (2003). *Seven keys to comprehension: How to help your kids read it and get it!* New York: Crown.

Children's Literature Cited

Brett, J. (1997). *The hat*. New York: Penguin Young Readers.

Cherry, L. (2000). *The great kapok tree: A tale of the Amazon rain forest*. New York: Harcourt.

Cowley, J. (2008). *Chicken feathers*. New York: Philomel Books.

Cronin, D. (2000). *Click, clack, moo: Cows that type*. New York: Scholastic.

Dadey, D., & Jones, M. T. *The adventures of the Bailey School kids* series. New York: Scholastic.

Day, A. *Carl* series. New York: Simon & Schuster.

dePaola, T. (2000). *Nana upstairs & Nana downstairs*. New York: Putnam.

Ehlert, L. (1991). *Red leaf, yellow leaf*. Orlando, FL: Harcourt Brace.

Ehlert, L. (1997). *Cuckoo Cucù: A Mexican folktale*. San Diego, CA: Harcourt Brace.

Ehlert, L. (2002). *In my world*. San Diego, CA: Harcourt.

Ehlert, L. (2004). *Pie in the sky*. San Diego, CA: Harcourt.

Ehlert, L. (2005). *Leaf man*. Orlando, FL: Harcourt.

Ehlert, L. (2007). *Wag a tail*. Orlando, FL: Harcourt.

Emberley, E. (1992). *Go away, big green monster*. Boston: Little, Brown.

Feldman, J. (1998). *Dr. Jean and friends*. Tampa, FL: Progressive Music.

Fleming, D. (1991). *In the tall, tall, grass*. New York: Holt.

Fleming, D. (1997). *Time to sleep*. New York: Holt.

Fleming, D. (1998). *Mama cat has three kittens*. New York: Holt.

Fleming, D. (2006). *The cow who clucked*. New York: Holt.

Fleming, D. (2007). *Beetle bop*. New York: Harcourt.

Fox, M. (2004). *Where is the green sheep?* Orlando, FL: Harcourt.

Frasier, D. (2000). *Miss Alaineus: A vocabulary disaster*. New York: Voyager Books.

Fyleman, R. (2001). Mice. In P. Richardson (Ed.), *Animal poems*. New York: Simon & Schuster.

Gibbons, G. (1991). *Monarch butterfly*. New York: Holiday House.

Gibbons, G. (2000). *Bats*. New York: Holiday House.

Harrison, D. (1999). *Wild country: Outdoor poems for young children*. Honesdale, PA: Boyds Mill Press.

Harrison, D. (2005). *Mountains: The tops of the world*. Honesdale, PA: Boyds Mill Press.

Harrison, D. (2006a). *Glaciers: Nature's icy caps*. Honesdale, PA: Boyds Mills Press.

Harrison, D. (2006b). *Sounds of rain: Poems of the Amazon*. Honesdale, PA: Boyds Mills Press.

Kellogg, S. (1988). *Johnny Appleseed*. New York: HarperCollins.

Laminack, L. L. (2002). *Trevor's wiggly, wobbly tooth*. Atlanta, GA: Peachtree Press.

Laminack, L. L. (2004). *Saturdays and teacakes*. Atlanta, GA: Peachtree Press.

Lewis, C. S. (2001). *The Chronicles of Narnia*. New York: HarperCollins.

Lies, B. (2006). *Bats at the beach*. New York: Houghton Mifflin.

Lobel, A. Frog and Toad series. New York: HarperCollins.

Marcovitz, H. (2007). *Pat Mora*. New York: Chelsea House.

Martin, B., Jr., & Archembault, J. (1989). *Chicka chicka boom boom*. New York: Simon & Schuster Books for Young Readers.

Martin, B., Jr. (2007). *Baby bear, baby bear, what do you see?* New York: Holt.

Mora, P. (1994). *Pablo's tree*. New York: Simon & Schuster.

Mora, P. (2000). *Tomas and the library lady*. New York: Dragonfly Books.

Mora, P. (2001). *Love to Mama: A tribute to mothers*. New York: Lee & Low Books.

Mora, P. (2005a). *Doña Flor: A tall tale about a giant woman with a great big heart*. New York: Knopf.

Mora, P. (2005b). *The song of Francis and the animals*. Grand Rapids, MI: Eerdmans Books for Young Readers.

Numeroff, L. (2000). *If you take a mouse to the movie*s. New York: HarperCollins.

Park, B. (1997). *Junie B. Jones is not a crook*. New York: Random House.

Park, B. (2001). *Junie B., first grader (at last!)*. New York: Random House.

Parkes, B., & Smith J. (1988). *The enormous watermelon*. UK: Gardners Books.

Provencher, R. (2001). *Mouse cleaning*. New York: Holt.

Root, P. (2004). *Rattletrap car*. Somerville, MA: Candlewick Press.

Schachner, J. (2003). Skippyjon Jones series. New York: Dutton Children's Books.

Shannon, D. (1998). *No, David!* New York: Blue Sky Press.

Sharmat, M. W. Nate the Great series. New York: Random House.

Simon, S. (1994). *Big cats*. New York: Harper Trophy.

Van Allsburg, C. (1985). *The polar express*. Boston: Houghton Mifflin.

Wiesner, D. (1997). *Tuesday*. Boston: Houghton Mifflin.

Wiesner, D. (1999). *Sector 7*. Boston: Houghton Mifflin.

Wiesner, D. (2006). *Flotsam*. Boston: Houghton Mifflin.

Zorfass, J. (2000). *Bella lost her moo*. New York: Harcourt.

Creating the Best Literacy Block Ever

Index

L

Ladson-Billings, G., *Dreamkeepers: Successful Teachers of African American Children, The*, 311–312

language development, literacy development and, 303–304

letter identification, assessment and, 230–231

letter-sound identification, assessment, 232

leveled text series, special needs, 271–272

Life in a Crowded Place, (Peterson), 10, 17, 194, 311

literacy, engagements with, 25

literacy block frameworks, 20

literacy blocks, 19

    community sharing and, 35-37

    defined, 21

    five components of, 22-23

    independent engagement and, 32–33

    intentional instruction and, 31–32

    peer interaction and, 34–35

    time, logistics and, 21–22

literacy development

    conditions for, 297–299

    evolution of, 295–297

literacy encounters with three rotations

    kindergarten literacy block, 72

literacy encounters with two rotations

    kindergarten literacy block, 71

Literature Circles Resource Guide, (Hill), 177

literature discussion groups

    first-grade literacy block, 109, 111, 115

    second grade literacy block, 139–140, 143, 150

    third grade literacy block, 175, 177, 182

literature extensions, stetting the stage for, 26

literature response journals

    first-grade literacy block, 111–112

    kindergarten literacy block, 87

    kindergarten literacy block and, 61–63

    third grade literacy block, 177–178

Long, R., 315, 317

M

McKenna, M., 244

Make it Real: Strategies for Success with Informational Texts, (Hoyts), 149, 179

Making Meaning (Studies Center), 50, 101, 166

Manning, G. and Long, R., *Theme Immersion: Inquiry-Based Curriculum in Elementary and Middle Schools*, 179

Manning, M., 231, 295, 302, 315

Manning, M., Chumley, S., and Underbakke, C., *Scientific Reading Assessment*, 18

Manning, M., Manning, G. and Long, R., 315

Marek, A., 142, 164, 170

Miller, D., 101

    Reading with Meaning, 50, 106, 132, 242

    Strategies that Work, 166

Mondo, special needs texts and, 272–273

Mooney, M., *Reading to, with and by Children*, 45

My Pedagogic Creed, (Dewey), 15

my reading responses form

    first-grade literacy block, 126

N

Nichols, M., *Comprehension Through Conversation: The Power of Purposeful Talk in the Reading Workshop*, 137

O

Oakapi, special needs texts and, 272

Observation Survey of Early Literacy Achievement, An, (Clay), 230

oral language development assessment, 233–234

oral text comprehension, assessment and, 238–239

Owocki, G., Comprehension, 18

P

parental involvement, 213–218

    author teas, 217